A
Time
to
Reap

A Time to Reap

The Middle Age of Women in Five Israeli Subcultures

Nancy Datan

Aaron Antonovsky

Benjamin Maoz

The Johns Hopkins University Press
Baltimore and London

The Johns Hopkins University Press, Baltimore, Maryland 21218
The Johns Hopkins Press Ltd., London

Library of Congress Cataloging in Publication Data

Datan, Nancy.
  A time to reap.

  Bibliography: pp. 185–88
  Includes index.
  1. Middle aged women—Israel—Case studies. 2. Subculture—Case studies. 3. Life cycle,
Human. 4. Menopause. I. Antonovsky, Aaron, joint author. II. Maoz, Benjamin, joint author.
III. Title.
HQ1728.5.D37   305.2'4'095694   80–26776
ISBN 0-8018-2516-4

Contents

Preface

In 1967 the research team of Datan, Antonovsky, and Maoz was created when Bernice Neugarten shared with me a U.S. National Institute of Mental Health proposal (P.L. 480 agreement no. 06-276-2) for a study of middle-aged Israeli women entitled "Sociocultural Patterns and the Involutional Crisis" and suggested that if I were interested, as she correctly suspected I might be, I should write the principal investigator, Aaron Antonovsky, to enquire about the possibility of joining the study. I did more: I wrote to the unknown Dr. Antonovsky to tell him that the hypothesis guiding his study was all wrong, that mine was better, and that if given a chance to participate in the research, I would prove it. Aaron rose to the occasion then as always, and took me on—as his partner, not as an adversary (as my letter might have warranted), nor as senior research assistant (the formal title available to me as an upstart M.A., a title which in no way constrained our partnership).

The team I joined included Aaron Antonovsky as principal investigator and Benjamin Maoz as co-principal investigator. Benjamin had worked as a family practitioner in an Israeli development town and rural district. His clinical observations of ethnic differences in coping with menopause, and the sparse data on involutional psychosis, had sparked his scientific curiosity. With the encouragement of Professor Henricus Wijsenbeek, director of the Gehah Psychiatric Hospital to which Benjamin had moved, he turned to Aaron, proposing a joint project. Aaron, a medical sociologist with a longstanding interest in cultural differences, suggested going far beyond the initial concern with pathology and maladaptation. Instead, the broad range of responses to menopause became the focus, an approach which Benjamin fully endorsed.

Bernice Neugarten played a very special role in our study: her own investigation of the responses of normal middle-aged women to the changes of menopause, the only such study at the time ours was conceived, was an important source of guidance; her role as U.S. project officer involved ongoing consultation and a generous involvement which went far beyond the call of duty; and somewhere along the way a piece of this study became my Ph.D. dissertation, and Bernice my dissertation advisor. Our research team owes her special thanks for inspiring and catalyzing this research; my own thanks are still more special.

Benjamin's Ph.D. dissertation also came out of the study; Henricus Wijsenbeek was an advisor. Special thanks are also due Henricus, project consul-

vii

tant, and whose generous investment of time and energy are much appreciated, and Helen Faigin Antonovsky, whose advisory role was to grow along with the project into full partnership during its active phase, a partnership which was vital to the study's growth.

I have given my colleagues no titles because the research team I joined was a partnership of persons, and for me positions were parenthetical in 1967. It was some years before I came to appreciate my own good fortune in finding distinguished senior colleagues whose view of rank was as generous as mine was naive; it will be many more years before my debt to their generosity is repaid.

For the three years of planning, fieldwork, and data analysis, the team of Antonovsky, Maoz, and Datan, with much help from Helen Antonovsky, worked at close quarters in Louis Guttman's Israel Institute of Applied Social Research, which provided an intellectual ambience where dialogue thrived, leading to the eventual interdisciplinary synthesis our team achieved. Looking backward, I find it easy to remember our ongoing debates, but impossible to recall who said what. With rare exceptions where our separate disciplines dictated our contributions—for example, the pilot and psychiatric interviews were conducted by Maoz, the survey research was designed by Antonovsky, the developmental model was mine—our collaboration was so close that we all did everything.

Although it is difficult to detect our individual contributions as we look back, it is easy to see the impact of our joint efforts on each of us individually as we have moved on. Aaron's *salutogenic* model of resistance resources and the sense of coherence in his book *Health, Stress, and Coping,* Benjamin's therapeutic cautions on the culture-specific meaning of work for middle-aged women, and my own writings on modernization and women's roles—and much more, detailed in the Bibliography of our publications which have proceeded directly or indirectly from this study—all point to the lasting effect this investigation has had upon our thinking.

In one important respect we were left unsatisfied as our study concluded. It seems obvious that the picture we had painted of middle age was only half-completed, and we proposed a complementary study of men—the husbands of the women of our study. But between the start and the completion of our study of women in five Israeli sub-cultures, funds for basic behavioral research had been cut back severely, our second proposal went unfunded, we never found out what middle age is like for the men in these five sub-cultures—and we still wonder.

At that point our research team disbanded, although our intellectual partnerships are unbroken. This book is the product of our joint efforts in thinking, planning, execution, analysis, and interpretation. It is jointly authored in every sense but one. I have put the sentences on these pages in their final form—though often a sentence itself, as well as the thought, will have multiple parentage. But the final say, as Aaron has continued to remind me, is mine: and every team member who has ever tried to sound a single note out of several voices will know why I thank him so wholeheartedly.

My personal efforts in the final stages of writing were complemented by the efforts of others. My daughter Merav translated Benjamin's follow-up psychiatric interviews from Hebrew, which is her native language, to English, which is mine, allowing me to scan for comparison in the selection of case histories. My secretaries, Rita Rendina of the Gerontology Center and Kris Grafton of the Department of Psychology, prepared the text and tables; their encouragement was as valuable to me as their assistance. Ray Koppelman, West Virginia University Vice President for Energy Studies, Graduate Programs and Research, and William Reeves, Director, Office of Grants and Contracts, gracefully arranged another last-minute miracle of assistance, at which I never cease to marvel, and for which, as always, my thanks are mixed with awe. Finally, the encouragement of Henry Y. K. Tom, Social Sciences Editor at The Johns Hopkins University Press, from the time of his first letter of inquiry through each of his delicate requests for progress reports—displayed in a position of honor on my refrigerator door—up to the final moment as the manuscript went into production, has been constant in every sense of the word, as is my gratitude to him.

Aaron, Benjamin, and I owe special thanks to our families. Their contributions are sometimes obvious: Helen Antonovsky was a partner in the active phase of the research; Merav Datan was a translator. But more often than not their contributions were intangible. For their patience and ongoing support when the planning, fieldwork, and analysis ran from dawn until well after dark, we thank each of our families; for the endless cups of tea which accompanied the writing of this book, I thank mine. Finally, for the privilege of writing this book and the many lessons in colleagueship which they have taught me, I thank Aaron and Benjamin yet once more—and not for the last time.

Nancy Datan

A
Time
to
Reap

Prologue

The Story of the Study

This is a study of women in transitions. These are women who have made the normative transitions of the life cycle from youth to maturity against a historical backdrop of geographical and cultural transitions. Most of the women in our study are Jewish immigrants to Israel; of them, the Central Europeans escaped or survived the Holocaust of World War II; the Turks, Persians, and North Africans migrated not only across space but through time, coming from cultures of tradition into a culture of change. The Israel-born Moslem Arab women, though they are not immigrants into a new country, have seen a new country come to life in the land where their villages stand.

Our study is concerned with the transitions of middle age—the normal changes of the biological and the family life cycles. But middle age is shaped by youth, and both are shaped by history. The progress of human history includes a process we call modernization, representing, among other things, a trend toward the mastery of nature, and, for women, increasing freedom from the constraints of the biological life cycle as well as the traditional role which evolved as one form of adaptation to biological constraints.

The central question of our study is this: How is a woman's response to the changes of middle age shaped by the culture in which she has grown? The cultures we have chosen in order to find our answer were selected to represent five points on a continuum ranging from tradition to modernity. Differences in cultures, then, are also differences in the degree of modernity. Thus our question can be rephrased as follows: What is the effect of the degree of modernity on a woman's response to the changes of middle age? And this in turn is a question reflecting a broader issue, one of the most significant social issues of our time: What is the effect of modernization and changing sex roles on the lives of women? While our study addresses the narrower question of the effect of the degree of modernity on women's responses to middle age, our findings, as we shall see, permit us to speculate about the broader issue.

In seeking an answer to this question, we found several. The irrevocable decisions of childhood, adolescence, and young adulthood shape the social con-

1

text of middle age, determining whether a woman will be surrounded by many children or by only one or two; whether she will be surrounded by grandchildren while she still has small children of her own at home; whether her family will still be her primary concern or if she is likely to seek an outside job; if she does seek work outside the home, whether she can hope for white-collar work or will be restricted by illiteracy to menial jobs. Each of these possibilities, as we shall see, can be found in one or another of the cultures in our study.

Furthermore, we can see culture, the biological life cycle, and history interact in the life histories of the women in our study. The women who were our subjects were born between 1915 and 1924; they were in their childbearing years during World War II and the Israel War of Independence. Childbearing was shaped, as we shall see, by the dominant cultural values in the country of their origin; these values were rarely affected by immigration to Israel. Thus women of the same age, bearing children at the same time and under the same historical circumstances, made quite different decisions. The Central European women restricted their families to one or two children, the Turkish women to three or four—and the Persian, North African, and Israeli Arab women bore families of eight, nine, ten, or more children. As a consequence, in middle age most Central European women and many Turkish women look back with regret for children they refrained from bearing during those difficult times, while the Persian, North African, and Israeli Arab women do not. Indeed, the Persians, whose migration brought them from traditional settings where large families were an economic asset to crowded city apartments where many children were a mixed blessing, sometimes regret today that their families are so large.

These predictable differences among cultures highlight our most remarkable finding, which is that of similarity of feelings among women from all five sub-cultures about one major change in middle age: menopause, and the loss of fertility. This change, a universal, maturational event which is sometimes thought to be the only developmental change of middle age, was welcomed by women in all five sub-cultures, whether they had borne fifteen children or only one or two. Even those women who looked back with longing for children they had not borne when they were younger did not now want to mother infants, or even to retain the potential for pregnancy. They seemed to be affirming a natural rhythm in the life cycle, reminding us of Ecclesiastes, who claimed that to every thing there is a season, a time to sow, and a time to reap.

But the universal truth of harvest in the middle years is shaped by what is sown in young adulthood. For some women, maturity brings new doors opening into worlds outside the home, along with the companionship that comes with long years of a good marriage, as the children grow up and leave home, creating new freedoms. For others, middle age may mean a sense of continuity between the generations, as grown children begin to provide support and grandchildren recreate some of the pleasure of early parenthood. And for some, middle age brings with it a sense of opportunities missed and gone forever; as we shall see, this is the story of the transitional women of our study, who grew up in the traditional cultures of Turkey, Persia, and North Africa, and who were transplanted by immigration to Israel into a modern culture where the traditional cues they had learned in young adulthood no longer served them. We shall suggest that each of these themes—the new freedoms of the modern women, the generational continuity of the traditional women, and the dislocations of the transitional women—is part of the experience of the transition to middle age: highlighted differently, perhaps, in different cultures, but potentially present in all.

A brief word on tradition, transition, and modernity. We shall be using *tradition* and *modernity* to represent the extremes of a continuum described in some detail in chapter 2, defined on the basis of selected demographic characteristics such as level of education, number of children, whether a woman's husband was chosen for her by her family or the choice was made by the woman herself. Our "modern" women, the Central Europeans, would be considered "traditional" by many young women in the Western cultures of the 1980s: they are middle-class housewives who have had high-school educations, who have borne one or two children, and who may or may not work outside the home. The modernity of the Central European women is defined in relation to the women at the "traditional" extreme of our continuum, the Moslem Arab villagers. Almost all of them are illiterate; they have been pregnant as often as twenty-five times; and despite spontaneous abortions, stillbirths, and the deaths of young children, many have ten or more living children, some of whom are still elementary-school age.

We have chosen the word *transitional* to describe the three sub-cultures—Turkish, Persian, and North African—which are intermediate between the modern and traditional extremes of our continuum. Not only is *transitional* an accurate description of the location of these sub-cultures on our continuum, but it is also a word with dynamic connotations. Though each of the sub-cultures we have studied is transitional—indeed, as we shall argue in our conclusion, we are all transitional—the processes of cultural transition and modernization are highlighted in the lives of the immigrant women from Turkey, Persia, and North Africa.

We located the Persian women at the center of our continuum, in the middle of transition; and at this writing, as the 1970s turn into the 1980s, events in Teheran bear out our decision and our choice of descriptor. The volatile Shiite Moslem clergy, whose history, as chapter 5 will show, is so closely bound up with that of the Persian Jewish immigrant women of our study, are once more arguing that "respect" for women requires a return to the veil. We shall see something of this rhythm of revolution and reaction in the lives of the Persian women in our study.

Our five sub-cultures represent points on a continuum between traditional and modern cultures, and it is tempting to see these points as representative of the process of modernization as well, a temptation which must be resisted. Each of our five sub-cultures is modernizing at its own rate and in its own way. Consider, for example, the lives the Persian women and their daughters might have led if they had not immigrated to Israel: a life of half-steps toward modernity alternating with full steps backward. Compare these women—for whom literacy was just slightly more probable than illiteracy—with the Israeli Moslem Arab women of our study, who are almost entirely illiterate—and whose daughters are high-school graduates: a remarkably swift and still more remarkably painless transformation. This single example, half-hypothetical, should suffice as a caution. If the reader is tempted nevertheless to speculate on the process of modernization—well, so were we. And though we have written within the limits of our data, which permit only comparative descriptions of the women of each of our five sub-cultures, we have often wondered beyond these limits, and we hope the reader will wonder, too.

Our study has its origins in an observed difference in cultural responses to middle age. While on his psychiatric residency, following family practice in Kiryat Shmona, a settlement town on the northern frontier of Israel, Benjamin Maoz observed that women who came from the countries of the Near East and North Africa were almost never hospitalized for involutional depression, while hospitalization was seen among women of European origin. Aaron Antonovsky, a medical sociologist, confirmed this difference in rate of hospitalization as characteristic of national health statistics for Israel. While involutional depression, a diagnosis which many have challenged as failing to represent a distinct nosological entity, affects less than 1 percent of the population, Maoz and Antonovsky speculated that the observed difference in rate of hospitalization for a relatively severe disorder might reflect cultural differences in stressful or supportive climates for middle age—differences which would affect all women, impeding or facilitating the transitions of middle age.

Three hypotheses were formulated to explain the differences in rate of hospitalization for involutional psychosis:

1. Differences in cultural patterns create varying degrees of stress in middle age; this stress is greatest for the modern, youth-oriented European culture, and manifest not only in the extreme response seen in involutional depression but also as nonpathological stress among normal women.

2. Stress may be more or less equal across cultures, but manifest as psychiatric complaints among European women and expressed as somatic complaints among Near Eastern women, since there are cultural differences in the permissable forms of expressed stress.

3. Stress may be more or less equal across cultures, but the diagnosis of involutional psychosis is made more often among the European women, due to some combination of the doctor's readiness to observe psychiatric symptoms and the woman's readiness to perceive and communicate psychic distress.

Antonovsky and Maoz proposed a broad-scale study to explore the consequences of cultural differences for women making the transition to middle age. Their general view was that greater stress could be anticipated among European women, who had planned and restricted childbearing, and who might therefore be seen as "denying" their femininity. Thus, the European women might view menopause as the loss of a potentiality which had never been fully expressed. The traditional women, by contrast, had fulfilled their feminine potential; they could be expected to welcome the relief from childbearing which would come with menopause, and would look forward to the raised status of the matriarchal role. Support for this view could be found in the psychiatric literature, where writers such as Helene Deutsch suggest that menopause is seen as a "closing of the gates" and an omen of aging and death.

Nancy Datan brought to the study a perspective from developmental psychology which led to a contradictory view: the European women, who had been involved in roles inside and outside the home, would find menopause and middle age a time of new freedom. Traditional women from Near Eastern cultures, by contrast, whose only role had been that of childbearer and mother, would find the loss of fertility both salient and stressful. Indirect support for this view was found in the developmental literature; direct support came from the study of Bernice Neugarten and her colleagues of 100 middle-class American women, who found the changes of menopause less significant than social changes, such as children leaving home, and who generally welcomed the cessation of fertility.

Our contradictory predictions about the relationship between tradition and modernity and the psychological well-being of women anticipated some of the debates over women's roles which began in the 1960s, have gained vigor in the 1970s, and promise continued vigor in the 1980s. It was our very good fortune to go into the field with sharply defined areas of disagreement; these helped prepare us to appreciate our findings, which, as we shall see, do indeed provide some answers to the question of the effect of the transition to modernity on the well-being of women.

Our study was designed to address two major issues:

1. What is the relationship between traditionalism or modernity and the psychological well-being of women in middle age?
2. What is the relationship between a woman's childbearing history—as shaped by the expectations of her culture—and her response to the loss of fertility?

Our study was carried out in four phases. The first phase was a pilot study during which semistructured psychiatric interviews were conducted by Maoz with 55 women of European, Near Eastern, and Israeli Arab origin. On the basis of findings from the pilot study, a closed interview schedule was constructed for the second phase of the study, a broad-scale survey among 1,148 women from five Israeli sub-cultures ranging along a continuum from modernity to tradition: immigrant Jews from Central Europe, Turkey, Persia, and North Africa; and Israel-born Moslem Arabs. The survey questionnaire dealt with aspects of middle age, including social roles and role satisfaction, attitudes toward menopause, menopausal symptomatology, self-reported psychosexual history, demographic information, and self-reported psychological well-being, broadly conceived to include the psychological, the social, and the somatic.

All women from the second phase of the study were invited to participate in the third phase, a medical examination. Of the 1,148 women who agreed to take part in the survey, 697 consented to the medical examination. There was somewhat more readiness to cooperate in the medical examination among women in the more traditional groups, but this difference was not statistically significant. The medical examination included a pregnancy history, a general physical examination, the woman's self-reported assessment of her physical and psychological well-being, and the physician's overall rating of her physical and mental health.

The fourth and final phase of the study consisted of follow-up psychiatric interviews with 160 women, sub-samples from each of the five ethnic groups in the survey who represented the high and low extremes with respect to self-reported psychological well-being. Among other findings, considerable agreement was seen between the women's self-report and the psychiatrist's diagnosis, although the psychiatrists had no prior knowledge of the women's responses. That is, a woman whose self-report indicated a high measure of psychological well-being was likely to be evaluated by the psychiatrist as well adjusted; conversely, women reporting low levels of psychological well-being on the survey interview were often independently evaluated by the psychiatrist as somewhat depressed. These findings were interpreted as a measure of support for the validity of the survey responses. A more detailed discussion of the four phases of the research can be found in appendix 1.

As we have seen, this study has its beginnings with clear, conflicting predictions. Antonovsky and Maoz anticipated that traditional culture would prove more supportive of the middle-aged woman, basing their argument on the negative valuation of aging in modern, youth-oriented cultures, and drawing support from traditional psychoanalytic views of menopause as a "closing of the gates," with femininity unfulfilled for the modern women, who planned and restricted childbearing. Datan rejected these views, arguing that the traditional woman's identity is bound up exclusively with the childbearing function, and is therefore diminished by the cessation of fertility, while the modern woman, with multiple roles and childbearing long since completed, would see middle age as a time of new beginnings. Put very simply, these conflicting predictions reflect a central theme in current debates over women's roles: whether a woman's "natural" place is in the home among her children, safe inside boundaries crossed only at her peril, or whether a woman's place is socially defined, and is now being redefined to permit her the broader horizons which are her "natural" right. And this, of course, is the broader question to which we have referred: What is the effect of modernization and changing sex roles on the lives of women? As we shall see, our study invites consideration of this question.

1 | The Faces of Eve

Comparative
Perspectives
on
the
Women
of
Israel

A mong the standard preworded telegrams available for dispatch from any
Israeli post office is the following statement, of Talmudic origin, a variant
form of congratulations on the birth of the firstborn: "A firstborn daughter is a
sign of many sons." No symmetry exists; sons are welcomed with the feast of circumcision, a celebration of such importance that it takes precedence over the fast
of the Day of Atonement—and nowhere is the birth of a firstborn son interpreted as the happy (or dismal) forecast of a series of daughters. It is difficult,
therefore, to avoid the conclusion that the intent of the Talmudists was to incor-
porate consolation into congratulations—perhaps adding, slyly, "Tough luck,
try again." Contemporary scholars seeking the roots of sex-role discrimination in
Jewish tradition need not look far.

It is a brief but thought-provoking ride from the central post office in
Jerusalem to the Knesset—the parliament of Israel, a government as barnacled as
most, with one exception: its response to the prospect of a woman prime minister
was a sign of political relief. Israel is a young country, though Judaism is an
ancient religion; this paradox might easily be seen as nothing more than a species
of cultural time-warp. Alternatively, and also correctly, this blithe political
egalitarianism can be viewed as part of the harvest of the kibbutz revolution for
the abolition of inequality between the sexes. Finally, of course, one may point to
the uniqueness of Golda Meir—there are no other women wielding comparable
power in the government of Israel—and propose that the national response was
simply a reflection of Machiavellian clarity of perception: at that moment, under

those circumstances, she was, so to speak, the man of the hour; and the government of Israel, a vulnerable political entity, could not afford to overlook her.

No doubt each of these efforts to explain away the peculiarities of female power in a state where Orthodox Judaism and Islam sit in the government side by side with the sons of the secular kibbutzim has its own measure of truth. Yet the paradoxes are more engaging than any explanation. Israel is a country where the face of a woman may be seen on a political campaign poster, or veiled for modesty in the vegetable market. Feminist reforms in mid-nineteenth-century Europe have made their effects felt among the European immigrants to Israel, as have the more recent reforms of Ataturk in neighboring Turkey on the immigrant Turkish women. At the same time, a sign in Mea Shearim, the Orthodox Jewish Quarter of Jerusalem, enjoins women to dress modestly—that is, in long-sleeved blouses and long skirts; pants are prohibited—and women who do not comply may be received with hostility.

Paradox and change are no less dramatic in the Moslem population of Israel. Polygyny was outlawed by the Israel government, and education for girls was made compulsory. Within the lifetimes of the women in our study, literacy—almost unknown among women in the villages—became universal. Almost none of the Arab women in our study can read or write; many of their daughters are certified high-school teachers. The close ties between the generations are a tribute to the strength of the traditional family, a strength easily ignored by those who welcome change.

The Equal Rights Amendment to the American Constitution has been a subject of concern and even bitter debate in the United States. From a cross-cultural perspective, this concern seems unnecessary. Israel has an equal-rights declaration which prohibits discrimination by race, creed, or sex; and a social critic is tempted to remark that without this proviso women's rights would be unprotected, for Israel is the land which gave Western civilization its traditions of male dominance and female subordination. The traditional sex roles are expressed in Genesis as Adam and Eve are expelled from the Garden of Eden: Eve is told, "In sorrow thou shalt bear thy children; thy desire shall be to thy husband, and he shall rule over thee," and Adam is told, "In the sweat of the face shall thou eat bread." With the passing of time, men's sweat has been mitigated by industrial technology, and modern medicine mitigates women's woe in childbirth; yet the roles of the working man and the homemaking woman can be seen as the enduring expression of biblical tradition, surviving in Israel today in the villages as well as in the cities—and challenged by the paradox of a woman's political rule.

Many traditions in Judaism and Islam are, according to most anthropological criteria, constraints on women and indicative of male dominance and female subordination. These include the traditional bride-price, ritual separation during menstruation, ritual periods of uncleanness following childbirth, and the fact that the period of uncleanness is twice as long for the birth of a daughter as for a son. Competing with the traditions of religion are the traditions of the secular ideology of the kibbutzim, founded by the immigrants of the Second

Aliyah, who came to Israel between 1905 and 1914, bringing with them a pioneering ideology, secular and egalitarian, which was perfectly suited to the circumstances of the land: dry or swampy or rocky, and available for redemption only through the marshalling of all available human resources. Radical changes in sex roles occurred during this time, well known to everyone who has taken an interest in the kibbutz: childrearing was collective, freeing women to share the duties of heavy labor and military defense. Men did not, however, take the primary responsibility for childrearing by becoming child caretakers; thus we may say that in a sense the kibbutzim, at least at first, masculinized everyone in the service of egalitarianism. The problems implicit in such a process have been expressed by women in the United States as well as in Israel as liberation for two jobs—work inside the home and out, with relief from neither. More than half a century has passed since the kibbutz experiment was begun, and this problem is not yet solved.

The pioneering kibbutzniks were joined by a subsequent wave of immigration from Central Europe in the 1930s; this second stream brought an alternate model of the emancipated woman, professional rather than farmer. A number of forces converged in the history of Israel at this point to support and further the emancipation of women from their traditional roles; and at the time of the founding of the State, fundamental laws were passed guaranteeing equal rights irrespective of sex. At the same time, however, coexisting with these pioneering women who are so familiar to us were groups of women who were quite traditional in many ways. They were devout, Orthodox Jews from Central Europe, who were as highly educated as their secular, pioneering counterparts, but who continued to observe religious ritual. There were Jews from Near Eastern countries, where no comparable movement for religious reform had occurred, and where the movement for the emancipation of women which had occurred in Europe 100 years ago was only beginning at the start of this century. Finally, there were traditional Arab Moslem villagers, whose lifestlye has been compared by Raphael Patai to that of the biblical Hebrews. In short, the unique circumstances which created the State of Israel brought together within a very small space and for a very brief time—for these striking differences across cultures were to disappear rapidly among their children and their children's children—women who represented not only different ways of life but also different points along a continuum as tradition yielded to modernity—or, more correctly, to new traditions.

The hope which guided our study was a hope of discovering something about the effects of modernization on the lives of women. It is said that in middle age one discovers the truth in cultural clichés: "We get too soon old and too late smart"; "If I had known then what I know now"; and the ultimate threat, "Wait until you grow up and have children of your own." The women of our story are grown up with children of their own; they have grown old enough and smart enough to know what they might not have known earlier; and the dramatic, changing historical circumstances of their growing up have ensured that they have seen alternatives to their own lives. Our study offers them a chance to tell us how their family life—that most sensitive barometer of social change—seems to them now, in the years when they reap the harvest sown in young adulthood.

As researchers, of course, we are not immune from the discoveries of truths in clichés; our questions grew from modest beginnings—the small puzzle of differential rates of hospitalization for an infrequent depression in middle age—to grander proportions. We hoped, as we began our investigation, to explore the effects of the degree of modernity on a woman's response to menopause and middle age. We wish, now that our study has been concluded, and now that we know what we didn't know then—the answers to our original questions—that we had asked other questions as well. Among our unasked and unanswered questions a few stand out. Of these, one is simple. We failed to ask the women of our study whether they used the ritual bath following menstruation, a ritual shared by Jews and Moslems, and an easy, precise, behavioral measure of the extent of traditional constraint on certain aspects of female sexuality, in a cultural tradition which identifies as the three chief sources of ritual impurity corpses, lepers, and menstruating women.

A second unasked question is more general. Our questions were phrased, often explicitly, to encourage women to respond in terms of their immediate cultural context. For example, we asked, "Compared to other husbands of women you know, how did your husband treat you over the years?" We did not ask the alternate version of this question, which might be phrased—now that we know what we didn't know then—as follows: "Israel is a land of many cultures. You've probably had a chance to see some of the many ways people from other cultures live. How would you compare your own family life to that of families of other cultures?" Questions of this sort would have represented a major undertaking, a new dimension to our research, if not an entirely different study. Yet the fact that these questions went unasked should not go unremarked.

Finally, we regret the fact that we could not have it both ways—a broad-scale cross-cultural normative study of women in middle age complemented by in-depth exploratory, descriptive interviews. The reader, we feel, will share this regret with us when we turn to our case histories, taken from our follow-up psychiatric interviews and used in this book to illustrate aspects of middle age in each of our five sub-cultures. These interviews served us as diagnostic measures, intended to help us assess the agreement between a woman's self-reported psychological well-being and a psychiatrist's independent diagnosis. They serve that purpose well, but they serve less well as illustrations: a summary statement by the interviewing psychiatrist makes us wish we could have eavesdropped, with the aid of a tape recorder, on the entire interview. Along with us, the reader will often want to hear the women of our study speak for themselves, and, as we have done, the reader will have to settle for percentages available in full in appendix 2.

Each of our unasked questions can be defended in the context of our research—which, like any other study, was carried out within the confines of a finite budget, and represented a negotiated compromise between the infinite and the feasible. Indeed, perhaps no defense at all is necessary, for our study would have been a failure if it had left us with no new questions. We invite the reader to share, along with our findings, our unsatisfied curiosity.

We shall proceed to an overview of the five sub-cultures of our study in chapter 2, highlighting the demographic contrasts among the women of these groups, and the modern, transitional, or traditional social contexts in which they live. The five succeeding chapters, chapters 3 through 7, will acquaint us with each of the five sub-cultures, proceeding from a brief history through a demographic portrait; a description of the social context of middle age; a view of sexuality, past and present; psychological well-being, which we define as the balance of joys and sorrows. Chapter 8 takes us beyond the bounds of our study to a cautiously speculative excursion into the meaning of modernization and the changing roles of women, as we now see these issues in light of the findings of our study as well as the new questions it has raised for us.

2 | Five Cultures
An Overview

The ethnic groups selected for our study were chosen to represent broad variation along a cultural spectrum ranging from traditionalism to modernity. Sampling is the art of the possible: our samples represent crude approximations to a continuum. As this brief overview will demonstrate, our five ethnic groups represent five points along a continuum marked at one end by the traditional woman, whose husband was chosen for her, who is illiterate, whose life has been given to childbearing, who is devoutly Orthodox; at the other end of the continuum by the modern woman, who chose her husband, who has had at least a high-school education and often beyond, who planned childbearing, and bore one or two children, who works (or wishes she did), who has moved away from religious orthodoxy, and may keep only a few traditions, or be completely secular. Between these two extremes our three transitional groups are found. Our demographic measures are rewardingly consistent with the order our five ethnic groups have been chosen to represent.

It is, therefore, essential to take note of the questions we cannot answer because of the populations we failed to sample. First, sampling constraints led us to select regions where a particular ethnic group was concentrated: thus our Central European women are middle class, as are most Central European immigrants of comparable age in Israel. As subsequent chapters will suggest, however, lower socioeconomic status among Near Eastern immigrants is a consequence of selective immigration to Israel and the harsh economy in the early 1950s, the period of large-scale immigration from the countries of the Near East. Thus, for these groups, ethnic identity, socioeconomic status, and degree of modernity are confounded.

Similar qualifications apply to the native-born Moslem Arab village women. Patai (1959) has suggested that folk life among traditional Arabs in the nineteenth- and twentieth-century Middle East is essentially comparable to the life of the ancient Hebrews as recorded in the Bible. This group was therefore selected to represent the extreme traditional end of the continuum. However, this selection excludes from our study modern, urban Moslem Arabs, an omission which should not go unremarked.

Furthermore, in choosing ethnic groups which approximate a continuum, we have had to leave unexplored many more subtle issues. For example, in the groups we have selected, demographically defined modernity is coupled with secularism. This is not invariably the case: there are groups of devoutly orthodox Jews and Moslems who obtain advanced education and professional training, as well as groups of uneducated nonbelievers.

Other omissions, which represent intriguing directions for inquiry, include such populations as kibbutz women, for whom the changes of middle age may be quite different, just as earlier events in the family life cycle are experienced differently; and Christian Arab women, whose religious traditions do not include the elaborate ritual menstrual taboos common to Judaism and Islam. However, our study attempts only a broad sweep across cultures, and we must leave the finer brushstrokes for future research.

Many of the traditional folkways seen in the Arab villages have also been preserved by observant Jews in the countries of their dispersion, and the mores governing sexuality and family life among the desert Hebrews were still being followed within the walls of European ghettos up to the present century. Thus, although there is great variation among the Middle Eastern and Central European cultures of this study, there is a common element of particular significance: many traditions, particularly the traditions which shape the sexuality of women, are fundamentally similar.

The foundation of the laws governing sexuality and family life is found in Leviticus. Jewish and Moslem writings, the Talmud and the Koran, subsequently interpreted and elaborated these laws; but despite these refinements, and some new practices added in the Koran and discussed in detail below, the network of ritual which governs the female sexual life cycle is essentially comparable for Jews and Moslems.

Leviticus prescribes a distinction between male and female beginning at birth; if a male child is born to a woman, she is "unclean" seven days, the child enters into the Covenant of Abraham (circumcision) on the eighth day, and she remains unclean thirty-three days. But if a female child is born to her, "then she shall be unclean two weeks, as in the time of her separation"—that is, the ritual separation for menstruation and seven days thereafter—"and she shall continue in the blood of her purifying sixty-six days." Thus the birth of a daughter is unmarked by any ceremony, the initial period of ritual impurity is likened to the routine ritual separation for menstruation, and the total period of impurity is double that for the birth of a son.

The laws governing menstruation set the menstruating woman apart as impure; she remains impure for seven days after the conclusion of menstruation; and she is made pure again only after a ritual bath. The ritual bathhouse, the *mikvah,* is constructed so that the bath consists of continually flowing water. During menstruation, a married woman is prohibited not only from sexual relations, but also from sharing her husband's bed: she moves to another bed during the menstrual period and for the seven days of ritual impurity which follow. Nor may she prepare his food, or touch his clothing, or have any other physical contact with him, either directly or indirectly, during this time. Sexual relations, even between husband and wife (and any other sexual relationship is prohibited and punishable by death), and even during the permissable days of sexual contact, render both man and woman ritually unclean: they must have a ritual bath, after which they remain unclean until the evening. While sexual pleasure within marriage is commended as part of the sacred marriage bond, it is subordinated to the greater good of procreation, preferably of sons.

Judaic interpretation of scriptural law, initially a body of rabbinical decisions which was deliberately handed on as "oral law" to distinguish it from the inflexible, divinely inspired Torah, was first codified and recorded in writing during the period between 200 B.C. and 200 A.D. These writings constitute the first division of the Talmud, the Mishnah; the second division of the Talmud, the Gemara, is a body of interpretations of the Mishnah. The Mishnah is divided into six orders, one of which deals with women; the tractates of this order treat levirate marriage, marital obligations, the revoking of these vows, the Nazirite vows, adultery, divorce, and betrothals. Menstrual taboos are treated elsewhere, as a tractate within the order dealing with ritual purity—which commences with the observation that the three chief sources of ritual uncleanness are corpses, lepers, and menstruating women. The summary of Talmudic laws which follows is no more than a brief overview of the most salient issues seen by the rabbis as requiring clarification. Within the Talmud exist prescriptions and proscriptions on almost every imaginable aspect of female sexuality. As will subsequently be shown, further elaborations are found in Moslem tradition.

According to the Talmud, a girl could be betrothed at as young an age as three days. Furthermore, the sages remarked that a man could marry her in any of the three prescribed ways: by giving her a ring, by reciting the marriage vows, or by having sexual intercourse. The marriage ceremony typically includes all three, but any one act by itself is sufficient for legal marriage. This discussion, in the tractate on Betrothal, is contradicted by statements in the tractate on the Menstruant, which make it permissable for a girl, even after betrothal, to refuse sexual intercourse if she has not yet menstruated or has not yet grown at least two pubic hairs. The statement that a three-day-old girl could be acquired in marriage by sexual intercourse is therefore most probably a symbolic indication of the general subordination of women to men.

In childhood, the primary sex-role distinctions were the strong emphasis on study for boys and the absence of any such emphasis (though study was not forbidden) for girls. Furthermore, while men sat apart from women when worshipping in a synagogue, girls less than twelve years old were permitted to sit with men. Entry into adulthood was marked by bar mitzvah ceremonies for boys at the age of thirteen; a girl's bat mitzvah—which, unlike a boy's, entailed no study of scriptures—was at twelve years, indicating the rabbis' awareness of different maturational rates in boys and girls.

After her twelfth birthday (or after menarche, if it occurred earlier), a girl could no longer sit among the men at worship. Furthermore, once she had begun menstruating, it was considered desirable for her to marry soon. Marriage involved paying a bride-price to the girl's father, as well as a ring, a marriage contract, and sexual intercourse. Orthodox Jewish marriage up to the present day has not altered these rituals, and since no other form of marriage in the Jewish community is recognized in Israel—where family law has remained within the religious communities since the Ottoman Empire—even nonbelievers must specify a bride-price on their marriage contract.

Because sexual intercourse alone was sufficient to legitimate marriage, sexual relations with any person other than the first partner—unless divorce intervened—constituted adultery, punishable by death. However, the sages recognized a woman's vulnerability to rape, and therefore her word was accepted if she claimed that sexual relations had occurred against her will—provided this happened outside the town, where "she might have cried out, but no one heard her." Such a case inside the town was more doubtful, some rabbis contending that she would be heard (and was therefore lying if she claimed otherwise), and others accepting her claim. However, if a woman accused a man of rape under any circumstances, generally her word was taken against his. Since adultery was a capital offense, and both men and women were liable to death by stoning, the willingness to accept a woman's claim over a man's constituted a major departure from the general pattern of male dominance. By contrast, in Moslem practice, often only women were punished by death for adultery, as will be discussed later.

A ritual bath at the conclusion of menstruation was prescribed for all women; however, in the case of the single woman, this was the only restriction, and, unlike the Moslem woman, she was permitted participation in any religious ritual where women had a part. For the married Jewish woman, menstruation also entailed avoiding physical contact of any sort with her husband, including preparation of his food or even directly handing him any object, which would instead be put on a table for him to pick up.

The rabbis paid considerable attention to the determination of a woman's menstrual status; a woman was supposed to inspect her body, and there was much disputation over what color a fluid must have to be identified as menstrual blood. Five colors were finally determined to be unclean: "Like the blood of a wound," "like the color of sediment," "the shade of the bright-colored saffron," "a color like that of water which has had the earth of the Valley of Beit Kerem stirred into it," and "the color of two parts of water mixed with one part of the wine of Sharon." The imagery of the sages, like the customs of the Moslem women in this sample, suggest that their concern was not sanitation, but rather a concern that the menstruating woman was potentially very enticing, to be avoided only through adherence to elaborate proscriptions.

Pregnant women were not unclean, though a bloody discharge required the same ritual exclusion and bath at cessation as did menstruation. Miscarriage rendered the woman unclean according to the prescriptions of Leviticus for birth: for a son, one week, followed by thirty-three days of purifying; and for a daughter, twice this period; while for a fetus whose sex could not be determined, the ritual purification lasted for a period equal to the time observed for a boy plus the time observed for a girl, in sequence. Rabbi Meir suggested that a woman who had weaned a child imparted uncleanness for the twenty-four hours just prior to the weaning, but his view was rejected and the lactating woman was considered unclean only at menstruation.

Menopause was defined by the majority of the sages as follows: "Who is deemed an old woman? Anyone over whom three periods have passed [without menstruating] at the time of her old age." A minority dissented, defining an old woman as a woman of any age who had missed three menstrual periods and was not pregnant. No role or status changes were associated with menopause in the Talmudic discussion, although the woman was naturally freed of all the taboos incumbent on the menstruant.

The Talmud dealt chiefly with possible violations of the law, such as theft, murder, or adultery, or ritual taboos, such as those concerning menstruation. There were, however, positive injunctions for fulfilling the roles of wife and mother, although these were brief and included in discussion of legislation against violations of the law. Wives were not to refuse their husbands sexual relations, nor were husbands to refuse their wives; sexual satisfaction was seen as a component of the marriage bond. In the case of polygynous marriage the husband was to divide his attentions with scrupulous fairness regardless of his own personal preference.

Mothers participated, though apparently only as role models for their daughters, in the often-repeated command to teach one's children diligently, and to keep the law, from generation to generation. In the main, however, the law was passed from father to son. A woman's role was that of maintaining a home and bearing sons for her husband (Mishanot: Nashim, Taharot); this changed little until the reform movement in Judaism developed in Central Europe, as we shall see in chapter 4.

The traditions of Islam evolved in part from biblical Jewish traditions, and many components of these rituals are shared. The menstrual taboos prescribed in Leviticus and described earlier in this chapter are repeated in the Koran: contact with a menstruating woman is forbidden, and following the conclusion of menstruation the woman must perform a ritual purification of her body; after bathing herself, she must immerse herself as many as seven times (depending on her caste) in pure water. Any bathing vessel will serve, however; no ritual bathhouse is required, as it is in Judaism. Moslem taboos extend to a prohibition on prayer, fasting, contact with the Koran, or any other religious act; Judaic taboos are confined to sexual contact between husband and wife.

Sexual intercourse, under Moslem codes, does not constitute a marriage bond. On the contrary, there is no prohibition against a man's premarital or extramarital sexual activity, so long as his partner is neither an unmarried girl or a wife, in which case he has committed an offense against the father and brothers in the first instance, or the husband in the second instance, and he and the woman are both punishable by death. In practice, however, it is often the woman alone who is killed, often by her father or brothers. This occurs occasionally even in Israel, where it is outlawed by criminal code and the father or brother knows he will easily be identified and brought to trial. The extreme harshness of this double standard for sexual activity is a dramatic example of the subordination of women to men even today (Patai, 1959).

In addition to religious commandment, there are customs which vary by locality. Sa'id Na'awi, public health officer at the Ministry of Health regional public health center which served the women of our study, described the customs followed by women in this locality. The woman was obliged to leave her husband's bed for the duration of menstruation, and she was not to approach him in his bed. During menstruation she dressed herself in old, soiled clothing, and did not comb her hair or make herself attractive in any way, so as to avoid wakening sexual desire in men.

During menstruation it was forbidden to women to visit mourners, to attend a funeral, or to enter a cemetery; it was forbidden to visit women in childbirth for fear of complicating the delivery; and it was forbidden to visit a woman who had recently given birth for fear of harming the baby or its mother's future fertility. It was also forbidden to step across the body of a sleeping or sitting man, for fear of causing him to break out in a rash. Finally, pregnant women were forbidden to visit a bride not yet married forty days, for fear of harming her future fertility. No special restrictions applied to lactation, but it had special significance in that a woman nursing another's child thereby created "milk-ties," the equivalent of blood ties between siblings, between her own child and the other child.

To sum up, Jewish and Moslem traditions closely circumscribe the sexual life cycle of women. Ambivalence over the enticing, dangerous, "unclean" menstruating woman is a common theme in both traditions. For the women in our study, modernity implies distance from religious tradition. As the brief comparative overview which follows will suggest, there are concomitant changes in the family life cycle, with accompanying differences in access to extrafamilial roles, which lead us to expect marked cultural differences among these five groups in the response to menopause and the changes of middle age.

Table 1 presents a comparison of the five ethnic groups in this study on selected social characteristics which are relevant as background to the study. This comparison serves as a preface to the more detailed descriptions which follow in chapters 4 through 8.

The modal Central European women in this study is at the modern end of the hypothetical continuum between tradition and modernity. She is comparatively well educated, and received her schooling—at least some secondary-school education—in her native country, and did not migrate to Israel until young adulthood. One-half of the women in our sample managed to escape Europe before World War II; the others came shortly thereafter. Thus the modal woman in our study is of veteran status in Israel, with the problems of finding housing, mastering Ḥebrew, and adjusting to an unfamiliar way of life all many

Table 1. Selected Social Characteristics by Ethnic Group (percentages).

Item	ETHNIC GROUP				
	Central Europeans	Turks	Persians	North Africans	Arabs
N =	(287)	(176)	(160)	(239)	(286)
Illiterate	0	29	61	60	96
Married before age 16	0	5	35	37	30
Married at age 21 or older	78	51	15	20	22
Husband selected by family	7	46	75	56	95
Conflict with family over choice of spouse	17	23	42	28	16
Seven or more pregnancies [a]	8	19	64	67	79
One-half or fewer of pregnancies brought to live birth [a]	47	17	6	4	4
Seven or more live births [a]	0	5	53	59	72
No children dead after birth [a]	92	77	52	42	22
Five or more living children	0	14	68	68	76
Five or more children currently living at home	0	3	29	36	53
Children now under age 14	16	30	47	57	56
Total childbearing span less than 7 years	70	35	13	20	10
Satisfied with number of children borne	28	47	39	48	59
Wishing to have borne more children	68	38	35	42	19
Wishing to have borne fewer children	3	16	26	10	22
Grandchildren	32	62	79	76	78
Working outside the home (full or part time, including family business or agriculture)	42	21	29	25	35
Feels "needed" by extended family member	46	60	62	51	17
Husband illiterate	0	25	49	53	66
Husband nonmanual worker	77	36	16	22	12
Currently religiously orthodox	21	30	57	85	98
Currently believe family should choose spouse	1	12	21	19	52

[a] Percentage based on medical sub-samples.

years behind her. She has settled in a large, affluent—by Israeli standards—town outside Tel Aviv.

She married in her early twenties. The choice of husband was hers rather than her family's; indeed, due to the Holocaust, many women had no family in the country when they married. Her husband, like her, is of European origin, and may have been slightly better educated; he is most likely a white-collar worker, and perhaps a professional.

Childbearing was planned by the European woman, and was typically restricted to one or two children. In retrospect, she wishes very much that she had borne a larger family, but says that economic conditions during her childbearing years kept her from having more children. Abortion is an available and acceptable technique for terminating an accidental pregnancy, and was used by many of the women in our study at least once or twice. Childbearing was delayed for some years after marriage, and thus the period of the empty nest is yet to come for most of the women in our study—and does not coincide, as is often the case for American women, with menopause. Most of the Central European women in our study still have children at home, either teenagers or unmarried young adults. Only one-third of the Europeans have become grandmothers. Two-fifths feel needed by a member of the extended family, often to maintain the only kin ties remaining after the Holocaust. About two-fifths work outside the home; of these, one-half work full time and the others part time, chiefly at clerical jobs.

Modernity can be seen in the high proportion—two-fifths—of Central European women who observe no religious ritual at all. An equally high proportion observe only some traditions, perhaps only keeping the major festivals. Only one-fifth of the Central European women describe themselves as devoutly Orthodox. Thus, both in values and in their lifestyle, these women represent a marked departure from tradition, as will be seen more clearly by contrast with succeeding groups.

The Turkish women in our study may be characterized as transitional in two ways. First, when we do see a modal Turkish response, it is less modern than the modal European response, but more modern than the three more traditional groups; second, on many items there is considerable internal variation, and in such instances responses can be found which are characteristic of modern, transitional, and traditional women.

The women in our study were born in Turkey just as Ataturk was initiating wide-scale reform and modernization. The modal Turkish woman is likely to have received some education and is probably literate, but she did not progress beyond elementary school. She married in Turkey at about the age of twenty. Just over one-half of these women chose their own husbands; close to one-half married a man selected by their family—sometimes reluctantly. Most immigrated to Israel during World War II as young adults, or during the 1950s, the years of mass exodus from Arab countries. Like the European, then, the Turk is a veteran in Israel; however, she is not as well-to-do. Her husband may have completed elementary school, but not likely more than that, and he may be a laborer, skilled manual worker, or, at best, of the lower middle class. She and her family live in Tel Aviv, the largest city in Israel, and affluence is all around them; but they are unlikely to move beyond the confines of their lower-income neighborhood.

Although there is variability in family size, the modal Turkish woman in our study has three children. Having married and begun childbearing sooner than the European, she is already a grandmother; at the same time—allowing for variations in childbearing span—considerable numbers of Turks still have school-age children at home, though none has small children now. Three-fifths of the Turks feel they are needed by some member of their extended family, usually for emotional ties. Only one-fifth of the Turks work outside the home, usually as unskilled workers, such as maids or child caretakers.

Although more of her life is given over to childbearing, and there are more traditional aspects in her background than in the European's, the Turkish woman's current values are clearly modern. She observes little religious tradition, and she does not feel the family should select a girl's husband, whatever her own experience. The modernization of religious and social influences on women's roles which took place a century ago in Europe, however, has taken place during her lifetime; if the European woman can take modern values for granted, the Turkish woman is learning modernization along with the society in which she has grown up.

The establishment of the State of Israel initiated a period of mass migration from Persia. An estimated 35,000 of a total of 90,000 Jews migrated between 1948 and 1955. Lacking both agricultural and white-collar skills, they were only slowly absorbed into the lower and lower middle classes of the urban Israeli population. In Tel Aviv, just as they had been in Persia, they are neighbors of the Turks; but they have failed, both as a nation and as a religious community, to make the strides toward modernization made by the Turkish Jews.

The modal Persian woman in this study has had little or no education, and she can neither read nor write. She married at about the age of sixteen; her family chose her husband, and she may well have opposed the choice. She bore a very large family, perhaps seven children or more, despite frequent miscarriages and deaths of children in early childhood. One-half of the Persian women still have children under age fourteen living at home; at the same time, 85 percent have become grandmothers. Nearly two-thirds feel needed by some member of the extended family, usually for emotional needs. About two-fifths of the Persians work outside the home, nearly always at unskilled manual work such as household help.

Like the Turks, the Persians are in transition toward modernity, but they have farther to go. More than one-half of the Persian women in our study consider themselves religiously Orthodox, and of the remainder nearly all observe some traditional practices. They do not, however, feel that a girl's husband should be chosen by her family, contrary to their own experience. More often than any other group, furthermore, the Persians now say they would have liked to have borne fewer children. Thus, though they have not abandoned religious tradition, their present attitudes toward marriage and childbearing suggest a rejection of traditional female role expectations—and perhaps of their own lifestyle.

Although they live side by side with the Turks in modern Tel Aviv, the Persian women are farther away from affluence and modernity. Their husbands, with less education, are most often unskilled laborers, and not infrequently welfare cases; their more meager income must be stretched for a larger family. It is probable that the tension resulting from disparities between a traditional life style and values which are shifting toward modernity—exacerbated by economic disadvantages which are to some extent related to their traditional life histories—is more acute for the Persians than for any other group.

In the mass exodus of Jews from North African countries which followed the establishment of the State of Israel and the accompanying rise in Arab nationalism, the upper stratum of North African Jewry migrated to France, while the uneducated, unskilled masses fled to Israel. The women of our study and their families came to Israel and settled in two adjacent towns. Located halfway between Jerusalem and Tel Aviv, where the foothills of the Judaean Mountains yield to the fertile coastal plains, the towns are isolated in an agrarian setting. Though both Tel Aviv and Jerusalem are near, the North African women are not surrounded by affluence or modernization. They live in crumbling Arab-built homes at the core of each town, or at the periphery of town in huge government housing projects built for economy and not for beauty. The pace of modernization is slower here than in the cities, and affluence, for the North Africans, is not next door but rather an inter-city bus ride away.

The modal North African woman in this study spent the first thirty-five years of her life in Morocco. She is likely to be illiterate, and she has had, at best, no more than elementary schooling. Nearly one-half of the North African women in this sample were married before the age of sixteen; in over one-half of the marriages the family determined the choice of spouse, usually with the girl's approval, and of those women reporting that the choice of spouse was theirs, most also report that their families approved. Instances of family choice of a husband urged upon a reluctant girl are considerably rarer among the North Africans than among the Persians, and slightly less frequent than among the Turks.

Childbearing took a major part of the life cycle for most North Africans. Three-fifths of the North African women in our study have borne seven or more children, and an even greater proportion (67%) have been pregnant at least seven times; however, both miscarriages and the deaths of children after birth were very common. At the time of our study, three-fifths of the women had children under age fourteen living at home; at the same time, four-fifths had already become grandmothers. About three-fifths of the North Africans feel needed by a member of the extended family, most often for emotional ties. One-quarter of the North African women are employed outside the home, usually at unskilled work but sometimes at semiskilled work.

The socioeconomic status of the North Africans is similar to that of the Persians: one-half of the husbands of the women in our sample are illiterate and are unskilled laborers or welfare cases. Nevertheless, their relatively disadvantaged status is not exacerbated by constant exposure to affluence: on the contrary, they reside in comparatively homogeneous towns made up of Near Eastern immigrants who cannot afford anything better. Without the stimulation—whether abrasive or not—of cultural pluralism, the North Africans have not shifted toward modern values as the Persians have. Most North African women describe themselves as religiously Orthodox (75%). Though some of their ways have changed—all but one-fifth now feel a girl should select her own husband—the North Africans are a fairly traditional group.

The Arab women in our study were born into the traditional setting of the village, and their lives reflect a traditional way of life. Born before compulsory schooling for girls, almost all (96%) are illiterate. They married somewhat later than the Persian and North African women—the median age at marriage for Arab women was seventeen. This difference may be due in part to the bride-price, higher in Israel than in neighboring Arab countries. The choice of husband was nearly always made by the family, and opposition was seldom reported by the women. This general acceptance is probably closely linked to the prevalence of arranged marriages in traditional Moslem Arab culture and their perception of this pattern as normative.

Childbearing has taken up a major portion of the lives of the Arab women in our study. Most have had seven or more live births. Miscarriages have been frequent, however, and, in addition, one-third of the group have lost three or more children after birth. At present, then, just over one-half have seven or more living children, as a consequence of the comparatively high mortality rate in early childhood. The bearing and rearing of a large family, therefore, required a very high number of pregnancies in order to compensate for the losses through miscarriage, stillbirth, and death of children in early childhood.

Over one-half of the Arab women in our study have five or more children living at home, and over one-half still have children under fourteen years of age. At the same time, four-fifths of the Arab women have already become grand-mothers. Thus, not only is there no drop in involvement with the maternal role as the Arab women reach middle age, but it remains on a level which is considerably higher than that in any other group in our study—while at the same time, most of the Arab women have also become grandmothers.

By contrast to every other ethnic group—and rather surprisingly, in view of the importance of the extended family in traditional society—less than one-fifth of the Arab women say they feel needed by any extended family member; and when they do, it is for instrumental tasks such as help in the home or child care, rather than for the emotional support reported by women in other groups. As will be discussed in chapter 7, we have surmised that the network of emotional support may be taken for granted by the Arab women in our study, and thus goes unremarked and unreported. Over one-third of the Arab women work out-side the home—a proportion higher than that seen among the transitional women—chiefly at agricultural work.

The Arab women continue to reaffirm traditional values, with less shift than in any other group. One-half of the women continue to feel the family should choose a girl's husband. Nearly all characterize themselves as religiously obser-vant. Although the Arab women of our study, like the immigrant Jewish women, have experienced the anxieties of three wars, they are the only group which has not undergone the dislocations of geographical mobility. While the land around them has changed dramatically in their lifetimes, within the villages change is taking place more slowly and without the discontinuity of migration.

As this brief overview has suggested, the five ethnic groups in our study represent broad variation along a continuum from tradition to modernity. Although they differ historically in many respects, the effect of a common religious and cultural tradition shaping the lives of women can be seen in every group—from the Central Europeans, among whom a movement took place to reform these traditions, to the Arabs, whose rituals add further restrictions to those inherited by Islam from Judaism, and who continue to follow their traditional ways. The following chapters will explore the consequences of these differences, commencing in childhood and shaping young adulthood, in women's responses to the changes of middle age.

3 | The Central Europeans

"I daydream of traveling abroad."

The Central European women in our study reflect a recent chapter in the history of the Jews of Europe, which is one of exile and persecution alternating with periods of peace and prosperity.* When the Black Plague devastated Europe in the fourteenth century, it left in its wake locked ghetto walls sealing off Jews from their neighbors. These walls, or their legal equivalent, were to remain until the French revolutionary spirit spread across Europe. The Jews of France were voted free and equal citizens in 1791; and, after a series of attempts which failed, equal civil rights were granted Jews by the Austrian constitution of 1849— only to be rescinded in 1851. The Prussian constitution of 1850 separated civil and political rights from religion, although discrimination in practice was not eradicated. Not until 1871, eighty years after the French emancipation, was full emancipation for the Jews proclaimed in the German Imperial Constitution, achieved under the empire of Bismarck.

A survey of the Jews of the Austro-Hungarian Empire in 1914, the start of the decade in which the women of our study were born, shows Jewish communities emancipated and their freedom formally guaranteed. In Hungary, despite a brief, intense resurgence of anti-Semitism in 1882, a Jewish population numbering almost one million felt the position of Jews to be legally secure, and their cultural and professional prominence to be equal to any Jewish community in the world. The 175,000 Jews of Austria were concentrated in Vienna, contributing significantly to the advance of the arts and sciences. The 360,000 Jews of Czechoslovakia included prominent artists and literary figures. Germany of 1914 was not free of anti-Semitic discrimination, but its 500,000 Jews contributed to the enrichment of German literature, science, and philosophy. The Jews of Central Europe, then, although still somewhat restricted, had achieved positions

*See Bibliography for sources used.

24

of distinction in the history of European culture by the turn of the century. But in 1914, just as the first of the women of our study were born, all this was about to change.

Following the devastation of World War I, several causes, such as the new nationalism in Czechoslovakia and postwar economic collapse in Austria and Hungary, revitalized latent anti-Semitism across Europe. During the same years Jewish immigration to Palestine, endorsed by the Balfour Declaration in 1917, increased. The community of 55,000 Jews in Palestine just after World War I was swelled by successive waves of immigration from Europe until it stood at 550,000 in 1939, on the eve of World War II. By this time, one-half of the women of our study had arrived in Israel.

The emancipation of the Jews of Central Europe and their rise to positions of prominence in European culture was accompanied by parallel activities leading to the emancipation of women and their participation in cultural life—activities which seem at times to foreshadow issues in the feminism of the 1960s and 1970s, while at times some recent issues in feminism seem to repeat the battles for equality fought more than a century ago in Europe.

In the middle of the nineteenth century increased urbanization and accompanying economic changes led to a strong movement for political, cultural, economic, and social equality for women, with an initial focus of concern on health and welfare for all women and children. In 1841 the German Jew Lina Morgenstern began her work in the field of child welfare; in 1864 Henriette Goldschmidt founded the Allgemeine Deutsche Frauenverein; in 1896 the International Women's Congress met in Berlin.

In Austria, as emancipated Jews became progressively more assimilated into Central European society, wealthy Jewish families began to bridge the social gap between the bourgeoisie and the nobility. The women of these families became hostesses in the growing salon society, and Jews came to dominate this level of Viennese society. These women were also professionally active, as doctors, lawyers, administrators, parliamentary delegates, teachers, writers, and painters.

Despite the high proportion of Jewish women active in the movement for women's emancipation, no specific large-scale Jewish women's movement existed until the beginning of the twentieth century, with the establishment of the Jewish Women's League in 1904. In the main these movements were organized along social class and sex lines, attempting to raise the status of the poor and to protect women and children from exploitation. However, Jewish organizations began to grow as anti-Semitism once more began to increase.

The processes of emancipation and assimilation affecting the Jews of Central Europe and the women of Central Europe were accompanied by a movement to reform Jewish religious practice—much of it discriminatory against women— which had its origins in Germany. The motivations behind the reform movement reflect the social forces affecting European Jewry and further differentiate European Judaism from the Judaism of the Near East, where no comparable movement for reform ever took place. The European movement for reform in

Judaism derived its impetus from two sources: on the one hand, the spirit of the Enlightenment encouraged the discarding of all religious practices not supported by reason and the needs of modern society; on the other hand, the Jews of Germany wanted to show their readiness to accept the responsibilities of German citizenship by eliminating such conflicting elements in Judaism as loyalty to Zion and a Hebrew liturgy. The movement toward Reform Judaism was strongest in Germany; and, though the reform movement later split between radicals and conservatives, a major transformation in religion—comparable to social and cultural emancipation—took place in Central European Judaism.

Despite great diversity in the various reform movements, there was a general liberalizing tendency: in the synagogue, the screened, secluded gallery for women was eliminated and men and women sat together for worship; the elaborate framework of sexual and menstrual taboos was simplified and reduced in the prescribed code of observance, and there was greater tolerance for individual variation in the observance of these rituals. Both by implication and in practice, then, these changes indicated a rejection of the subordinate status of women as it had been set out in biblical codes.

The Jews of Central Europe were the most thoroughly acculturated in the world, and just as their emancipation was most complete, so was that of the women of these communities, who held positions of prominence in most professions and in many areas of European cultural life. And the Jews of the countries of Central Europe, the most completely assimilated of any Jewish community in the world, were the first to be attacked by the Nazis.

The Nuremberg Laws were enacted in Germany in 1935, prompting many Jews to immigrate to Israel—among them families whose daughters would be among the subjects of this study. Austria was taken in a bloodless coup in March, 1938. In September of the same year the Sudetenland was ceded to Germany, and in March, 1939, the remainder of Czechoslovakia was invaded. Action toward the destruction of these Jewish communities was not taken, however, until relatively late, subsequent to action against the Jews of Poland; mass extermination of the Jews of the Greater Reich was carried out in 1943. During that year 180,000 German Jews, 60,000 Austrian Jews, and 243,000 Czech Jews died. In March, 1944, Nazi troops entered Hungary, and 100,000 Jews were exterminated within a few months.

The British Mandate Government in Palestine enforced the restrictions on European immigration set out in the White Paper of 1939. From the time of the White Paper, throughout the years of World War II, until the establishment of the State of Israel in 1948, Jews succeeded in reaching Israel only by way of complex escape routes from Europe and illegal immigration ships making secret night landings on the coast of Israel. The survivors of Nazi Germany were not able to immigrate openly to Israel until 1948.

The scars of European history are woven into the rhythm of developmental change in the case history of one of the European women. Born in Hungary in 1921, she was the third of eight children in a devout Orthodox family whose home was a small village, where her father owned a company which manufactured church decorations. She completed ten years of schooling. During the war she married and moved with her husband to a large city—a move which saved her life; her entire family died in the Holocaust. Her own survival was not simple: first her husband, then she, were taken to forced labor camps, and their daughter was sheltered by a Gentile family.

The family was reunited at the end of World War II and managed to immigrate to Israel in the wave of "illegal immigration" carried out against British opposition. They reached Israel in 1946, and settled on a kibbutz. In Israel's War of Independence, her husband was killed at the age of thirty-three.

Since that time her life has been dedicated to her daughter. She never remarried, and her life has been a constant struggle for adequate income and economic support. She is bitter about the Ministry of Defense and its insufficient support for widows. The effort to survive occupies all her time.

The psychiatrist's summary is brief: "Tragedy. It is hard to talk about emotional pathology or about 'disturbances in femininity'—these are the consequences of a terrible life. Perhaps the single neurotic element is that after the death of her husband in 1948 she was never encouraged to remarry. Instead she struggles on for the sake of her daughter, who is now twenty-two; who knows what will happen when the girl marries?"

As we shall show, the shadows of European history can be seen to interact with the developmental rhythms of the life cycle for the women of Central Europe.

DEMOGRAPHIC CHARACTERISTICS

Just over half of the 287 Central European women in our sample were born in Germany and Austria, over one-third in Czechoslovakia, and the remaining 14 percent in Hungary. Their birthdates cluster around the end of World War I and the disintegration of the Austro-Hungarian Empire.

The Central European women are at the pole of modernity on the continuum represented by our five ethnic groups. They are a relatively well-educated group: over three-quarters had at least some secondary education, obtained by almost all in their native countries despite the adverse social and political climate of their youth. Most of these women came to Palestine after the age of eighteen, and just over one-half managed to leave Europe before the outbreak of World War II. Slightly over one-quarter of our sample—that is, half of those who did not succeed in leaving Europe before war broke out—went through the concentration camps. Not one of our sample is a new arrival in Israel; all but seven arrived prior to 1952.

Almost all the Central European women married, at the median age of twenty-three. As modern women do, many (40%) chose their own husbands, with the family blessing; but many others (39%) married under the cloud of

World War II, with no family around to bless or to blame. Finally, some chose their husbands in the face of family opposition (14%). The traditional pattern of "matchmaking" has almost entirely vanished in this population, in the wake of women's emancipation—and the war.

Most of these women married peers, men not more than five years older than themselves; only rarely (14%) was the husband older than his wife by a decade or more. While almost none of the women married non-European men, the effects of the turbulent interbellum period and of migration are reflected by the fact that almost one-half of the women are married to men born in a country other than their own country of origin. Three-quarters of the ever-married women are still married to their first husbands; despite the dislocations of war in Europe and in Israel, only 13 percent have been widowed, and more than one-half of those have remarried. Divorce (9%) is less frequent than widowhood, and has almost always been followed by remarriage.

The European women have small families, and childbearing is generally planned through contraception, coitus interruptus, or the abortion of unwanted pregnancies. Almost three-quarters have no more than one or two children; only 17 percent have three children; and childlessness is more common (7%) than a family as large as four children (3%). However, one-half of our subjects have been pregnant four or more times, while only 3 percent of the women have given birth to four or more live babies. The medical histories* suggest that for this group much of this loss is due to induced abortion. By contrast with early termination of pregnancy, however, pregnancy brought to term in this population meant excellent chances for the child's survival; 92 percent of those women with at least one live birth had no children who died thereafter. This association of pregnancy with planning and the happy news of a live birth is very much a phenomenon of modernity, as we shall see by contrast with our four more traditional groups.

Central European women are still involved actively as mothers; four-fifths of those who bore children still have at least one child living at home. The "quickening" of the family life cycle which is characteristic of modernization can be seen in the timing and duration of childbearing: most of this group (87%) bore their children within nine years or less. And for more than one-half of the women, the youngest child at home is at least eighteen, while not a single woman has a child under six years old. The children are, for most, nearly but not quite grown up: more than one-half our women do not yet have married children. Some do, however; and one-third are already grandmothers.

Like their middle-class wives, not one husband of the women in our sample had less than four years of school; more than one-half had some secondary school; and one-quarter had some university education. One-third of the husbands are professionals, or owners or managers supervising at least ten

---

*The data in this paragraph are based on the medical examinations. As can be seen in appendix 1, those examined are representative of the total group.

employees—which in Israel is a substantial enterprise—while only one-fifth are manual workers, almost all of them skilled.

Being middle class and modern go together: two-thirds of these women report spending almost all their leisure time with their husbands, while almost none rarely or never spend time together. These women anticipate autonomous partnerships for their daughters, too; all but three women feel a girl should choose her own husband, though it is hoped that the family will agree. The cultural values implicit in these behaviors and attitudes represent not only a move toward sexual equality but also a move away from tradition, which is reflected in our subjects' religiosity. Two-fifths of the sample describe themselves as completely secular, another two-fifths report just some traditional observance, and only the remaining one-fifth characterize themselves as Orthodox or devout. Measuring modernity independently of ethnic identity, we found four-fifths of these women to be at the extreme modern end of our index.*

The typical Central European woman, born during the collapse of the German and Austro-Hungarian Empires, is the demographic prototype of the middle-class, modern woman of her generation. She was likely to have grown up and received her schooling—at least some secondary education—in her native land, and did not migrate to Israel until young adulthood, just before World War II—or as a survivor, shortly thereafter. She married at twenty-three; her husband, just a few years older than herself, had perhaps a bit more education than she did, but the disparity was not great. Unlike their shared socioeconomic background, there was a fair chance his national background would be different from hers. There was little question that the choice of spouse was hers: often, she was without family when she married. Her marriage was stable, though widowhood and divorce were not unknown among her friends. She was very unlikely to have more than one or two children, in a relatively brief period of childbearing. Although accidental pregnancies might occur, abortion was an available and acceptable technique for terminating a pregnancy. Once born, a child's chances for survival were very good. Her few children were not born immediately after marriage, and so she still has children at home, as teenagers or older, but probably not yet married. When they do marry, she feels it should be to partners of their own choice, though she would like to approve. She is not at all devout, though she observes some religious traditions. Her free time is amost always spent with her husband, when he too is free from his office work.

The themes of modernity find expression in the case history of one of the Central European women. Born in Czechoslovakia in 1915, she was only six months old when her family moved to Berlin. Her father, a businessman, responded to the changing political climate by moving his family—a wife and three daughters, of whom our subject was the middle-born—to Israel in 1934, when she was twenty.

She married a lawyer in private practice, like herself an immigrant to Israel,

---

*This index, along with all other indexes, scales, and typologies, is described in appendix 1.

but born in Bialystok. They live comfortably with their two daughters: the older, 22, began law school upon completing her army service; the younger, 19, is presently in the army.

Although she is currently managing well, she is apprehensive about the period of the "empty nest," after her daughters leave home for good. She intends to respond by going out to work. She already assists her husband with office work, but she wants very much to be fully occupied, and plans to solve the problem of the "empty nest" with full-time work.

THE SOCIAL CONTEXT OF MIDDLE AGE

The European woman finds her role as spouse is stable, satisfying, and central. Most women (61%) say they need their husbands a great deal; even more (71%) feel greatly needed by their husbands. There are very few women who feel they do not particularly need their husbands, and even fewer who do not feel needed by their husbands. For more women (63%), the spouse role, as measured by their perception of their husband's need for them, has been stable over the past ten years; if not stable, it has been increasing (30%). The perception of need in the marital relationship seems to be somewhat greater for the Europeans than for women in our other ethnic groups, although the differences are not great. When it comes to what the women feel needed for, however, the difference becomes dramatic. The affective component of the marital relationship is its core for most European women (65%), and its importance is not rivalled by any other category of response. This may be why the overwhelming number (85%) feel satisfied with the extent to which they are needed.

While the role of spouse is stable or even increasing in importance, the role of mother is on the decline. The children of the European women, as we have noted, are grown, but not all are grown up, and the period of the empty nest is around the corner, if not already in sight. The European women see themselves as moving out of the mother role with some rapidity, almost one-half saying they are needed less by their children now than they were at the age of forty, and few saying they are needed more. Two-thirds unequivocally reject the suggestion that they are sorry to see their children becoming more independent, while three-quarters feel their children appreciate them. And the large majority disagree (58% disagree strongly) with the idea that children nowadays do not pay much attention to their parents.

The European woman's response to her children's diminishing need for her seems to reflect her security in her role as well as her perception of the nature of motherhood. When asked what her child needs her for, two categories stand out as characterizing the Europeans: affective and cognitive. As a mother she seems to feel that what she is needed for is the emotional tie which, though its character might change, need not be attenuated over time; or, on the other hand, guidance, advice, help in studies, which might be expected to promote autonomy and independence and thus ideally bring about a diminished need in time.

If motherhood is on the decline, grandmotherhood is on the increase. Less than a decade ago, almost none of our European women had grandchildren; almost one-third do have grandchildren now, while another 14 percent have married children and may be expecting grandchildren. At middle age, then, the role of grandmother is just beginning for the Europeans, while for more traditional groups grandchildren have been around for a while.

Almost two-thirds of those with grandchildren see them at least once a week. For most the primary tie is a modest one: just visiting, knitting and sewing for them, giving presents. A few report their primary function as babysitters, some even caring for the grandchildren while the mother goes to work. Overwhelmingly, the role—not an extensive tie for most—suits them well. No more than a handful feel grandchildren either demand too much of them or, on the contrary, prevent them from doing things they would like to do. On balance, most women express a satisfactory and increasing involvement in grandmotherhood. To these must be added the women in our sample who are not yet grandmothers, but look forward to it soon.

Changes in the homemaking role seem to reflect concurrent changes in family roles. Homemaking was intentionally defined as going beyond routine household activities to include "things you do to improve the house, knitting and sewing, work in the garden, and so on." One-half of the Europeans spend quite a large part of the day in homemaking activities; very few (11%) have hardly any involvement in homemaking. However, it is a declining role, perhaps related to the fact that the children are growing up: 43 percent say they spend less time in these activities than they did when they were forty. The decline does not seem to bother most: a majority are satisfied with the time spent in homemaking.

Other family relationships parallel that with the spouse, though of course on a much smaller scale. Just under one-third of the European women reported that they were very much needed by at least one relative outside the nuclear family, while another third felt somewhat needed; for some (22%), this is a growing role in recent years. However, almost one-third report no relatives who need them; of those whose relatives need them, 43% feel no change since the age of forty. Finally, a small minority feel burdened by the demands of this role (17 percent of those who feel needed at all). For most, the relationship is evidently satisfying: three-fifth of the women see their relatives at least weekly. Role satisfaction may come from the nature of the tie: it is—as is the case in other roles—essentially affective rather than instrumental. As we shall see, in more traditional groups this tie is more often task-oriented than emotional.

The European women as friends and neighbors do not fit either of two common stereotypes: neither the supposed anonymity of the urban, middle-class housewife nor the kaffee-klatsch culture of the suburbanite. Less than one-third "get a chance to really chat with friends and neighbors almost every day"; for almost equal numbers, such encounters are rare. For a plurality of the Europeans, then, this role is relatively minor; furthermore, its importance has diminished in recent years. One-third of the women now spend less time with friends and neighbors than they did at age forty; only 13 percent report an increase. This decline parallels the decline of the mother role, and suggests the possibility that young children around the house tend to keep the mother in the neighborhood, in turn creating greater opportunity for such informal contacts. While almost two-thirds of the women are satisfied with the amount of time they have with friends and neighbors, this decline is unwelcome for some, who would like to have more. As we shall see below, this is not the only role in which a significant minority seeks greater involvement. What is more, in considering interpersonal relationships, it would appear that blood is thicker than water: friendship is a less satisfying role than spouse, relative, or grandmother, in which we see satisfaction and stability if not increased involvement; it is also less satisfying than motherhood, in which there is a decline which is not unwelcome. By contrast, almost one-third of the European women would prefer more involvement with their friends than they presently have.

Institutional arrangements in Israel are far more convenient for the woman who wishes or has to work than in most other countries, and indeed many European women take advantage of the opportunity. More than two-fifths of our sample work, half of these full time. Of those who work, one-fifth are in professional and managerial occupations, more than two-fifths in clerical and sales positions, and almost all the remainder are skilled manual workers (for example, seamstresses). Since age forty, there have been some changes: some work now who did not work then, and vice versa; some work more now, and others less. But the overall change is in the direction of a slight decline in participation in the labor force; and as a group, the European women are not happy about this decline. One-quarter of the women work and find pleasure in their work; another quarter do not work and do not wish to; but more than one-third do not work and wish they did.

To the extent that any of our five ethnic groups participates in avocational activities, such as volunteer work or adult education, the European women do. But even among the Europeans it is uncommon, involving less than one-fifth of the group. Organized avocational activities are not a norm in Israel, even for middle-class women like our European subjects; however, as we shall see, the low rate of involvement does not necessarily reflect a lack of interest. While there is no evidence of volunteer activities having increased for our subjects, looking to the future it is possible to anticipate an increase, at least if attitudes are indicative of future behavior. Almost without exception, the women engaged in volunteer activities are happy about them; and more than one-half of those not so engaged today indicate, with varying degrees of enthusiasm, that they would indeed like to be doing something of the sort. Only one-third are uninvolved and satisfied. Like work, volunteer activities attract a substantial minority of the European women, and may reflect a desire to fill the increasing free time as children grow up and leave home.

To sum up, the dominant role for the European woman is that of wife; it is a central tie and is expected to stay that way. As the children grow up and leave, immediate involvement in the mother role is declining, although this tie is seen as one of affection rather than deeds, and is expected, therefore, to continue. Grandchildren may have arrived or be expected soon; the European women anticipate this role with pleasure. Involvement with relatives outside the nuclear family is not great, although there has been some recent increase; not much change in this role is expected. Concurrent with changes in the nuclear family, there has been some decline in involvement with homemaking, but no dissatisfaction with this change.

By contrast, there is a general sense among the European women that more time could be spent outside the home, at work, with friends and neighbors, or in volunteer activities, and there is a measure of dissatisfaction with the present level of involvement in these roles, perhaps reflecting the increase in available time and energy as the children grow up and leave. However, looking across changes in all roles, we do not find that horizons are narrowing for the European women. For more than one-half (58%), at least four roles have remained the same or demanded increased involvement; and three-fifths of our subjects express satisfaction with the nature and extent of their involvement in at least four of these eight roles.

The social context of modernity is suggested by the case history of one of the European women, who was born in Germany in 1919, the younger of two children from a secular, middle-class home. She completed twelve years of school, although she did not graduate. In 1938 she immigrated to Israel, where she lived for three years on a kibbutz.

She has been married for twenty-seven years to her second husband, after a brief first marriage. Her husband, fifty-six, runs a tourist agency. He has suffered three mild cardiac attacks. She herself is healthy; she is employed in a children's nursery. The couple has three children: the oldest, twenty-six, is a chef in the United States; the two younger children are twins, aged twenty-three, the son an accountant and the daughter a beautician. All three completed secondary education.

She reached menarche at thirteen, completed menopause at forty-six, and reports no symptomatology; she was glad to finish up with menstruation. Her full-term pregnancies and births were normal; in addition, she reports eight induced abortions, having become pregnant very easily.

She worries, with reason, about her husband's heart condition. They have abstained from sexual relations recently because of his condition, and she misses sex a little.

Sometimes she still longs for the wealth they had and were forced to leave behind in Germany; she daydreams about winning enough money to permit her to travel abroad. Meantime, in addition to working, she is part of a small social group which meets twice a week to play cards and sometimes gets together to watch television, still a social novelty in Israel. Notwithstanding the current stress of her husband's illness and the past dislocations of war and immigration, she is a cheerful, open, contented woman, moving easily into the changes of middle age.

SEXUALITY: PAST AND PRESENT

A woman enters her sexual maturity with the first menstruation, an event which takes its meaning from her cultural context. For the European women, menarche signifies the beginning of adolescence; as we shall see, for women in more traditional cultures, sexual and social maturity come together.

Asked to recall their feelings at the first menstruation, the European women offered a tempered recollection of menarche. One-third chose only positive or positive and neutral words from among the choices offered; just one-quarter chose only negative words; for most, feelings were mixed and muted. Our pilot interviews suggested that preparation for menstruation was frequent, though not universal; we surmise that this played some part in their response.

The recollection of adolescence, on the other hand, was generally positive. Despite the fact that for so many this period was marred by the rise of Hitler, very few recall adolescence in negative terms. Three-quarters of the European women remembered adolescence in positive, or positive and neutral, terms.

Menstruation was rarely problematic for the European women; by and large they report no special unpleasantness, either in adolescence, young adulthood, or after age forty. A minority recall some difficulty, such as irregular or lengthy menstruation; but on our summary scale, the European women cluster in the low-difficulty scale types.

If there is any norm among the European women's spontaneous responses to questions about menstruation, it is one of affective neutrality. Asked about the best thing about menstruation, just under one-third said it was good for physical health or cleansed the body. One-fifth saw menstruation as proof that one was not pregnant, or still fertile. Another fifth simply said it was "natural." Fifteen percent had nothing good to say about menstruation, and the remaining responses were too diverse for classification. As for the other side of the coin, most, when asked, found something unfavorable to say about menstruation. Forty percent spoke of physical discomfort; 11 percent mentioned limitation of activity; 9 percent spoke of some emotional discomfort. Not many (8%) mentioned uncleanliness, though it will be recalled that in traditional Judaism the menstruating woman is in a state of ritual uncleanness which limits her interaction with her husband and is the basis for excluding her from full participation in religious rituals. It would appear, then, that among these modern European women, a variety of historical antecedents—including religious reforms and a general emancipation of women—combine to yield what might be called an increasing distance between the biological life cycle and the social life cycle.

Adult sexuality, for the European women, is marriage and motherhood. The quality of the marital relationship, for most of the European women, is one of a pacific tie. Most (60%) see their husbands as more considerate of them than is the case in other marriages; and very few feel that they have been treated worse than other wives. Quarreling is infrequent: one-third say they hardly ever quarrel, and almost none report considerable quarreling over the years with their husbands. Within the sexual relationship, satisfaction is more common than dissatisfaction among those responding (up to 11 percent of the women did not answer one of the four questions). Roughly one-quarter of the women described themselves and their husbands as "very satisfied" with their sexual relationship, over the years as well as now, with little difference between wives' and husbands' satisfaction. At the other end of the scale, there were few "not satisfied" responses, although here there is a slight suggestion that wives see themselves as more dissatisfied than their husbands, and that dissatisfaction has increased slightly over the years. We may sum up, however, by noting that the marital history scale indicates that a substantial majority of the European women describe a satisfactory marital relationship, while less than one-third of the sample fall in the negative scale types.

Natural childbirth in hospital, with delivery by a trained midwife, is the general rule in Israel, where most of the babies of these women were born. The European women have coped successfully with problems of pregnancy, childbirth, and infant care. For most, the first pregnancy was without difficulty; only one-fifth miscarried or aborted their first pregnancy, or had predominantly negative feelings about it. Similarly, the first childbirth was typically problem-free; three quarters describe a normal labor, and less than one-tenth report such problems as premature or Caesarean birth; stillbirth was very rare. Adjusting to the new baby was no problem for most; only 15 percent report difficulty. Speaking of later pregnancies, most (all but 17 percent) felt their pregnancies were easier, or no more difficult, than other women's; an even larger proportion felt this way about subsequent deliveries. Four-fifths reported no particular problems in infant care with later children. Looking back, then, most European women found childbearing and motherhood a source of gratification; few remember difficulty.

It is this largely positive experience, perhaps, that can explain a common source of regret in this group. Most of the European women (68%) now wish they had borne more children; almost none (3%) wish they had borne fewer. Asked to explain their feelings about desirable family size, a majority (56%) responded by speaking of the pleasure children bring. One-quarter spoke of the reasons which had kept them from bearing the children they now wish they had had: the difficult circumstances they faced during those years, including, of course, the disruptions of World War II, as well as the economic austerity in Israel during their childbearing years. Only 16 percent mentioned the physical demands of bearing and rearing children.

To sum up, the modal middle-aged Central European woman looks back on the sexual dimension of her young adulthood with satisfaction. Her major regret—a regret tempered by a recognition of objective reality, and not a sense of personal failure—is that she did not have more children. This regret, however, is one which might be expected to have considerable bearing on her response to the changes of menopause—among them the loss of fertility and any chance of bearing additional children.

One-third of the Central European women are postmenopausal; for another 10 percent, menstruation ceased after surgery. About one-quarter are currently in menopause; finally, one-third still menstruate regularly. The median age reported for menopause is 48.4 years, highest of all groups, perhaps as a consequence of advantages in nutrition and general health enjoyed by the European women, who are clearly the healthiest group, with the lowest reported menopausal symptomatology. There is no support for our initial expectation that the European women might tend to report more psychic or psychosomatic than somatic symptoms: each of the three types of symptoms contributes just about equally to the total symptomatology score.

Menopause has many meanings to the European women. Spontaneous responses to an open question about "the most important thing to you about menopause and middle age" (in Hebrew, literally "the age of transition") did not produce a consensus. One-fifth had no answer at all; one-fifth of those responding said there is nothing important about it. The most frequent response (35%) reflected concern over physical health and bodily changes. Almost one-fifth expressed concern over possible consequences for emotional health, a proportion which, though low, is higher than that in other ethnic groups, indicating that there is a measure of relative salience—though it is less than we expected—for the psychological consequences of climacterium in the perceptions of modern women.

Asked to describe the best thing about menopause, 29 percent of the European women had no response. Of those responding, 21 percent cited freedom from child care and greater independence. A larger proportion responded when asked to describe the worst thing about menopause: almost two-fifths who answered spoke of the sense of aging, and a few mentioned an awareness of death. Another 20 percent mentioned problems in physical health which accompanied or followed menopause; only 22 percent had no response.

In addition to open questions calling for spontaneous answers, we asked a series of twenty-three closed questions about changes related to general areas associated with menopause and middle age: loss of fertility, cessation of menstruation, physical health, emotional health, and social and personal changes. Here we found consensus, but it was not what we had anticipated. The strongest agreement was expressed on the questions dealing with the loss of fertility, which, to our surprise, was welcomed. We had thought these women, who so often expressed regret that they had borne so few children, might also regret the finality of menopause. This was not at all the case. Consistently, some three-quarters of the respondents agreed with statements expressing pleasure at the cessation of fertility, and disagreed with statements expressing regret. The summary score of the five items dealing with the loss of fertility shows 73 percent of the European women in the two most positive categories—a finding which is particularly remarkable when we recall, first, that pregnancies were planned in this group, and second, that the period of childbearing has been over for some time for these women. It would appear that the potential for childbearing has meaning which goes beyond the experiential likelihood of bearing children at this age—and, what is more, that its meaning in middle age is no longer positive, since the cessation of fertility is so emphatically welcomed.

Consistency was also seen in the European women's responses to the implications of menopausal changes for the marital relationship. The dominant response to this category of questions was a lack of anticipated change. Menopause, the European women seemed to be saying, makes little difference in my relationship to my husband. This could be seen in several ways. Nonresponse to these items was about as frequent as to the open questions described earlier; and those who did respond generally disagreed with the items, whether phrased positively or negatively. Thus most women disagreed with the suggestion that husbands are more interested in their wives at middle age; they also disagreed that husbands are less interested in their wives at this time. Most also disagreed with the notion that a woman's pleasure in sexual relations changes, either for better or for worse, although a substantial minority (40%) expected some change—about equal numbers forecasting improvement and decline. But the dominant picture was one of continuity and absence of anticipated change in the marital relationship. This was reflected in the summary score, which showed most European women clustered around the neutral and muted positive points on the scale. These responses are consistent with our earlier discussion of the marital relationship; as we have seen, the dominant characteristic of this relationship is its stability.

The other areas we questioned yielded a more complex picture with less consensus, even across items in a single area. This is clearly seen in responses to the items we have grouped together under the heading of physical health. Two items dealt directly with the cessation of menstruation. To our surprise—since our pilot interviews had suggested that this perception of menstruation was found predominantly among more traditional women—a substantial majority (76%) of the European women felt that the cessation of menstruation might be undesirable; they agree that "so long as she is still menstruating, a woman's body is released every month from pressure and harmful materials." Nevertheless, a majority (59%) are pleased "to be finished with the unpleasantness of menstruation." Most do not agree that menopause brings better health and more energy; furthermore, more than half agree that menopause may be a cause of weakness and disease. In general, then, the European women feel that menopause brings with it a decline in physical health, although many are glad menstruation is over. The summary score in this area shows a negative balance: 58 percent of the European women are found in the two most negative categories.

Questions on the emotional consequences of menopause provoke ambivalence, tipped toward a slightly negative balance. Almost three-quarters of the European women agree that a woman becomes more nervous and moody as a result of menopause; almost as many disagree with the suggestion that menopause is followed by greater peace and tranquility. Finally, a substantial minority (41%) agree with the rather extreme assertion that "as a result of

menopause, a woman may go crazy." The summary score reflects this polariza-
tion: 43 percent of the European women are represented in the two most negative
categories; 38 percent are found in the two most positive categories. This, then, is
an area of strong feeling but little agreement; and, though the European women
do not spontaneously speak of emotional distress, and do not themselves report
psychological menopausal symptomatology, if asked whether such consequences
are possible, many agree.

Finally, the area we have called social and personal change elicits a picture of
mixed gains and losses. Most European women do not feel menopause brings a
change in social status, either for better or for worse: the great majority reject the
two statements which suggest increase or decrease in the social status of
postmenopausal women. On the other hand, two positive statements find considerable agreement among the European women: almost two-thirds agree that
"at middle age a woman has more chance than before to take good care of
herself and her appearance," and more than two-fifths feel that a woman is freer
at middle age to do the things that attract her. These gains, however, are offset by
the sense of loss expressed by the considerable minority (43%) who agree that "a
woman begins to age suddenly during change of life." The summary score,
which shows a dispersion, reflects these mixed feelings.

To sum up, the salient—and surprising—finding is that European women,
who planned, began, and completed childbearing long ago, and who look back
with regret on the children they did not bear, nevertheless welcome the loss of fertility. There is general agreement that menopause and middle age do not alter the
stable marital relationship most women enjoy. However, most European women
tend to see middle age as the beginning of a period of decline in physical health,
although many see some compensation with the cessation of menstruation. Questions on emotional health suggest ambivalence, with both positive and negative
feelings. Finally, in the realm of social and personal change, the European
women see a generally balanced picture of compensatory gains and losses.

The interaction of history and individual development as it affects the family
life cycle is dramatically highlighted by the case history of one of the European
women, who was born in 1914 in a small village just south of Budapest. She was
the middle-born of three children in a secular home, and she completed eleven
years of school. Her first menstruation was at age fifteen, and would continue
regularly until it ceased when she was forty-two.

In 1940 she married a mathematician who had been a child prodigy since the
age of ten and was a university professor at the time of their marriage. On the eve
of World War II he traveled on a lecture tour to France, and from there he
escaped to Persia, and she after him. In Persia they married and their daughter
was born; from Persia they moved to Bagdad in 1950, where they were not
known to be Jews. In 1951 they managed to immigrate to Israel by way of Italy.

The pregnancy and birth of her daughter were normal; in addition, she ter-
minated two pregnancies with induced abortions, and two more pregnancies
ended in spontaneous abortions. She wanted more children when circumstances

became more favorable, but was unable to bring her two attempted pregnancies to term; today she looks back on this with regret.

She coddles her prodigy husband like a child. Shortly after his arrival in Israel, he became part of the nation's academic elite, a career not without stress; four years ago he had a nervous breakdown. She endures his temperament and avoids arguments and stress.

Menopause was difficult, with hot flashes which she refused to treat with medication, managing instead on the self-discipline of a survivor. Things are easier for her now, and her health is improved. Her chief sorrow is that she did not have more children.

PSYCHOLOGICAL WELL-BEING: BALANCING SORROW AND JOY

"Psychological well-being" is a fair approximation but an inadequate translation of the emotional dimensions we attempted to capture with questions in the category we have called *tsoris* and *naches,* Yiddish words anemically rendered into English as *trouble/grief* and *joy.* The American constitutional right to the "pursuit of happiness" expresses a one-dimensional notion which few would accept in the Middle East, where idioms are rich with the anticipation of a rhythm of pleasure and pain, and where life is, indeed, often difficult, though struggle (and sometimes good luck) may bring rewards.

Our questions reflect the cultural context in which they were asked, and attempt to measure the balance between worries and pleasures. The modal Central European woman shows a clear net positive balance in this realm, a finding consistent with the picture which emerged from the study of the social context of her life and the dimension of sexuality.

When we asked about pleasures and problems in role relations, we found one role which seemed to be a source of almost undiluted pleasure to the European women. Those who were grandmothers overwhelmingly enjoyed grandmotherhood (83%), with almost no troubles at all (81%). Motherhood was not so easy: a majority (62%) enjoyed their children to a very great extent—but only one-third felt their children were not a source of worry. Marriage, too, was a source of worry along with pleasure for most: 41 percent were at the positive extreme in describing their husbands as a source of happiness, but only 39 percent felt that this relationship was free of worries.

By contrast to family roles, task-oriented roles were less often a source of pleasure, though it was also true that these roles were not a source of worries either. For those who were gainfully employed, work was viewed positively, but without strong enthusiasm. More than one-half (55%) had almost no trouble with their work, but only one-third reported that they enjoyed it to a very great extent. Finally, housework was no trouble at all for most (71%); but very few (15%) reported enjoying it.

The modal European woman, then, sees herself functioning happily, on balance, in her five major roles. She is wholly enthusiastic about being a grand-mother; pleasure is dominant for her in her role as mother and wife, but it is not unmixed with worries and problems. She is considerably less enthusiastic about employment, and gets little or no enjoyment from housework; by the same token, however, these roles are not a source of problems for her. The summary score, based only on those three roles occupied by the great majority of the sample, shows that most (56%) derive more pleasures than worries from their roles; for another one-quarter, pleasures and worries balance out; and only one-fifth feel their worries outweigh their pleasures.

Though, as we shall see, the Europeans describe fewer worries than women in other groups, their lives include the problems of day-to-day existence in a country at war. Our fieldwork was carried out in 1969, during the "War of Attrition"—a period of daily border skirmishes and frequent terrorist attacks, a time when people paused, each hour, to hear the news, and often gathered closer to hear the names of the dead. The European women described general concern over national security; to this was added the personal worry over a family member in the armed forces. These concerns were dominant: even after responses had been given to eight closed items in these areas, responses to an open question about "any other worries" elicited mention of war and its costs from 39 percent of these women. Among the eight closed items, the only question prompting a comparable response was worry over the husband's health, mentioned by just over one-half of the women as a cause for considerable concern. The woman's own health, debts, financial problems in general, and unspecified worries about death were issues that concerned only about one-quarter of the women. Not more than 15 percent of the European women expressed much worry about growing old. The dominant worries of the Europeans, then, are the safety and well-being of family in a country at war—realistic worries in hard times.

Our final series of items dealt with less tangible indicators of well-being, and the European women's responses confirm the image of the modal Central European woman as well-adjusted. Moreover, there is a suggestion of stability, with a touch of optimism: there has been no decline in well-being over recent years, and the future may even bring some improvement. To be sure, there are some women whose lives are quite troubled, but they constitute a small minority.

We asked whether "you feel you might really break down under your problem," and although one-quarter had indeed felt this way sometimes, 62 percent had never felt like this. On the other hand, asked how they feel about what they have gotten out of life so far, one-third are substantially satisfied, and only one-fifth go so far as to say they are not so satisfied. There is no sense of constriction: over one-half feel very free to do the things they wish to do, and only one-fifth feel bound to any extent. Furthermore, most see no change since age forty, and 29 percent feel even freer than they did at forty; only 12 percent feel more tied down. Finally, notwithstanding our earlier finding that many European women believe a woman begins to age suddenly during change of life, 44 percent were satisfied by their own personal appearance, another one-third felt neither satisfaction nor concern, and only one-fifth expressed concern.

These responses seem to suggest that the European women feel a fair measure of satisfaction with their lives; about one-third would seem to feel (as suggested by the summary score) even more positive. At the other extreme, a minority (between 10 and 20 percent) present a quite troubled picture. This generally favorable picture is supported by the three "mood tone" questions. The feeling of having nothing to do, which we take to reflect a sense of emptiness, is very rare: it afflicts only 12 percent sometimes or often, while four-fifths of the women say they never feel this way. About one-half report that they begin and end the day in a generally good mood; only about one-tenth begin and end the day feeling low.

The relative optimism among the European women also appears in their responses to the request to locate themselves on a rung of a ladder whose top represents the best possible life, and the bottom the worst. The mean score shows this group to be contented with the past (at age forty, mean rating 6.2, with a possible maximum of 9) and equally contented in the present (mean rating 6.2), while they forsee a slight change for the better in the next five years (mean rating 6.9). Only 13 to 21 percent ranked themselves, for any of the three time periods, on the four lowest rungs of the ladder. One-third saw themselves at the two highest rungs for the past and the present; this proportion came close to one-half with regard to expectations for the future.

Both the optimism of the European women and an indication of their struggle to achieve it is expressed in the case history of one of these women, who was born in Czechoslovakia in 1920, the seventh of eleven children—whose happy childhood came to an abrupt end not long after she completed high school. Her family was taken to an extermination camp, and she is one of only four who survived. Her own good health—and luck—aided in her escape, which she managed alone.

She met her husband—like herself a Holocaust survivor—in the refugee camps of postwar Europe. They immigrated to the newborn state of Israel in 1949. They have been married twenty-five years, and their relationship is a close, companionable one: she accompanies her husband on all his business trips. He is an engineer, she a housewife.

Her first menstruation occurred when she was fourteen, and brought no surprise; her own two daughters were more shocked than herself when they reached puberty. Her menstruation is still regular, and she is pleased: "Thank God." It is no bother, and it is a sign of health. Her health is still good: she sleeps well, and appetite is "too good"—she cannot keep herself on a diet. But in speaking of this she recalls the extermination camp and cries, admitting that she eats now because she remembers the hunger of those days, and how she used to tell herself, "If only just once I could have enough to eat, I could die content." The memory of those years is still with her, especially at night, when dreams bring back the waking nightmare.

But life is good to her today: a handsome husband and carefree sexual relations; she was pregnant only twice, and bore the daughters of whom she is so proud. "They know everything from piano to *sponga*"—the arduous technique for keeping Israeli floors spotless—and she believes this comprehensive education which her daughters received is far superior to her own impractical childhood, which left her a spoilt child, unready for the rigors of the concentration camp. She herself learned the duties of a housewife with difficulty, and she is happy her daughters can manage anything from a home to the jobs they hold.

She sums up with a note of contentment: she has great satisfaction from her life today, from her husband and her daughters. But her final words cast a shadow; not yet fifty years old at the time of this interview, she declares, "If I die, I die content and at peace."

The European women are survivors; not only the substantial proportion (more than one-quarter of the sample) who were in Nazi concentration camps, or those—thirteen percent—who survived the war by hiding out, but even those who came to Israel before World War II: all can be said to be refugees from the Holocaust. "Psychological well-being," a positive balance between sorrow and joy, is something they have had to struggle to achieve. That is has been won back by so many leads us to suppose that without the catastrophes of young adulthood, a happy middle age would have been within the reach of many more.

4 The Turks

"I tasted nothing of life."

The geographical division of Turkey between Europe and Asia is perhaps symbolic of the transitional state of the Turkish women in our study. In his comparative study of modernization among the countries of the Middle East, Lerner remarked that "Turkey is not yet a modern society in our sense, but it is no longer a traditional society in any sense" (1958). Lerner's measures of modernization were the separation of religious and secular law, representative government, mass education, and the unveiling of women—with its attendant connotations of emancipation from the very strict confines of the traditional female role. These steps toward modernization were changes initiated by Ataturk when he came to power in 1924, and thus took place in the infancy or early childhood of the women of our study. In other words, the modernization of cultural traditions shaping women's roles which took place a century ago in Europe has taken place during the lifetime of the Turkish women in this study, who may thus be said to be transitional in two ways: as participants in a transitional period in Turkish history, and as immigrants from a modernizing society into a modern society.

The process of modernization initiated by Ataturk's reforms spread most rapidly through the concentrated urban sectors of the population, where Jews were found in disproportionate numbers. In 1927 over one-half the Jewish population lived in Istanbul and another one-quarter in Izmir and Edirne; thus, in all likelihood, most of the women in our sample came from the urban centers in which modernization was taking place most rapidly.

The non-Moslem minority communities were well advanced over the Moslem majority with regard to the education of children. This paradoxical advantage was a consequence of the Ottoman government, which had opposed mass literacy over the centuries, producing a disparity in education between Moslem and non-Moslem which can still be seen. The Jewish communities of Turkey were well organized in the early part of this century, and the Alliance

Israelite Universelle established a broad network of schools, making education
the rule rather than the exception. As a consequence, Jewish women were advan-
taged—by contrast to the transitional Persian women, who met double
discrimination, as women and as Jews—and this advantage can be seen in their
relatively high literacy rate: two-thirds of the Turkish women in this study are
literate, while Lerner reported in 1958 that only fourteen percent of the women of
Turkey were literate.

The position of women in Turkey is quite advanced by Middle Eastern standards. In 1926 polygamy was made illegal, and women received equal rights in
divorce; in 1933 they were granted political rights. Unveiling was accomplished
by example and persuasion rather than by decree, and the veil in Turkey gradually disappeared. This successful transition is highlighted by contrast to the events
in neighboring countries: Persian and Afghanistani leaders, impressed by the
pace of social change in Turkey under Ataturk, returned home and decreed the
unveiling of women. In both cases opposing conservative forces reinstated the
veil, which persisted until the time came when more basic educational and social
reforms created an atmosphere in which unveiling could be accepted—unstable
reforms which have yielded once more to revolution and reaction.

Despite the relative emancipation of the Turkish woman, Moslem traditions
are still very strong, and they exerted an influence on the Jewish communities in
Turkey as well. The family is an important and powerful institution, as in every
traditional society, and is governed by the father and elder brothers. But the pattern of male authority is slowly yielding to egalitarianism: although the position
of the Turkish woman is still inferior to that of the European, it is the most
advanced of any Middle Eastern woman but the Lebanese.

The near-equal standing of the Jewish community in Turkey was abruptly
altered in 1942 with the introduction of the "varlik," a capital levy on property
and excess profits which was arbitrarily fixed. Though the tax was abolished after
a year, property and funds were never returned, and the Jewish community suffered heavy losses. No official anti-Jewish measures were taken subsequent to the
"varlik," but latent anti-minority feelings erupted from time to time. With the
establishment of the State of Israel, close to one-half of the Jewish community
emigrated from Turkey. The taxes required for permission to emigrate left many
without financial resources; prohibitions on landowning in Turkey had kept
them from acquiring agricultural skills. Those who came to Israel settled, for the
most part, in lower-income neighborhoods of urban communities, like those in
which the women of our study live.

To sum up: the Turkish women of our study were born into a period of
cultural transition, which would see women slowly emerging from the subordinate status symbolized by polygyny and the veil. In their lifetimes they would
experience a second transition: migration from a modernizing culture to a culture
of modernity. The process—and the price—of these transitions is expressed in
the case history of one of the Turkish women, who was born in Turkey in 1920 to
a family of seven children. Her father tried his hand at many trades, with relative

success in the garment business; her mother was a housewife. She herself went to school in Turkey for a short while; she also worked briefly for a furrier before her marriage, at age nineteen, to a husband two years older than herself.

She was divorced in Turkey from her first husband, however, after seven years of marriage: she remembers him as a coarse, ignorant man, an unsuitable mate for her; she describes herself as more sensitive and gentle. She has one daughter, her only child, now twenty-nine, married, and the mother of a little girl whom she loves very much.

She and her daughter immigrated to Israel in 1949, where she worked at a variety of menial jobs, ranging from maid to fruit-picker. Ten years after her first marriage, she remarried. Her present husband is several years older than she is, and their life, she says, is "okay." She has never stayed home; her years of independence accustomed her to earning her own money, and today she is a seamstress.

She describes herself as a patient woman who keeps things inside herself until she explodes: "That's how God made me." Life is a struggle for her, and always has been; her feeling is that she owes her strict conscience as well as her strong personality to the hard life which has been hers since birth. Her relationship to her daughter is a good one—"That's what I have in my life"—and she hopes for more grandchildren as well.

She owes her social life to her husband's initiative, though she adjusts well and has friends. Their sexual relationship, however, is not a close one; and she remembers her first marriage as no better: in seven years there was almost no sexual contact: "I couldn't stand him—and especially not in bed." This dimension of her life seems unfulfilled: she looks toward old age, asking from God only to see some peace, and looks back on her years of marriage without the sustenance of sexuality with regret. "I tasted nothing of life," she says; perhaps these are the words of a woman who was led by the broadening horizons of transition to expect a little more.

DEMOGRAPHIC CHARACTERISTICS

The Turkish women, like the Central European women, were born during years which marked the decline of their native land from the status of imperial power. Turkey, however, was soon to embark on a period of modernization comparable, in certain respects, to that which had occurred perhaps half a century earlier in Central Europe. The progress—not always smooth—toward modernization can be seen in the demographic characteristics of the women in our study.

For the great majority of the 176 Turkish women in our study, the years prior to adulthood were spent in Turkey. It was in Turkey that those in this group who received any education at all—just two-thirds of these women—went to school, rarely beyond the elementary level. While their level of literacy, as we have pointed out, is high by contrast to the Moslem majority in Turkey—as well as by comparison to the more traditional groups in this study—29 percent of these women are illiterate. This number must be compared not only to the more traditional, less educated groups, but also to the Central European women, where illiteracy is unknown, and probably unthinkable. The universality of education in modern societies may cause us to forget that it represents a social victory—and one which is not complete, particularly for women in traditional cultures.

Some changes in the family life cycle, reflecting the transition toward modernity, can be seen among the Turks. Most of the Turkish women were married in Turkey, and very few (15%) were married before the age of eighteen. The median age at marriage was just over twenty; quite a few (26%) were not married until age twenty-five or later. In more than one-half of the cases the woman chose her own husband. Nevertheless, tradition had not disappeared: for close to one-half the girl's family chose her husband for her, and she did not always accept their choice willingly. For most, the age difference between husband and wife was not great; however, a large minority (39%) married husbands six or more years older than themselves. The Turkish women's marriages are quite stable: 83 percent of the ever-married Turkish women are still married to their first husbands, and only 12 percent have been widowed, while even fewer (5%) have been divorced; most of the widows and divorcees have remarried.

Considerable migration from Turkey took place before World War II: almost one-quarter of the women in our sample reached Palestine before the start of the war. Another one-quarter managed to immigrate during the war despite the British White Paper restricting Jewish immigration. After the war, immigration slowed to a trickle; but within the first years after the declaration of the State of Israel, an additional 38 percent of the women in our sample arrived. The Turkish women, then, are of veteran status, almost as longstanding as the Central European women: only 11 percent of the Turks arrived after 1952.

Most women, then, were married by the time they reached Israel; in these cases, their husbands were also born in Turkey (72%). Those who had come to Palestine in their youth, however, married men who may not have been born in Turkey, though in all likelihood they were of Middle Eastern origin (20%).

The Turkish women's families are just a little larger than the families of the Central European women: 70 percent of the Turks have between two and four living children. Only children are quite unusual (5%), though childlessness is not (10%); families as large as five or more, unknown among the Europeans, can be found among the Turks, though they are far from common (15%). Finally, deaths of children after birth are, in this group, not at all rare (23%).

Childbearing, among the Turkish women, reflects this group's transition toward modernity. For some, the "quickening" of the family life cycle characteristic of modernity—normative among the Europeans—can be seen: 35 percent completed childbearing within a period of six years. It was more often the case, however, that childbearing went on over a decade or longer (41 percent of those who ever bore children). This lengthy childbearing period means that today almost three-quarters of the Turkish women have married children, and most of them (62%) have grandchildren; at the same time, a few still have children under age six at home, some (28%) have children aged six to thirteen, and more (35%) have adolescents, aged fourteen to seventeen. For these women, motherhood is by no means over, although grandchildren have come for most; only a minority (27%) still have no married children.

The husbands of the Turkish women have had more education than the women themselves; but, like their wives, they have not gone far. Only one-fifth went as far as secondary school; most (56%) only had between four and eight years of school, and one-quarter had less than that. In turn, their occupational achievements are not great: unskilled or irregular manual labor is most common (38%), followed by some who advanced to lower middle class or small business (29%); skilled manual work was the third most frequent category (18%).

The attitudes and behavior of the Turkish women show that they are moving toward modernity, but have not yet arrived. Almost one-half of these women married husbands chosen by their families, but only 12 percent today feel this is right. The great majority (78%) think this should be a choice made by the girl, with her family's approval; 10 percent even go so far as to say that the family need not approve. Religious traditions are kept only minimally by the majority (60%); another 10 percent describe themselves as completely secular. The great majority (86%) spend their leisure time together with their husbands.

The modal Turkish woman is transitional in two ways. First, when there is one modal response in this group, it is intermediate between modernity and tradition. Second, this is a group with internal variation greater than that found among the Central European women; measures of central tendency do not reveal those women who are more modern than most, and likewise conceal those women who are still fairly traditional. In our description of the modal Turkish woman, these qualifications should be borne in mind.

The Turkish women in our study were born just as Ataturk was initiating wide-scale reforms and a program of social changes which would be particularly important for the lives of the women of Turkey. The modal Turkish woman in this sample was likely to have received some education; if so, she is literate, but she did not progress beyond elementary schooling. She married in Turkey at about the age of twenty. She is just as likely to have had her husband chosen for her by her family as not—and if so, she probably accepted the chosen spouse reluctantly. She may have come to Israel during World War II, as a young adult. Like the Central European woman, the Turkish woman is a veteran in Israel; however, she is not as well-to-do. Her husband may have completed elementary school, but it is not likely that he went much beyond that; and he may be a laborer, a skilled manual worker, or, at best, lower middle class. She and her family live in Tel Aviv, the largest city in Israel; affluence is visible to them, but they are unlikely to move beyond the confines of their lower-income neighborhood.

Although there is variability in family size, the modal Turkish woman in this study has three children—and it may well be that a child of hers has died. Having married and begun childbearing sooner than the European woman, she is already a grandmother; at the same time, she is very likely to have school-age children still at home with her. While more of her life is given over to childbearing and childrearing, and her traditional origins can be seen in her educational disadvantages and perhaps in the family constraints which affected her choice of husband, the Turkish woman's current values are clearly modern. She observes little religious tradition, and she does not feel the family should choose a girl's husband, though this may contradict her own experience. The modernization of religious and social forces affecting women's roles which took place a century ago in Europe has taken place within her own lifetime, perhaps broadening her horizons without bringing her hopes to fulfillment; she may see further changes in her children's generation.

Some of the processes of transition can be seen in the case history of one of the Turkish women, who was born in Turkey in 1922, the younger of two children. Her father was a peddler and her mother a housewife during her early childhood. She completed three grades in elementary school, but her father died when she was ten and her mother went out to work, and her schooling came to an end.

She married at twenty-one; she had known her husband for six months prior to marriage. One daughter was born in Turkey; this child is now twenty-three years old. The family, including her mother, who presently lives with them, immigrated to Israel in 1949. Her husband is a carpenter; she feels fortunate that she has never had to work in Israel.

Her youngest child is only seven years old, a child born reluctantly as a result of family pressures, some nine years after her third child. In addition to the four births, which were fairly easy, she had two miscarriages and two induced abortions. She has entered menopause and is pleased; she is a grandmother, and it would frighten her to see menstrual blood at her age. In addition, she wants no more children, and the certainty of menopause frees her from this anxiety.

She manages her home well; she is quite attached to her mother, although this is often a source of conflict with her husband. Her home is in general a place of equilibrium, however; and she is very pleased to be a grandmother.

THE SOCIAL CONTEXT OF MIDDLE AGE

Marriage, for the Turkish women, is generally a stable and satisfactory relationship, though it does not have the centrality that the Europeans describe. The perception of mutual need between husband and wife is somewhat less intense than that reported by the European women. Although most Turkish women feel very much needed (67%) by their husbands, and feel they need their husbands almost as much (53%), this proportion is slightly lower than that seen among the Europeans. At the other extreme, it is rare for a Turkish woman to report little or no need in her husband's feelings for her, but this percentage is slightly higher than among the Europeans. This difference between the two groups is greater—though it is still very slight—for that small percentage of Turkish wives who feel little or no need for their husbands. Like the Europeans, the Turkish women see little change in the marital relationship since age forty, and they are generally satisfied; but the small percentage of Turkish women who feel their husbands now need them less (13%), or who wish their husbands needed them more (14%), is double the proportion of dissatisfied European women. Consistently, then, the Turkish women describe their marriages as stable and satisfying; but there is also a consistent, though slight, drop in satisfaction when the Turkish women are compared to the Europeans.

It is the content of the marital relationship which differentiates the Europeans from the Turks, however, and marks the Turkish women as the more traditional group. Affective ties between husband and wife were mentioned by two-thirds of the European women, while less than one-fifth of the Turks give this response. The Turkish marriages are more similar to our three more traditional groups than to the European marriages: one-third of the Turkish women feel they are needed as housekeepers, another third "as wives," and 6 percent feel they are needed as the mother of children, a category which was not mentioned at all by the Europeans. In short, the Turkish marriage differs only slightly from the European marriage in the perception of the intensity of need, but the husband's need, as the women see it, is more often for a homemaker than for a comrade.

The Turkish women are not yet experiencing any contraction in the maternal role. They report that their children need them very, very much (48%) or quite a lot (20%); furthermore, the children's needs have not changed, for the most part (53%), since the women were forty; indeed, their needs may even have increased (22%). This pattern is more or less characteristic of every group except the Europeans, who, as we have seen, for the most part feel their children now need them less. The longer childbearing span among the Turks, as among the more traditional groups, means that for most women there are still school-age children in the home; the perceived sense of increasing need for some seems to bear out the folk wisdom, "Little children—little problems; big children—big problems."

As was true of the marital relationship, the content of the maternal relationship is more often traditional among the Turks than among the Europeans. The Turkish women are more often needed by their children for homemaking chores (29%) and less often needed for affective ties (17%) than are the European women; cognitive needs, commonly mentioned by the European mothers, are rarely (5%) cited by the Turks. Perhaps this is part of the reason the Turkish women have little or no regret (84%) about the prospect of their children's independence. Along with most women in the study, the Turks feel their children appreciate them; and they reject, though less firmly than the Europeans do, the notion that children nowadays do not pay attention to their parents.

Grandchildren have come along for the majority of the Turkish women (62%); for most, this is a relatively recent change. Some, however, did have grandchildren when they were forty (26%); of these, a little more than one-half say they see their grandchildren less frequently nowadays than when they were forty. However, contact with grandchildren is very frequent for most of the Turkish women: of those with grandchildren living in Israel, all but 8 percent see the grandchildren at least weekly, and one-third see them daily—contact which, for most (80%), involves presents, cooking, or sewing. Like the Europeans, the Turkish women generally find their relationship with their grandchildren satisfying (77%). Only a few (11%) feel their grandchildren demand more than they want to give—again, however, this discontented minority is twice as large as it is among the European women.

Homemaking takes up much or most of the day for many Turkish women (60%), but takes less of their time now than when they were forty (54%). This change satisfies most (61%), and may reflect the fact that their children are growing up and leaving—though with their larger families and longer childbearing span, some children still remain at home.

Other family relationships are important for many Turkish women: one-third feel greatly needed, and another one-third needed, by a relative outside the nuclear family. Unlike the needs of husband and children, relatives' needs are described by the Turkish women—as by the European women—primarily in affective terms (61%). These needs have been stable for most (55%) since age forty. The great majority are satisfied by their family ties (80%), which are fairly extensive, involving weekly contact for more than one-half, and at least once or twice a month for another one-fifth.

The Turkish women spend somewhat more time with friends and neighbors than the Europeans do: close to one-half (43%) of the Turks report almost daily contact. Still, many (39%) report a decline since age forty, and about the same number wish they had more time for friends and neighbors. Once more, the Turkish women's responses resemble those of the European women—with discontent just a little more common among the Turks.

Unlike the Europeans, the Turkish women do not often work outside the home (22%), and those who do not work rarely wish they did. This is not surprising, since of those Turkish women who are employed, more than one-half work at unskilled jobs, such as domestic labor. Finally, volunteer activities are very rare (7%), and nonparticipants are, for the most part, uninterested.

The modal Turkish woman, then, feels she is needed by her husband, children, and grandchildren; but she is needed for the daily round of household duties more often than for affection, companionship, or advice. Affective ties are more often salient with relatives outside the immediate family circle. Although the modal Turkish woman has had grandchildren for some time, she still has children around the house; if there is any change in family roles, it is expressed by a slight decline in homemaking activities. On the whole, the Turkish woman is satisfied by her family roles—but perhaps not quite as satisfied as her European counterpart.

Unlike the European woman, however, the modal Turkish woman has little or no desire to work outside the home, or to participate in volunteer activities. In the first place, her work horizons are limited by her relative lack of education, so that the jobs most likely to be open to her are unattractive. And in the second place, while the family is not so demanding as in more traditional groups, the Turkish woman, for the most part, is still fully occupied at home.

The social context of transition is illustrated by the case history of one of the Turkish women, who was born in Russia in 1922 but spent all of her early years in Turkey, until her immigration to Israel in 1936. The early years in Israel were difficult: her father peddled candy, her mother was a housewife, and she herself worked as a maid for two years.

At fifteen, she married a man five years older than her, who was employed in a factory. Her early marriage was without any prior sexual instruction, and her first encounter with sex on her wedding night was shocking and painful. She has remained frightened by sex to this day, and if she and her husband have intercourse, it is always a result of his threats.

Her first child, a son now thirty years old, was born when she was only sixteen. In addition, she has sons aged twenty-five and twenty-three, and daughters aged twenty and ten. Two other children died after birth; two premature births did not survive; she miscarried twice, and had one induced abortion.

She has adjusted herself to her husband, who is a private man and does not like to go out and enjoy himself. She does love to go out and have a good time, but to avoid conflict, she has accepted things as they are: "I am the sort who takes what comes, and takes it for the best."

She is the one with complete responsibility for the household, and manages everything by herself. Her chief source of pride is that she is already a grandmother.

She still menstruates regularly, and speculates that "maybe afterwards the problems start. But if menopause is no bother, it may as well come. Of course everyone wants to stay young, but there is no asking for what you can't have."

SEXUALITY: PAST AND PRESENT

The first menstruation marks a woman's entrance into adult sexuality, an event which takes its meaning from the social context. For the European women, sexual maturity precedes social maturity; for some of the Turkish women, sexual and social maturity coincide. Together with this, the Turks have remained closer to a tradition which defines the menstruating woman as ritually unclean. These factors may help to explain the shift in feelings as menarche is recalled by the Turks, a shift from the generally neutral feelings reported by the European women to the predominantly negative feelings (56%) reported by the Turks—a shift which becomes more pronounced with successively more traditional groups. Like the Europeans, however, most of the Turkish women (78%) describe their teenage years in positive terms.

The Turkish women rarely report difficulty with the menstrual cycle: menstruation was generally regular (83%), and for most (78%) was largely or completely free of any unpleasantness. Like the more traditional groups— though somewhat less frequently—the Turkish women felt that the best thing about menstruation was its beneficial effects on physical health (60 percent, more than twice the proportion of European women giving this response). Not many Turkish women mentioned emotional health (8%), but this proportion was equal to that of European women, whereas this response was extremely rare in more traditional groups. Only 8 percent of the Turkish women had nothing good to say about menstruation.

By contrast, almost one-quarter of the Turkish women said there was nothing bad about menstruation. Of those who did have something bad to say, most (37%) mentioned physical discomfort. More than one-fifth of the Turkish women—nearly three times the proportion of Europeans giving this response—described menstruation as dirty. This seems to bear out our suggestion that menstruation takes its meaning from the cultural context—in the case of the Turks, a culture which defines menstruation as unclean.

Adult sexuality, marriage, and motherhood came sooner for the Turks than for the Europeans, coinciding for some with the teenage years. Almost one-half of the Turkish women married husbands chosen by their families, a choice they did not always accept willingly. For the most part, however, the Turkish women seem to be at peace with their husbands nowadays. Nearly one-half describe their husbands as better than most; but, on the other hand, close to one-fifth feel their husbands have treated them less well than most husbands treat their wives; extreme dissatisfaction, though reported by only 8 percent of the Turkish women, is almost unknown among the Europeans. The Turks do not often voice their dissatisfaction in quarreling, however; few (8%)—again, however, more than twice the proportion of European women—report very frequent quarreling, and 35 percent, slightly more than the Europeans, almost never quarrel.

The sexual relationship in Turkish marriages is for the most part a satisfactory one. The Turkish women report that sexual relations are generally satisfactory for their husbands, though there has been a slight recent increase in dissatisfaction (from 5 percent dissatisfied over the years to 15 percent presently dissatisfied). The Turkish women more often report that they themselves are dissatisfied with the sexual relationship; this has risen from just under one-fifth to just under one-third. As we have seen when the social context of marriage was considered, then, the sexual dimensions of the marital relationship is reported by the Turks to be generally satisfactory—but the incidence of dissatisfaction, while small, is consistently higher than that reported by the Europeans. Like the European women, however, the Turkish women report their own sexual dissatisfaction about twice as frequently as their husbands', and a substantial minority of wives (31%) are currently dissatisfied.

If sexuality is slightly less satisfying for the Turkish women than for the

Europeans, pregnancy and birth are somewhat easier, at least with the first child. A majority of the Turks (53%) have only positive recollections of the first pregnancy; two-thirds gave birth without any special difficulties. However, stillbirth, though very rare (5%), occurred twice as frequently as it did among the Europeans; this proportion, we shall see, remains low, but increases regularly with decreased modernity. Most Turkish women (57%) made the adjustment to motherhood quite easily. Subsequent pregnancies were described as easier or about the same as most women's pregnancies by all but one-fifth of the Turkish women; even fewer reported any special difficulties with later births, and just over one-fifth described problems in adjustment with later babies, a proportion just slightly larger than that found among European women.

For the Turkish women as for the Europeans, then, childbearing was a generally positive experience. It is therefore probable that it is the larger families of the Turks which create the difference between their feelings and those of the European women regarding desirable family size. While a large majority of the European women wished they had borne more children, nearly one-half of the Turkish women were satisfied with the size of their families, and some (15%) went so far as to say they wished they had borne fewer children. A sizeable minority (38%) would indeed have wanted more children—a proportion which is almost constant across the three transitional groups, although family size is not constant—but it is fair to say that the Turks are generally satisfied with their family size; by contrast, the majority of the Europeans are not.

The Turks cite physical (24%) or economic (30%) factors as determinants of family size somewhat more often than the Europeans do, while emotional demands (21%) are mentioned somewhat less frequently by the Turks than by the Europeans. Thus the Turkish women see family size as the outcome of the same factors—which may be characterized as instrumental role demands—which define the maternal role. As we shall see, however, differences in childbearing history and present feelings about desirable family size appear to have little direct effect on the Turks' attitudes toward menopause.

Most of the Turkish women (56%) are postmenopausal, rarely (5%) as a consequence of surgery; almost one-fifth are currently in menopause. Only 26 percent still menstruate regularly. The median age at menopause in this group is 46.9. Reported menopausal symptomatology is slightly higher among the Turks than among the Europeans, a difference which may reflect the higher proportion of Turks who have reached or passed through menopause.

For the Turkish women, as for the Europeans, spontaneous responses indicate that the most important thing about menopause is its effects on physical health (35%); next in importance is emotional health (15%), followed by implications for family or other social relationships (11%). Explicit mention of the cessation of menstruation is not frequent (9%), but is more often heard among the Turks than any other group.

Asked to name the best thing about menopause, the Turkish women gave a variety of answers, such as a sense of personal health and liberation (19%), more freedom from children (14%), freedom from pregnancy (11%), or freedom from menstruation (16%). Only 19 percent had nothing good to say about menopause.

There was more consensus on the negative side: one-half of the Turkish women felt changes in physical health were the worst thing about menopause. Just under one-fifth—compared to twice this proportion among the European women—associated menopause with aging and death. Only 10 percent expressed concern over emotional health: however, this proportion is twice as large as in the more traditional groups. Only 6 percent had nothing bad to say about menopause.

The Turkish women's responses to the twenty-three closed items asking for attitudes toward specific aspects of menopause and middle age were generally similar to the responses of the European women. Like the Europeans, the Turks welcome the cessation of fertility, though slightly less emphatically; like the Europeans, the Turks feel menopause has deleterious consequences for physical health. The Turks and the Europeans agree that emotional health may suffer at this time, and the Turks are the most extreme of all groups in agreeing "definitely" that as a result of menopause a woman may go crazy (17%).

Almost two-thirds of the Turks feel that middle age brings greater personal freedom, and a similarly high proportion feel that a middle-aged woman is given more respect than before; the latter view, one which is characteristic of the more traditional groups, is one which the Europeans do not share. Finally, while most Turks expect the marital relationship will not be much affected by menopause, a majority agree that a woman's sexual pleasure diminishes after menopause (59%)—a view European women reject.

To sum up, the sexual dimension of the modal Turkish woman's life complements the picture yielded by the study of her social context. The modal Turkish woman is slightly but consistently less satisfied with her sexual relations with her husband, both now and looking back over the past, than is the European woman. Furthermore, the Turkish woman is likely to believe that menopause will diminish her sexual pleasure even more.

On the other hand, the Turkish woman has little regret about the number of children she bore—some women even wish they had not borne so many—and is glad to see menopause bring an end to fertility, though she worries about its effect on her physical health, and occasionally about her emotional health as well. These losses are compensated to some extent by her feeling that middle age will bring her greater personal freedom and more respect than she has had up to now.

Among the transitional Turkish women, those whose lifestyles resemble the more modern European women often seem to have captured a comparable mutuality in the marital relationship. This can be seen in the case history of one of the Turkish women, who was born in Turkey in 1915, the firstborn in a family of three daughters, who enjoyed being the only child in the family for the first ten years of her life. Her father was a businessman and her mother a housewife.

She menstruated for the first time at the age of fourteen, with friends her only source of knowledge; at home sex was very much taboo. Her feeling has always been that menstruation is natural, and her response to it is generally favorable. She never suffered premenstrual discomfort of any sort.

She married at the age of twenty-one. Her husband too is Turkish. He is a tailor by trade, and she helps him in his work; she has never worked independently outside the home. She bore her three children in Turkey; only two of them survived, a daughter, now thirty-three, married with two children; and a daughter, twenty-five, also married with two children. Between her daughters a son was born, but he died at the age of only a year and a half.

Her pregnancies were easy, and the babies were very much wanted. She felt well during pregnancy and gave birth easily. She nursed her babies several months, although a breast abcess halted the breastfeeding of her firstborn daughter after four months.

Menstruation ceased three years ago, when she was fifty-one. She knows there are generally symptoms which accompany menopause, but she never experienced any of them. She was concerned when she missed a period, thinking perhaps she was pregnant; but she went to a doctor who told her it was simply change-of-life, and since then she has not menstruated—"and that's that."

She denies any particular reaction to the changes of middle age. Some of her friends have had menopausal symptoms, but she has none. Indeed, she is glad menstruation has stopped, because she no longer experiences the cyclical tension—"either a period comes, or I'm pregnant"—and, in addition, feels cleaner. Without menstruation life is without the anxiety and fear of pregnancy.

Her relationship with her husband has always been excellent, marked by mutuality and reciprocal understanding. Neither, she says, dominates the other, and they share the work of the household. Their sexual relationship is also good, although of course her husband now is middle aged, with something of a decline in potency. Like her, he was pleased when menstruation stopped, because they can have intercourse whenever they want.

Now that the girls have grown up and left home, there are no worries—they're married. One daughter lives close by and sees her mother every day; the other lives a little farther away, in a neighboring city, and they visit once a week. With the girls married and settled down, health is the couple's only worry—her husband suffers from high blood pressure. Until now their worries were about their girls; now they can give thought to themselves. They enjoy a round of social activities, and are well integrated into their community.

PSYCHOLOGICAL WELL-BEING: BALANCING SORROW AND JOY

When the Turkish women are asked to describe their pleasures and worries in role relations, their responses confirm our sense of a somewhat traditional woman, as we have seen in the social and sexual perspectives on the marital and maternal relationships, who describes a less intense interpersonal relationship and greater emphasis on the household duties of wife and mother than does the European woman. Unlike the Europeans, a majority of Turkish women take pleasure in their housework (61%), and two-fifths also find housework a source of worry—responses which are consistent with their greater emphasis on the instrumental component of the wife and mother role. Unlike the working European women, however, those Turkish women who work outside the home do not often get pleasure from their work (19%). Women's work, they seem to be saying, is in the home, and part of the daily rhythm of life's ups and downs.

Like the European women, however, the Turks take very great pleasure (71%), unmixed with worry, in their grandchildren. This large majority is somewhat lower than the corresponding percentage of Europeans, perhaps reflecting the fact that for many Turkish women, grandchildren—though dearly loved—are no longer a novelty. Children too are a source of very great pleasure for most Turkish women (58%), but, like the Europeans, the Turks' pleasure in their children is somewhat more subdued, and is mixed with at least some feelings of worry for more than three-fifths of the women.

The relative proportions of pleasure and worry tip still farther away from unmixed joy as the women consider their husbands, who are not as often enjoyed to a very great extent (29%), while the proportion who view their husbands with worries—more than three-fifths—is just as high as that found among the Europeans.

In short, the Turkish women's family feelings resemble the European's: grandchildren are easy to love, but are somebody else's worry: the more intimate relationships with husband and children more often evoke mixed feelings of pleasure and worry. The Turks, however, are somewhat less often happily married; and, as in other contexts, this can be seen as they balance worries against pleasures.

The Turkish women are disadvantaged economically by comparison to the Europeans; this may explain why they are consistently more worried than the European women about finances (47 percent extremely or quite worried) and debts (51%). Moreover, health—their own (58%) as well as their husbands' (61%)—aging (35%), and death (46%) trouble the Turkish women quite a bit more frequently than the Europeans. The Turks share with the Europeans a high level of concern for national security in Israel (96%) and for family currently serving in the Israel Defense Forces (87%).

Spontaneous responses to an open question on any other worries also reflect the lower socioeconomic status of the Turkish women: over one-quarter mentioned finances again, and this was the largest single category of worry for this group. Other worries included such family matters as children leaving home (21%), family in the army (15%), or their own health (14%)—the latter a problem which, in one form or another, is mentioned more often by the Turks than by the Europeans.

Like the European women, then, the Turkish women's worries include the problems of day-to-day life in a country at war. But the balance of concern, for the Turks, is with the problems of day-to-day life itself. It is not surprising, therefore, to find that the Turkish women are less optimistic about their lives than the Europeans. While the majority (68%) are satisfied, to some extent at least, by what they have gotten out of life so far, this proportion is smaller than it is for the European women. Together with this, nearly one-half of the Turkish women—twice the proportion of Europeans giving this response—have felt, sometimes at least, that they might break down under their problems. They do not, however, feel confined by life; most, like the Europeans, feel free to do the things that attract them, and quite a few (30%) feel even freer now than they did when they were forty.

Nevertheless, the emotional climate of the Turkish women's lives is not quite so sunny as the Europeans'. The feeling of having nothing to do is a little more frequent among the Turks (24%), and they more often begin the day in a bad mood (28%) or end it in a bad mood (15%) than do the European women. The same pattern is seen in their own evaluation of their lives, as expressed by their self-ranking on the ladder scale, just past the midpoint between the bottom (worst) and top (best of all possible lives)—a mean ranking of 5.4, representing a slight decline since age forty; the future, they expect, will bring little more than a return to the status quo (5.9). This pattern is quite unlike the European women's higher overall ranking, presently stable, and anticipated overall improvement. The Turkish women seem to have had more of a struggle than the Europeans with their day-to-day lives.

Joy and sorrow are located at home for the Turkish women, in family relationships and in worries about health. These are illustrated by the case history of one of the Turkish women, who was born in Turkey in 1922, into a family of six children. She hardly knew her father; he died when she was only two years old. Her mother went out to work to support the family.

She was in school only until third grade; then she too went out to work in a sock factory, contributing to the family's support. She worked until her marriage, at the age of twenty-one. Her husband, a butcher, is a year older than she is. Their relationship is excellent: "We were happy even before we married, and I wish my daughter happiness like mine." From her words, one gets the impression of a sensitive husband.

She is the mother of three children, now aged twenty-five, twenty-two, fifteen. The youngest was born after her immigration to Israel in 1950. Her relationship with her children is a good one. She stays in close touch with them, and they get along well. She also gets on well with her second son's wife, and very much enjoys her grandson.

Neither she nor her husband wanted to leave Turkey; they immigrated to Israel because her mother did. The first years in Israel were difficult ones; along with so many other Near Eastern immigrants, they lived in one of the many tent cities, the best accommodation available during that period of economic austerity in Israel. Her health suffered at the time; she had fainting spells and difficulties breathing, which were treated by a doctor at her home.

Since the first breakdown in her health, at the time of her immigration to Israel, she has never really fully recovered. She has suffered intermittent headaches and pains in the pelvis for the past three years; a while ago, a cardiac irregularity also appeared. She describes a feeling of indifference toward these problems, "maybe because of the aging." She is also indifferent toward menopause: "Leave it to nature to decide." It is possible to detect behind her words some fears about the approach of old age.

As this case history suggests, though they are not survivors of the Holocaust, the Turks have been sojourners. And they too bear the scars of history, perhaps more often expressed by the small erosions of day-to-day living. Born at a time of rapid modernization, immigrants from a modernizing society into a modern society, the Turkish women have come a long way toward modernity—but they have not yet come all the way.

5 | The Persians

"Don't
take
me
out
of
my
kitchen."

The long history of the Jews of Persia began in the sixth century B.C., during the reign of Cyrus. This community was part of the ancient Babylonian Jewish community, the center of creativity from which the Talmud sprang. The early history of the Persian Jews, however, in which creativity and prosperity were only rarely interrupted by persecution, came to an end with the rise of Islam. The Shiite Moslem clergy instigated persecutions which were to continue from the sixteenth century until the revolution in 1920. For centuries Persian Jews were forced to choose between conversion to Islam and costly ransoms; both alternatives progressively impoverished the Jewish communities of Persia. In 1920—around the time the women of our study were born—the Jews of Persia were granted equality under the law. But ancient customs and traditions of discrimination were little affected; indeed, strong social ostracism by the Moslem majority even increased with the rise of nationalism.

In the first part of the twentieth century the low economic status of the majority of the Persian Jews was further exacerbated by the development of industry and modern networks of communication, processes which crowded out the many peddlers and small tradesmen. At the same time, anti-Semitism increased in the villages, causing Jews who had traditionally lived as shepherds to immigrate to the large cities—adding to the squalor and overcrowding of the ghettos, and to the number of beggars who lined the streets.

Within these city ghettos the Jews lived in poverty, in primitive, unsanitary housing, often crowded to a density of ten to fifteen persons to a room. Eye and skin diseases were endemic, and malnutrition was more common than not. The majority of the ghetto inhabitants were sickly and shortlived, earning an inadequate living or none at all.

The illiteracy, poverty, and disease which characterized the lives of the Persian poor showed their cumulative effects in the lives of women and children. The rate of illiteracy was higher among women, and their health hazards were multiplied by early marriage and frequent pregnancies, and the endless work both in the home and out of it. Women very often worked outside the home as maids and laundresses, while their husbands were beggars. The status of women was inferior to that of men, and wives were under the absolute authority of their fathers and husbands. The standard of education was low and the system of education disorganized, with the result that girls seldom went to school at all—allowing little hope that they might improve their lives.

The traditional segregation and seclusion of Persian women was symbolized by the veil. In 1935, attracted by Ataturk's program of social reform in neighboring Turkey, Riza Shah decreed the compulsory unveiling of women. His decree, however, was lacking the necessary support of an underlying social climate of liberalization such as that prevailing in Turkey. Immediately following his abdication in 1941, conservative opinion reasserted itself and large proportions of women returned, without protest, to the veil. The practice of veiling and the accompanying social restrictions on women were strongest among the poor. Unlike the Turkish Jews, the Persian Jews had no strong community organization, and the Persian Jewish women suffered from the inferior status of women, compounded by the inferior status of the Jew.

The establishment of the State of Israel opened up a period of mass migration from Persia. An estimated 35,000 of a total of 90,000 Jews migrated between 1948 and 1955. Lacking both agricultural and white-collar skills, the Persian Jews were only slowly absorbed into the lower and lower middle classes of the urban Israeli population. In Tel Aviv, as they had been in Persia, the Persians and the Turks are neighbors; but the Persian Jews have failed, both as a nation and as a religious community, to make the strides toward modernization made by the Turkish Jews.

The price of this failure seems to be greatest for women, as we can see in the case history of one of the Persian women, who was born in Persia in 1924, the daughter of a peddler who had two wives. She is the daughter of the first of these wives; her mother died when she was only two.

She never went to school, working from early childhood weaving rugs. She married at sixteen; her husband is five years older than she is. She began her childbearing in Persia and has eight living children; two additional pregnancies miscarried and two were aborted. Her children bring her worry rather than joy: when they were young, she worried about their marrying, and now that many are married, she worries about her daughters giving birth, and about their problems in rearing children. Her life, it seems, has always had an undercurrent of fear.

The family immigrated to Israel in 1952. Her husband had been a building laborer, but after an accident at work he has been an invalid. She has been employed intermittently weaving rugs in Israel as well.

She describes her relationship with her husband as usually good. Toward sex, however, her feeling is one of total indifference. She is ready to claim that if any marital problems arose between them, they would be due to her husband's minimal educational level; like her, he is illiterate.

The family is Orthodox, but religion seems to be a matter of keeping the rituals rather than a source of personal comfort. She has had problems with her health for the past seven or eight years: "Every day I have something different. The head, the legs, the stomach, a feeling of weakness. . . ." For the past two years her physical complaints have been compounded by depression. She does not sleep well at night; sometimes she cannot sleep at all. Sometimes she goes out to work at her weaving, simply so she will not have to stay at home alone.

Her chronic depression and anxiety have been complicated by the very recent death of her father's second wife, the stepmother who reared her. Thus, to her general fears for her children's well-being and her own health, there has recently been added a fear of death.

DEMOGRAPHIC CHARACTERISTICS

The years of birth of the 160 Persian women in our sample cluster around 1919, shortly before Riza Pahlavi came to power. However, there is little evidence that this revolutionary leader's efforts toward modernization had much impact on the lives of these women. Almost three-quarters of the Persian women had less than four years of schooling, and most of these are illiterate. Very few went beyond the eighth grade. Marriage came early: 22 percent of the Persian women were married before age fourteen, and another 37 percent by age seventeen. For most of the Persian women, marriage reflected the family's choice of spouse (75%). In the relatively few cases where women did choose their own husbands, this often occasioned conflict with the family. Moreover, almost one-half the women whose husbands were chosen by their families report retrospectively that they did not accept their family's choice willingly.

Most husbands (63%) are at least six years older than their wives, and even greater age discrepancies are not uncommon. Relatively few husbands are not of Persian origin; presumably these are the husbands of those few women who came very young to Israel. Marriages, though not always made willingly, rarely broke up. Today 82 percent of the women are married to their first husbands; another 6 percent are married for the second time; 10 percent are widows, and 2 percent divorcees.

Almost two-thirds of the Persian women have been pregnant seven or more times, and only a minority (14%) had four or fewer pregnancies. Most gave birth to seven or more live infants (53%), though the majority (51%) failed to bring all their pregnancies to live births. Finally, almost one-half the women who had live births suffered the loss of one or more children after birth, a toll exacted by the disadvantaged socioeconomic status and its consequences for health, as well as the frequent pregnancies. Despite the rate of miscarriage and childhood deaths, however, almost two-fifths of the Persian women now have seven or more living children.

Childbearing started early and continued for many years for most of the Persian women, covering a span of thirteen years or more for 56 percent. Thus 47 percent of the women still have children at home aged thirteen or younger—indeed, 10 percent have children aged five or even younger—and 9 percent have as many as seven or more children still living at home. On the other hand, most (85%) have married children, and almost all of these women have grandchildren as well.

The demographic characteristics of the Persian women are, in general, those of traditional women. The Persians, however, are traditional women who immigrated to a modern society quite some time ago. One-quarter of the Persian women immigrated to Palestine before the founding of the State of Israel; almost one-half came just a few years thereafter; hardly more than one-quarter can be considered new immigrants. Most immigrated as adults: 63 percent immigrated between the ages of twenty-five and forty, and only one-fifth immigrated before age nineteen.

Immigration to Israel in the early years of statehood offered the Persians relief from anti-Semitism but very little opportunity to improve their socioeconomic status. The great majority of the Persians are lower class. Almost one-half of the husbands of the women in this group had less than four years' schooling; another 44 percent had only four to eight years in school. Just over one-half the husbands are unskilled laborers, and almost one-fifth are on welfare.

Although their socioeconomic status reflects the disadvantages of their traditional origins, immigration to modern Israel has had its effect on the traditional values of the Persian women. Only 57 percent still keep Orthodox religious traditions, though almost none define themselves as completely secular. Furthermore, although three-quarters of these women married husbands chosen by their families, only 21 percent still believe today that this is the way things should be. Finally, the traditionally separate lives of husband and wife seem to have merged in this group: 69 percent report that they spend their leisure time together with their husbands.

The modal Persian woman, then, is a traditional woman transplanted from a difficult life to a world she never made and to a life that has not been much easier. Born in 1919, she never went to school, and can neither read nor write. Her role was wife and mother; and she was soon married off by her family, at about age sixteen, whether or not she opposed her family's choice of husband. Despite its inauspicious beginnings, the marriage was very unlikely to end in divorce, and widowhood is also uncommon. Over a period of close to two decades, she became pregnant at least seven times. Despite miscarriages, she bore at least seven children, one or more of whom were likely to die subsequently. She has school-age children—perhaps some even younger—still at home; and, at the same time, she already has grandchildren.

She came to Israel shortly after the founding of the State, when she was already about thirty years old. Her husband, also of Persian origin, is clearly lower class. If not on welfare, he is likely to be an unskilled laborer. She herself keeps religious traditions, though many women she knows are moving away from religious tradition. The days when a family determined a girl's choice of husband, as well as the times when husband and wife spent leisure time apart are, in her opinion, long gone.

The ties to tradition can be seen in the case history of one of the Persian women, who was born in Persia in 1920 to a family of five children. Her father was a shopkeeper and her mother a housewife. She did not go to school at all, and married at the age of thirteen, to a husband who was then twenty-four. He was a peddler in Persia, but since their immigration to Israel in 1953 he has been without a trade and has worked at jobs supplied by the Ministry of Welfare.

Immigration to Israel was accompanied by considerable financial difficulties. The couple lived for twelve years in a shack in one of the *ma'abarot,* the transit camps built in the early 1950s to house the many penniless refugees from the countries of the Near East. Recently their grown children have been able to help them a little, and they now own an apartment in Tel Aviv.

She is the mother of eight children, ranging in age from twelve to thirty-four; her oldest child was born when she was only fifteen. Her pregnancies and childbirths were without any special difficulty. Those children born in Persia were nursed as long as two years; in Israel she nursed her babies only six months.

Menstruation ceased a year ago, and she has had some symptoms of menopause, including chills and hot flushes. Her feeling is that menstruation is healthy, and if it stops too soon, that is not healthy. But once menstruation ceases, "thus it has to be." She has been somewhat nervous recently, but does not feel this is a consequence of menopausal changes. She believes her nervousness is due to the illness of one of her sons, and to the family's precarious finances.

Her relationship with her husband has always been normal. Her youth did not interfere with their sexual relationship, which continues to this day to be normal. They observe religious traditions, including the custom of *niddah,* the ritual separation of husband and wife during the wife's menstrual period, no longer necessary now that her own menstruation has ceased.

Three of her children are married; the rest are still with her at home. She does not speak of the freedom which comes with the children's departure. On the contrary, for her it is hard to part with the children when they marry—but one accepts it, and, in time, gets used to it.

THE SOCIAL CONTEXT OF MIDDLE AGE

The Persian women's marriages, which not infrequently were made against their will, are, by comparison to marriages in our other groups, the least rewarding.

While many Persian women are indeed satisfied by the marital relationship, a substantial minority—larger than in any other ethnic group—is not.

Most of the Persian women (66%) feel that their husbands need them at least quite a lot, most often for housekeeping tasks (35%) or simply "for everything" (36%). While only 12 percent state that their husbands do not need them, this figure is higher than in any other ethnic group. The other side of the coin is more striking: less than one-half the Persian women feel they need their husbands at least quite a lot, and one-fifth say they do not need their husbands—again, a figure higher than in any other ethnic group. In other words, not only do some of the Persians deny dependence on their husbands, but their perceptions of their own needs and their husbands' needs are more often different than in any other group. On the assumption that a gratifying relationship between adults is based on mutual exchange, whatever the coinage, this difference suggests a problematic relationship for a substantial minority of the Persian women.

The suggestion of some problems in the marital relationship is borne out by the Persians' responses to questions on their satisfaction and on recent changes. The proportion of women who are satisfied by the extent of their husbands' need, though it represents a majority (61%), is the lowest of any group; the Persians, strikingly more often than any other group (25%), wish their husbands needed them more. Paradoxically, looking at changes in the marital relationship since they were forty, many (42%) report no change in their husbands' need, and almost as many report that their husbands now need them more. One-fifth—again, the highest figure of any ethnic group—say they are needed less now than when they were forty. Reading between the lines of these responses, we are tempted to wonder whether the Persian women, whose husbands may need them more nowadays, are somehow telling us that they wish they were needed for something else—though they may not be able to say just what they wish this might be.

Motherhood is still a demanding role for most of the Persian women. More than two-fifths of the Persians still have four or more of their children living at home with them—a figure which underscores the traditional salience of childbearing when we recall that almost none of the European women and a minority of the Turkish women bore this many children. Thus, in middle age, many Persian women are *currently* surrounded by more children than most of the more modern women ever had.

Almost one-half of the Persian women have at least one child of elementary-school age; another 31 percent have children aged fourteen to seventeen. It is not surprising, then, that a majority (61%) say they are very, very much needed by at least one of their children. Many feel their children need them "for everything" (43%); another third mention the instrumental tasks of motherhood, such as cooking and cleaning. Most say their children's needs have not changed since they were forty; those who feel they are less needed now (25%) are hardly more numerous than those who feel more needed now (22%).

The Persian women are nearly unanimous in their feeling that the growing independence of their children brings no regrets at all (75%), or very little (15%). Most do feel their children appreciate them, but one-third do not; almost as many agree that children nowadays do not pay much attention to their parents. For the Persian women, then, motherhood, which began early and has taken so much of their lives, occupying a major portion even of their middle years, may not have brought them rewards which are proportionate to the demands.

One-third of the Persian women had grandchildren by the time they were forty; today, an average of a decade later, fully four-fifths of the Persians are grandmothers. Grandchildren, then, are not new for the Persians, though the role may be relatively recent for some. There has not been much change since age forty for those who did have grandchildren then. Some two-fifths of the Persian women see their grandchildren once or twice a week, and close to one-third see them even more often than that. The Persian grandmother's role is chiefly (80%) instrumental: feeding, cooking, sewing, or giving presents. Only one-tenth mention their grandchildren's affective needs. Another tenth are mother-substitutes, providing daily care for their grandchildren, perhaps while their daughters go out to work. By and large the Persian women seem satisfied with this moderate role; few feel that it is too demanding or, conversely, that there is more they would like to be doing.

Like the Turks, the Persian women spend most (29%) or quite a bit (33%) of the day keeping up with the demands of homemaking. These demands have dropped, since age forty, for one-half of the women, though they have remained unchanged for just over one-third. About one-half are satisfied by the time they give to homemaking; some (30%) give less time than they want, while others (24%) feel they give too much. Unlike any other ethnic group, then, a majority of the Persians—a scant majority, to be sure (54%)—express dissatisfaction with the time they spend on homemaking, feeling it is either too much or too little. Whether this reflects the demands of a large family or is somehow indicative of more general dissatisfaction, the Persians, consistently more often than other groups, convey a sense of discontent.

Dissatisfaction is more common than satisfaction in another role which might serve as a source of emotional support, that of friend and neighbor. Nearly one-half of the Persian women, the highest proportion of any group, wish they had more time for friends and neighbors; this proportion outnumbers those who are satisfied (43%), and is the converse of the pattern seen in every other group, where satisfaction is considerably more frequent than dissatisfaction. The Persians are not a socially isolated group: one-quarter get to "really chat" with friends and neighbors almost daily. However, an equally high proportion almost never do; this proportion is exceeded only by the North African women, who—unlike the Persians—are in the main quite satisfied.

Most of the Persian women are not employed outside the home. Of those (30%) who do work, most work part time, for the most part at unskilled manual work, often as domestic help. There has not been much change in the proportion of working Persian women since age forty. As we have seen, maternal and homemaking obligations have not diminished very much, but even when free time does increase as the children leave home, there is little indication that the Persian women will want to fill this free time with outside employment: those who work have few complaints, but of those who do not work, most do not want to work. Hardly any Persian women are engaged in volunteer activities, and few wish they were.

The new horizons which may appear in the lives of middle-class women as their children grow up and leave home, then, are largely absent for the Persian women. Most, without experience or skill of any sort, are unlikely to enter the labor market at this stage of the life cycle unless compelled by economic necessity. As for avocational involvements, in recent years there has been a return to higher education by women who interrupted college or professional training to rear their families. But the Persian women, who started with very little education or none at all, are unlikely to begin their schooling in middle age; and those who are illiterate are unlikely to find themselves attracted to—or, for that matter, eligible for—any sort of volunteer work.

The social context is the family for the middle-aged Persian woman. This is seen in the case history of one of the Persian women, who was born in Persia in 1920, an only child whose mother died giving birth to her. Her father was a shopkeeper who married her mother's sister after his wife died, and raised the girl. She attended school for six years, from the age of nine until she was fifteen.

At the age of sixteen she married a man six years older than herself, a machinist. Five of their eight children were born in Persia, before their immigration to Israel in 1950. Immigration brought financial difficulties; her husband worked at odd jobs, and she was a housewife. Things were harder at first, but have improved as the children grew up; two of her children are now married, though six are still at home with her.

She had exploratory surgery four years ago for a possible growth in the abdomen; although nothing was found, menstruation ceased at that point. She was advised to take medication, but refused—she was glad to reach menopause, didn't want any more children, and declared, "Enough! Every three years I've had a baby."

Her pregnancies, like her menstrual cycle, were free of difficulties. She breastfed each child for two years, which may have aided in delaying the next pregnancy; they are an Orthodox family, and used no other form of contraception.

Her feeling about sexual relations is that this, like her role as a homemaker, is part of the burden which is laid on a woman from the day of her birth. Her relationship with her husband reflects a similar resignation. She describes him as a closed, contained, and rather irritable person. As for herself, she describes herself as quiet and calm. She finds some compensation in her social life: she loves to go out and meet people.

Her youngest child is only eight years old, a third-grader. This child was conceived when her oldest daughter became pregnant; and the two of them, mother and daughter, gave birth on the same day in the same hospital, side by side.

SEXUALITY: PAST AND PRESENT

Among the Persian women, the interval between sexual maturity and the social maturity signified by marriage has narrowed considerably; indeed, in this group there were cases of women who married as young as ten years old, prior to menarche. For the modal Persian woman (46%), the recollection of menarche is a memory of fear, unpleasantness, or shame. Fewer than one-fifth of the Persian women characterized first menstruation as a positive or even a neutral experience. The teenage years, by contrast, bring happier memories; these women, often brides during their adolescence, choose "hopeful" or "carefree" as often as more neutral terms. Fewer than one-fifth have predominantly negative memories of these years.

Menstruation, when not interrupted by their frequent pregnancies, has been regular for over four-fifths of the Persian women, although close to one-half— more than any other group—report the duration of a menstrual period as six days or longer. For the majority (57%), menstruation has occasioned little or no unpleasantness at any time in their lives.

Physical well-being, for the Persian women, is the salient consequence of menstruation. The best thing about menstruation, for 76 percent of the Persian women, is the release of physical pressure, the cleansing of the body, making one feel better. Asked about the worst thing about menstruation, more than one-quarter had nothing bad to say, and another two-fifths spoke of the physical discomfort and pain. Menstruation, then, is a bodily event for the Persian women, with generally positive significance.

The marital relationship, for the Persian women, is a realm of psychosexual development which has been less gratifying than for other groups. Over one-fifth of the Persian women were willing to tell our interviewers that they had quarreled considerably with their husbands over the years. One-quarter felt their husbands have not treated them as well as most husbands treat their wives—a figure higher than that in any other group. Similarly, fewer Persian women than any other group—only one-third—felt they were better treated than most wives.

In the sexual relationship, clear evidence is seen of the relative deprivation of the Persian women, relative to their own husbands as well as to women in other groups; what is more, this relationship is worse now than it has been over the years. While the Persian women report that their husbands may well have been very satisfied over the years (54%), only a minority of wives (35%) were very satisfied. Furthermore, only 7 percent of the husbands were dissatisfied over the years, compared to more than one-fifth of the wives. This has worsened with time: fewer (30%) of the husbands are now seen as very satisfied, and even fewer (19%) wives. The proportion of women presently dissatisfied has risen to 40 percent.

Most striking about these figures is not the absolute proportions expressing dissatisfaction in sexual relations, but rather the discrepancies between perception of one's husband's sexual satisfaction and one's own experience of satisfaction—as well as the steep decline over the years perceived in the satisfaction of both marital partners. The undercurrent of discontent found in the social and interpersonal dimensions of the marital relationship among the Persian women is, then, even more strongly expressed in the intimacy of the sexual relationship.

Though a majority of the Persian women feel they have coped well with problems of pregnancy, childbirth, and infant care, again there are substantial minorities who feel they have not managed so well. More than one-fifth of the Persian women, responding to six descriptors of the first pregnancy, remembered this pregnancy in negative or ambivalent terms. More than two-fifths—a figure higher than that in any other group—had some special difficulty with the first birth; one-quarter—likewise the highest proportion of any group—reported some difficulty in adjusting to the needs of the new infant. Asked about subsequent pregnancies, births, and adjustment to infant care, about one-fifth consistently recalled some particular difficulty.

Only two-fifths of the Persian women are satisfied by their family size. Dissatisfaction is more frequently expressed by women wishing they had more children (35%) than by those who wish they had had fewer children (26%). The latter figure, however, is higher than that in any other group—and we may speculate that it is not easy for a woman to say, after the fact, that she would have wanted fewer children. Understandably, the Persian women most often mention economic problems as their reason for wanting fewer children, and almost as often mention the physical demand of bearing and rearing children.

To sum up, the sexuality of young and middle adulthood seems to have been less than completely satisfying for a substantial minority of the Persian women. It is reasonable to ask whether this dissatisfaction will be reflected in their responses to questions about menopause and middle age. One-half of the Persian women are postmenopausal, 10 percent as a result of surgical intervention; 17 percent are currently in menopause, and one-third still menstruate regularly. The median age at which menstruation was reported to have ceased completely is 45.7 years (a figure which would be raised by excluding those who underwent surgery and eventually including the women who are now menopausal or premenopausal). As we have noted, the median age at menopause in the five groups is roughly parallel to their degree of modernity: the Persian women reach menopause earlier than any group except the Arab women.

The Persians are clearly the group with the highest level of reported menopausal symptomatology. This seems to be reflected in their responses to an open question about the most important thing about change of life. While one-third had no answer, fully three-fifths of those who did reply spoke of the physical consequences and changes associated with menopause, a proportion almost double that of any other group. No other category of response elicited more than 8 percent of the replies.

The same concerns were expressed in the Persian women's answers to the question about "the worst thing . . . in connection with menopause and change of life." Again some three-fifths of those replying spoke of the consequences for physical health. Bodily change was also the dominant theme in response to the best thing about menopause: one-quarter mentioned the cessation of menstruation, and 13 percent seemed to feel this might improve health. In addition, one-fifth felt menopause might improve emotional health by bringing greater freedom, a response which may reflect feelings about the cessation of fertility, as we shall see.

The responses of the Persian women to the twenty-three statements describing possible consequences of menopause and middle age suggest that this is a period of considerable salience for them. As we have noted earlier, a substantial minority of the Persians, who so often bore so many children, now say they wish they had borne fewer children. This may be a difficult statement to make; it seems to be easier to declare "good riddance" to pregnancy and childbearing, and a majority of the Persian women did just that. The loss of fertility was seen by most as an unmitigated blessing. Close to three-quarters of the Persian women are found in the two most positive categories of the summary score based on these five items. While a similar proportion of European women had equally positive feelings, they have long since completed childbearing, and the loss of fertility, it is reasonable to speculate, signifies only an end of anxiety over a possible unplanned pregnancy—one far more likely to end in induced abortion than childbirth. For the Persian women, by contrast, menopause means not only an end to fertility but an end to pregnancy, childbirth, and infant and child care.

But if menopause means a welcome end to fertility, the Persian women also feel it brings highly undesirable consequences for physical health. Almost all the Persians agree that the cessation of menstruation means that the body will no longer be cleansed regularly of its accumulated poisons, although a majority (61%) are pleased to be finished with the unpleasantness of menstruation. If there is some ambivalence about the cessation of menstruation, consensus is almost complete regarding the deleterious consequences of menopause for physical health. Not only is there extensive disagreement (80%) with the suggestion that a woman feels stronger and healthier after menopause, but an even larger proportion (85%) agree with the statement that "at change of life, a woman begins to suffer from weakness and disease." Like most women, the Persians feel that menopause has generally negative consequences for physical health: 68 percent are found in the two most negative categories of the summary score, a percentage which would have been higher but for the ambivalent feelings about the cessation of menstruation.

There is general agreement among the Persian women that menopause has adverse consequences for the marital relationship. Two-thirds agree that women enjoy sex less after menopause, and the possibility that after menopause women enjoy sex more is generally rejected (78 percent disagree), despite—or perhaps because—the possibility of pregnancy no longer exists. One-half of the women agree that a husband becomes less interested in his wife at middle age; even more are willing to reject the possibility that the husband's interest increases. The minority—one-third—who agree that a woman might be sorry after menopause because her husband would have wanted more children—suggest traditional aspects of the marital relationship: the European women, just as pleased as the Persians by the end of fertility, almost unanimously rejected the suggestion that their husbands might want more children while they did not. The summary score for this set of items shows that the Persian women feel that, on balance, the effect of menopause on their marriages is negative—a view shared only by the North African women.

The Persian women, like the more traditional groups, do not often antici- pate negative changes in their emotional health as a consequence of menopause. Indeed, a majority look forward to greater peace and tranquillity, while very few (20%) agree that "as a result of menopause a woman may go crazy." Never- theless, some two-thirds do agree that menopause may make a woman more ner- vous and moody. The summary score indicates that a plurality (48%) of the Per- sian women associate menopause with some improvement in emotional health, although a substantial minority (35%) feel things may change for the worse.

Finally, the social and personal changes associated with menopause are judged by the Persian women to be generally positive. A large majority (69%) feel that middle age marks a time when the woman is accorded more respect than before, and almost as many reject the opposite statement ("less respect"). Middle age, for most Persian women, also means more of an opportunity to take care of oneself, and more freedom to do as one wishes. The final item in this category may have been interpreted by the Persian women as a measure of physical change, rather than an estimate of the social value of youth: 70 percent of the Persians agree that "a woman begins to age suddenly during change of life."

To sum up, the sexual dimension of the lives of the Persian women seems to highlight certain issues suggested by the social context. For the Persian women—compared to other groups—marriage has less often brought pleasure, and the quality of the marital relationship, particularly the sexual bond, is thought to decline in middle age. Childbearing has sometimes been difficult, and the cessation of fertility which comes with menopause is welcomed by most. Other aspects of menopause and change of life are also salient: most Persian women expect a decline in physical health, though they anticipate some change for the better in their emotional health. Finally, as traditional women generally do, the Persians expect that middle age will bring them greater respect than they had had before.

A common theme among the Persian women is sexual dissatisfaction. This is underscored in the case history of one of the Persian women, who was born in Persia, the middle of five children. She married at eighteen, and the couple immi- grated to Israel in 1949, before any of their children were born. Her husband is a peddler.

Their sexual relationship has always been a source of tension rather than mutual gratification. She wanted no more than her three children (now aged fifteen, eleven, and seven); two were born after pregnancies that lasted more than nine months. She aborted three subsequent pregnancies, refusing to bear additional children.

Sex occurs only as a consequence of her husband's demands, and since the three children were born she insists that he withdraw before climax. She has not felt well and so often refuses sexual relations; he has sometimes responded by demanding or threatening her. He continues to demand sex from her nowadays, so much so that even her son tells his father to leave her in peace.

She feels that the day he stops demanding sex, she will be halfway to health. "If only the period would already stop, because I suffer from it. Sometimes blood pours, and it's tiring. There are those who say it isn't good for menstruation to end, but it weakens me so that I'm just waiting for it to end," she says, adding that her husband's sexual demands have brought her to thoughts of murdering him; menopause, she says, will put an end to his demands.

PSYCHOLOGICAL WELL-BEING: BALANCING SORROW AND JOY

An undertone of malaise could be detected in the responses of the Persian women to questions on the social context of middle age and on past and present sexuality. This tone is somewhat stronger in the Persians' responses to questions which call for self-reported measures of satisfaction and psychological well-being.

The intimate family relationships with husband and children reflect the mixture of feelings already seen, perhaps amplifying the negative note somewhat. While almost two-thirds of the women very much enjoy at least one of their children, just about the same proportion feel their children bring more than a little worry: indeed, 39 percent, more than any other ethnic group, report worries to a great extent. The Persian women's husbands give them even less pleasure and even more worries: no more than one-quarter say they are very, very happy with their husbands, while almost as many (21%) say "not so much" or "almost not at all"—an admission which, in the quasi-public situation of an interview, may be quite revealing. As for the other side of the coin, those who say they have almost no worries about their husbands (26%) are outnumbered by those with quite a few worries: 41 percent, the highest proportion in any ethnic group. In short, the problematic family relationships suggested as characteristic of a substantial minority of Persian women take their highest toll in reported psychological well-being. Grandchildren, however, are a compensatory source of joy. More than four-fifths of the Persian women say they very much enjoy their grandchildren, and no more than a handful see them as a source of trouble.

Homemaking is, if anything, satisfying: one-third of the Persian women enjoy homemaking, and for most it causes no problems at all. Those who are employed have little to say about their work; it brings no special pleasures, but it brings no special problems either. Outside the immediate household, however, additional worries are seen. Worry about the security situation in the country— certainly realistic in 1969—was almost universal (98%). Although this proportion is higher than in any other group, it is at least in part explained by the fact that 89 percent of the Persian women expressed concern for a family member in the armed services. While no other cause of concern had equal salience, a majority of the Persians were quite or especially worried by their husband's health (62%), their own health (63%), finances (61%), and debts (54%). Growing old bothered fairly few (24%); the same was true of death (34%). Finally, asked about "any other worries," many Persian women (33%) mentioned their families once more; this was the largest category of response among the Persians, and, in addition, the Persians gave this response more frequently than all but the Arab women, whose children are not drafted into the Israeli Army.

As might be anticipated, the more general questions about psychological well-being confirm the recurrent theme of discontent among the Persians. Perhaps the most telling item is the question "Do you sometimes have the feeling that you are likely to break down under your problems?" A majority of the Persian women, in proportions higher than any other group, have felt this way: 17 percent very frequently, 15 percent frequently, and 28 percent sometimes. We would suggest that a group of women of whom close to two-thirds are willing to admit that their problems sometimes come close to breaking them is a group which, though it is holding on, faces a constant press of burdens without assurance that they will continue to bear up.

While the thought of breakdown may occur briefly and pass over, the Persian women's responses to a more general question suggest a more general sense that life is lacking. Asked if they are satisfied "by what you have gotten out of life so far," the Persians more often answer no (39%) than yes (26%), expressing less satisfaction and more dissatisfaction than any other group.

There is no indication that the Persian women feel their lives to be confining: most (57%) feel free to do what they want, and for most (58%) this sense of freedom has not changed since they were forty. It may be possible, however, in light of earlier responses, to surmise that freedom, for the Persian women, means fewer tasks rather than new opportunities. This, perhaps, helps to explain their response when asked if they ever feel they have nothing to do. We intended this question to suggest a sense of emptiness; however, the proportion of women reporting that they feel this way "very often" or "sometimes" increases steadily with increased traditionalism, and may well reflect, for the traditional woman, the feeling that the household is at peace. This response, in any event, is coupled with responses about mood in the morning and evening, and neither indicates negative feelings.

Finally, as the Persians try to evaluate their lives overall on a ladder ranking, they see their present lives—as do the other transitional women, the Turks and the North Africans—barely above the midpoint (a mean response of 5.6). Moreover, life was no better at forty (a mean response of 5.6, lowest of all five groups). Perhaps most telling of all, the Persians, alone of all our groups, expect the future to be no better (a mean response of 5.8).

Like the Turks, the Persian women are in transition; but they have farther to go. The transitional women, born in countries where the transformation from folkways to modernity was taking place fairly rapidly, were then transplanted to a country where modernization was complete, and their relatively traditional lifestyles were outmoded. The undercurrent of discontent running through the responses of the Persian women may reflect the fact that the transition they made was the most extreme, bringing with it the stress of meeting the demands of a modern environment with traditional responses. Perhaps the Persians have lost the benefits of traditional folkways while not yet deriving any of the benefits of modernity.

The sense of transition is strong in the case history of one of the Persian women, who was born in Persia in 1920 to a family of seven children. Her father was a shopkeeper and her mother a housewife. She completed elementary school in Persia. She married at the age of fourteen and finished high school after marriage. Her first child was born when she was fifteen. Each of her five children was breastfed two years; her pregnancies and births were normal.

Their sexual relationship is, for her, part of the obligations and duties which a wife must meet. Like her other duties, this too is fulfilled, but she has no reactions of satisfaction of her own, and nothing approximating sexual pleasure.

Her social life is confined to the family circle. She finds no friends in her neighborhood because none are her intellectual equals. She reads widely, especially in Persian literature, and no one around is on her level. Nevertheless, her education—and perhaps her private aspirations—are reflected in the education her children have received. All five of the children have completed high school, no ordinary accomplishment in Israel, where free compulsory education at the time of our fieldwork ended with the eighth grade, and high school required payment of tuition.

She does not permit herself broader personal horizons. In this way she keeps herself from neglecting or abandoning her home and the children who need her—and the husband who is able to give them nothing. She sums up this commitment (and perhaps a well-controlled longing for something more) by saying, "Don't take me out of my kitchen."

6 | The North Africans

"I have patience without end."

The history of the Jewish communities in North Africa dates back to antiquity. Jewish settlement, it is believed, began with Jews who came to North Africa together with Phoenician colonizers, to be joined later by exiles from Palestine after the destruction of the Second Temple in 70 A.D. The Jews of North Africa, moreover, were the first to return to settle in *Eretz Yisrael* after the destruction of the Second Temple; since that time there have been successive small waves of immigration from North Africa to Israel, particularly during periods of persecution.

With the Moslem conquest of North Africa, old Jewish communities revived and new communities were born. During the Middle Ages, North African Jews immigrating to Israel included such noted scholars as the Rabbi Moshe ben Maimon (Maimonides). Jews expelled from Spain swelled the community of scholars in Morocco. During the years in which Moslem culture flourished, Jewish culture and intellectual life flourished together with it. With the decline of Moslem culture, the aristocratic Jewish communities sank into squalor. Furthermore, the Moslem decline was compounded for the Jews by Moslem persecution. The status of the Jews was that of "dhimmi"—nonbelievers with a protected but inferior status. The spiritual climate which had once produced scholars and sages dwindled to insignificance in the centuries of persecution, and most of the Jews of North Africa sank into illiteracy.

Until the beginning of the twentieth century the Jews were subjected to severe oppression and discrimination, sometimes amounting almost to conditions of slavery. They were employed at compulsory labor and subjected to humiliating regulations: they were forced to wear distinctive black clothing and skullcaps, and upon leaving the Jewish quarter—the *mellah*—were made to remove their shoes. The *mellah* was surrounded by walls, and its gates were

74

locked at night. Within its streets and houses, overcrowding and abysmal sanitary conditions prevailed.

With the establishment of the French Protectorate in North Africa in 1912—shortly before the first of the women of this study were born—a number of changes were introduced which made it possible for Jews to leave the close confines of the *mellah* and its centuries-old squalor and to enter the newer parts of the city, where they took up trained professions and positions in the civil service. However, at the same time that mobility into the professional classes was growing, there was increased migration from the small, primitive villages of the interior; and this unskilled Jewish population poured into the *mellah*. In this way two social strata were created; the upper, modernizing stratum became increasingly subject to French influence and lost contact with the community of the *mellah,* while the lower stratum remained within the confines of its walls and its traditions.

Within the *mellah* living conditions were very difficult. Inadequate housing, with six to ten persons in a room, was the rule. Skin and eye diseases were endemic, and blindness resulting from untreated trachoma was frequent. Infant mortality was high, and chronic illness was seen among young and old. The Jews of the *mellah* who could find work were small merchants or peddlers, tailors, cobblers, harness-makers, and workers in precious metals. Many lived by begging.

The position of women was clearly subordinate to men. Bigamy was common in the past, decreasing only recently. In the cities work for women was rare, except for a small number of seamstresses and governesses, and a few women who lived as prostitutes, a recognized trade. Village women had no opportunity at all for employment outside the home, and indeed were forbidden to go out alone, or to speak with any man not closely related to them.

At about the time the women of our study were born, education was the prerogative of boys, and at that constituted no more than a few years of *heder* (religious schooling), at a primitive level, and no general education at all. The number of women at the turn of the century who received any education was infinitesimal.

This situation was to improve steadily through the efforts of the international Jewish community. Schools were established by the Alliance Universelle Israelite, and trade schools were created by the Organization for Rehabilitation and Training. During the childhood of the women in this study, major strides toward universal education were made, but few of our subjects profited by these developments, either directly—their level of education is very low—or indirectly, through their husbands' education or occupation.

Family life was that of the traditional patriarchy, and women were entirely under their husbands' authority, tied to the traditional roles of childbearer and homemaker. From early childhood, when they helped their mothers at household tasks, to adulthood, their lives centered around the duties of the home. Indeed, women were kept at home, and did not even go outside alone.

Marriages were arranged, and arrangements were often completed while the girl was still a child, though the marriage was not consummated until puberty. During pregnancy and childbirth, women were thought to be weakened and subject to the influence of the Evil Eye, a custom absorbed from the surrounding Moslems and Berbers. Attempts to ward off the Evil Eye, and to ensure the birth of a boy, motivated many ritual practices. After menstruation and after childbirth women went to the *mikvah,* the ritual bath of purification.

A woman's life, in short, was one of ritual and tradition throughout, from the very earliest efforts, prior to her birth, to ensure a male child, through every stage of development. This very traditional woman was, during the generation of women in our study, slowly to be replaced by a woman increasingly exposed to education and to the influences of Western culture.

It was not, however, the modern women who immigrated to Israel. In the mass exodus of Jews from North African countries which followed the establishment of the State of Israel and the accompanying rise in Arab nationalism, the upper stratum of North African Jewry migrated to France, while the uneducated, unskilled masses fled to Israel.

The women of this study and their families came to Israel and settled in towns which had been occupied by Arabs until they were abandoned in 1948. Located halfway between Jerusalem and Tel Aviv, where the foothills of the Judaean Mountains yield to the fertile coastal plains, the towns are isolated in an agrarian setting. Though modern, bustling Tel Aviv and eternal Jerusalem are not very distant, the North Africans are not surrounded by affluence or modernization. They live in crumbling, Arab-built homes at the core of the two towns, or at the periphery of town in huge government housing projects built for economy and not for beauty. The pace of modernization is slower here than in the cosmopolitan cities, and affluence, for the North Africans, is not next door but rather an inter-city bus ride away.

The sense of tradition is strong in the case history of one of the North African women, whose family of five daughters is a disappointment to her. Her firstborn was a son who died of a fever at eighteen months, during a period of conflict between herself and her mother-in-law, when, she says, "the milk was like poison, and the child died." Her mother-in-law petitioned the local rabbinate, who found in her favor and determined that her son and daughter-in-law leave her home and live on their own, to let the neighbors determine whether she was an adequate wife.

When the family immigrated to Israel they brought their conflicts with them; now her mother-in-law says she doesn't deserve a solar hot-water-heater—that she should bear a son first. Her own feeling, however, is that it is her mother-in-law who brings the influence of the Evil Eye to bear on her, keeping her from additional pregnancies and the birth of a son. Indeed, she believes that when she passes women in the street carrying their sons in their arms, they turn into their houses for fear that the evil will fall on them too.

Her relationship with her husband is complicated by his close contact with his mother, who often speaks against her. Nevertheless, though he also very much wants a son, since he now has no one to help him out in the store, he sometimes comforts his disappointed wife by saying that perhaps it's a blessing that they have no sons, who would only have been killed in the war.

Their daughters, however, cause problems for her. They go out at night and come home late—she doesn't know what to do with them, and threatens, in the hope of frightening them, to call the police. Her oldest daughter, twenty-three, is already married; she wishes very much that the eighteen-year-old would marry already, so she would have less worry.

Both still hope to have more children, but, though her husband has been receiving treatment for two years, she has not become pregnant since the birth of their youngest daughter, who is now twelve years old. Besides the death of her young son, one daughter was stillborn, the result, she thinks, of her mother-in-law's influence through a visit her husband paid on his mother two days before the child was born dead.

Her oldest daughter, however, has a son, and this is some comfort to her, making her feel as though she too has finally had a son of her own. But she still regrets that she bore none of her own, and recognizes that the approach of old age puts an end to any remaining hope: "Sometimes I think I'm going to die. I'm old now; we're finished."

DEMOGRAPHIC CHARACTERISTICS

The North African Jews who immigrated to Israel were those with nowhere else to go. Middle-class Jews leaving Morocco, Tunisia, and Algeria turned to Paris rather than to Tel Aviv. Furthermore, the relatively traditional North African Jews who came to Israel often settled, as the families of the women of our study did, in fairly homogeneous and rather isolated towns, setting them apart from daily contact with modern urban life. As we shall see, the demographic data suggest that the North African women are nearer to tradition than to modernity.

The great majority (72%) of the 239 North African women in our study were born in Morocco; 26 percent were born in Tunisia, and only five women were born in Algeria. Their ages are evenly distributed across the decade of birth—from 1915 to 1924—chosen for our study. Schooling was rare: 60 percent of the North African women are illiterate, and only 36 percent had four or more years of school—almost none beyond elementary school.

Marriage—universal in this group—came early. Seventeen percent of the North African women were married before they were fourteen years old, and another 20 percent were married in the next two years. By the age of twenty-one, 80 percent of the North Africans were married. All married in their native countries; a majority (56%) married husbands chosen by their families, usually a choice they approved. A total of 43 percent chose their own husbands, and most (30%) had their families' approval. Husbands were born in the wife's country of birth. Most were older than their wives by six or more years; 17 percent were older by eleven or more years. Marriage, for most, was stable; but the age difference between husband and wife is now reflected in the proportion of widowed women (17%). Divorce was not unknown (9%). Some women have remarried; today 83 percent are married, 13 percent are widows, and 4 percent are divorcees.

Education (if there was any), marriage, and childbearing preceded immigration to Israel. Almost none of the North African women came to Israel before the founding of the State. One-third came in the years of mass migration just after 1948; another 42 percent arrived between 1953 and 1962, and another fifth came in 1963 or later. Most (55%) were between the ages of twenty-six and forty when they arrived in Israel; 36 percent were older. This, then, is a population of new immigrants whose traditional lifestyles were shaped before their entry as full citizens into a modern state.

Barrenness is traditionally a curse, and the North African women could consider themselves blessed with fertility. Most (86%) were pregnant at least four times; 67 percent were pregnant seven times or more. Foetal wastage was not great: 59 percent of the North African women had seven or more live births; indeed, 58 percent brought all their pregnancies to live births. Miscarriage occurred, however, for 36 percent. Deaths of children after birth were considerably more common: a majority (58%) of these women lost at least one child after birth. As a consequence, 43 percent of the women now have seven or more children.

North African women bore children over many years; more than one-half of these women (57%) have a span of thirteen or more years between their oldest and youngest living children. Indeed, some (17%) have as many as seven or more children now living at home, and most (57%) have children thirteen years old or younger—some (9%) aged five or younger. The great majority of the North African women (84%) also have married children; of these, most now have children of their own.

This is a population at the bottom of the socioeconomic ladder, as can be seen from the educational and occupational characteristics of the husbands of the North African women. More than one-half of these men spent only three years or less in school; another one-third had four to eight years' schooling. Only 22 percent are presently in nonmanual occupations; most (49%) are unskilled laborers, and the remainder are on welfare.

The traditional pattern seen in the demographic characteristics of the North African women is also reflected by their religious practices: the great majority (85%) keep all or most of the religious tradition, and only one woman describes herself as secular. However, there has been some shift away from traditional values. Although 56 percent of the women reported that their own husbands had been chosen by their families, today only 19 percent feel this should be the way marriages are made. Furthermore, 71 percent said that they spent most or all of their leisure time together with their husbands, a step away from the traditional separation of the worlds of women and men.

The modal North African woman in this study was born in Morocco in 1919. She had little or no schooling and is illiterate. By the time she was seventeen, her family had chosen a husband for her, like herself a native of Morocco, and probably more than six years older than her. She soon began childbearing, and bore at least seven children. Miscarriage was not common, but she did suffer the loss of at least one child after birth. Today she is still absorbed by the demands of motherhood and is very likely to have children under the age of thirteen at home. Her older children, however, are already married, and she has become a grandmother. While she is still married to her first husband, she has a good many friends who are widowed, and some who are divorced.

She came to Israel as an adult, at the age of thirty-five, arriving after 1953; she probably feels herself to be a new immigrant. Her husband was unlikely to have had more than three years of school in Morocco. In Israel, he is an unskilled manual laborer. The North African woman still keeps religious tradition today, but she has departed somewhat from her parents' way of life: she generally spends her leisure time together with her husband, and she believes that her daughters should choose their husbands for themselves.

The traditions of the past can be seen along with the process of transition in the case history of one of the North African women, who was born in Morocco in 1918. Although she has eight living children and miscarried three pregnancies, she wanted more children, and was disappointed when she ceased to become pregnant.

Her husband was chosen by her family when she was twenty. She was happy with the match, and they still get along today. Although he is sometimes tense—and less patient with the children than she is—she feels this is a consequence of their financial problems, which have grown somewhat worse recently. They have a fish store, and she works there for a few hours every day.

Just as her parents chose her husband, she helped her daughters choose their husbands; but, she says, it is impossible to be sure if the choice was wise. One of her daughters married a man who seemed devout and good, but it turned out that he was sickly and nervous, and has been hospitalized more than once. She very much wants her daughter to divorce him, but her daughter claims he is good to her and refuses to divorce him on account of his illness. Fortunately, her other married daughters have been luckier. She doesn't always get to visit her children as much as she would want, but she always enjoys the holidays, when the whole family is together.

Her principal worry is the older of her two sons, now doing his regular army service in the Sinai. The problems of national security trouble her very much; she listens constantly to the news and is very worried when she hasn't seen or heard from her son for a while. This worry is compounded by the fact that her younger son, now in high school, will be drafted in just a few months; this thought is very hard for her.

On the other hand, her son's accomplishments in high school are a major source of pride. She herself never went to school at all; until she married, she was at home helping her parents. Although her home was happy and her memories of childhood and adolescence are likewise happy, with each mention—and she makes mention frequently—of her son's work in high school, she also expresses some regret that she herself never had a chance to go to school.

THE SOCIAL CONTEXT OF MIDDLE AGE

The North African women, like other traditional women, often married husbands their families chose; unlike the Persian women, however, the North African women seldom recalled the choice of husband as an occasion for conflict with the family. Whether their early experiences helped to determine their subsequent feelings, or their present feelings temper their recollections of the past, the relatively harmonious entry into marriage is congruent with the North African women's present descriptions of marriage as a stable and satisfying tie.

Most North African women (63%) feel their husbands need them quite a lot or even more, a need most often described in general terms, "as a wife," or "for everything" (43%). Specific needs were less often mentioned by the North African women than by any other group; the instrumental component of the marital relationship was mentioned less by the North Africans than by any group except the Europeans (where the affective tie was dominant); specific mention of affective ties was even more uncommon (10%). Childbearing and mothering, though not mentioned frequently (13%), were cited more often by the North Africans than by any other group, a point which may bear on the sexual dimension of the marital tie, as we shall see. Moreover, the salience of childbearing and childrearing may also be reflected in the North African women's relationship to their growing children.

The feeling of need in the marital relationship is described as mutual by the North African women. Although, like all women in the study, they describe their husbands' needs as somewhat stronger than their own, one-half (51%) need their husbands quite a lot or even more. Hardly any describe little or no need for the spouse, and this proportion is the same when wives describe their husbands' needs and their own (8%). Their husbands' needs are usually stable (53%) or growing (31%); and the great majority (78%) are satisfied with this relationship.

Most North African women still have quite a few children living at home with them; over one-half have four or more children at home as young as elementary-school age. Most (62%), as we might expect, still feel needed to a great extent or even more. However, need is not a simple function of the number and ages of children at home, since the Persian households are not very different, and the Persian women report a higher extent of need. While the Persians say they are needed for household chores, however, the North African women are needed "as a mother" or "for everything" (54%).

Like intensity of need, stability of need is not a consequence of the number of children. More often than any group but the Europeans, the North African women see their children's needs as having declined since they were age forty (39 percent, a proportion equal to those who see no change). This perception of declining need may be due, in part, to the North African women's fondness for small children, for they—unlike any other group—are sorry more often than not to see their children grow up and become more independent. Evidently this is not because their children have been a disappointment but because they are sorry to see a rewarding relationship come to an end: most North African women (72%) feel their children appreciate them, and most (62%) reject the suggestion that children nowadays don't pay attention to their parents. One way or another—first, as we have seen, with the relatively high number who mention childbearing and motherhood as part of the marital tie, and next with the numbers who are sorry to see their children grow up—the North African women express a special pleasure in small children. This theme, as we shall see, recurs.

Most (76%) North African women have grandchildren, and it is no surprise that more than half see their grandchildren several times a week, if not every day. Most (73%) say they knit, sew, or cook for their grandchildren; 10 percent help out with child care, as mother substitutes. For those (56%) who had grandchildren by the time they were forty, there has been little change in the extent of their contact with their grandchildren. And for most (72%) the relationship with the grandchildren is just as it should be—though the direction of dissatisfaction among the minority who are not content is the reverse of that found in other groups: more North Afrian women would like to be doing more for their grandchildren (12%) than feel too much is demanded of them (8%). This difference between the North Africans and all other groups seems to bear out the suggestion that they have a special, lasting fondness for small children, a suggestion which is not based on any one single set of responses but rather on similar responses to different issues.

Like the other traditional women in this study, the North African women give much or most of the day to homemaking (64%), though this has declined for some two-fifths of the women since the time when they were forty. Most (58%) are satisfied by the time they spend at homemaking; less than one-fifth feel that it takes more of their time than they want to give.

Many North African women are needed by relatives outside the immediate family, at least to some extent (51%). Like all but the Arab women, the North Africans most often describe this need as affective (68%). The role is stable for many (51%) and satisfying for most (68%); however, like the Persian women, a substantial minority of the North African women (23%) would like to feel more needed by their relatives. More than half the North African women see their relatives rather infrequently—no more often than from time to time. Indeed, the reported frequency of contact with the extended family drops with increased traditionalism, contrary to what might be expected. This finding, however, may be due to the dislocations of migration, or for that matter might reflect the heightened salience of family contact among more modern ethnic groups.

Although the North African women live in smaller communities than those of the Europeans, the Turks, or the Persians, they do not report a proportionately higher frequency of contact with friends and neighbors. Indeed, although some 37 percent do get together several times a week or more, the very same number almost never get time with friends and neighbors—the latter proportion higher than in any other ethnic group. For most (56%), things have not changed since they were age forty; but if there has been change, it has usually meant a decline (36%). Still, those who are satisfied with things as they are (59%) outnumber those who wish they had more time with friends and neighbors (37%).

Most North African women do not work (75%). Of those who do, most work as domestics or in some other form of unskilled manual labor. Although those who work say they enjoy their work more often than not, those who do not now work do not wish they did, perhaps as a consequence of the lack of attractive employment opportunities for this largely unskilled group of women. Hardly any North African women participate in volunteer activities, and most do not want to begin.

For the North African women, then, the social context of middle age is the immediacy of home and family, a home which still has happy memories of small children and close ties to grandchildren. The sense of family is strong in the case history of one of the North African women, who was born in Algeria in 1917. She was married at fourteen, and her first son was born hardly more than a year later, but this child died at the age of three. A second son died when he was only six days old. A third pregnancy ended in miscarriage. Finally, a son was born to her who lived; he is her only child.

She very much wanted more children, but was afraid to become pregnant after her last child was born. She and her husband went to many doctors, and some suggested shots, but her husband was opposed to this. In his opinion, a son has to come naturally, and if no son comes, this is God's will: "God gave and God took."

The family immigrated to Israel, together with her parents, in 1951. Life in Israel, she says, is very different from life in Algiers. There the woman had to sit at home and help her parents; she worked at home and didn't have much to say. Although her own childhood memories are happy, she never went to school in Algiers, and in Israel she has begun to learn to read and write. Still, she is not jealous of the opportunities young people have today: "The world is like that. The world is not made for people; people come and go, and the earth remains the same."

Her husband, who is her cousin and was a close neighbor before their marriage in Algiers, is an excellent husband—"there's enough income"—and he gives her his paycheck without asking her to account for the family budget. They go out together quite a lot.

She is very close to her son and daughter-in-law. They both work, and they decided it would be better for their children, a girl aged four and a boy aged one and a half, to be with her than with a stranger. She enjoys the care of her grandchildren, though sometimes she finds it a little harder than she expected: "I'm not used to running after little ones every day; it's been a while for me." Indeed, sometimes the work and the noise they make annoys her, but it quickly passes. She feels that the grandchildren are like her own, and it helps to compensate for the children she lost. Her son and daughter-in-law come to her home to eat every day. Family relations are very good.

She worked fifteen years in a cigarette factory, from the time they immigrated to Israel, a period of hard times when they both worked hard. And she knew that after a day's work she still had to go shopping and clean the house. She is glad now to be at home and enjoy some peace and quiet. Even when the grandchildren are not there, she is never lonely and always has something to do. Besides, she has many neighbors to visit, and if she does not visit them, they visit her. The only tense spot is the daily news; as she listens, she is sometimes very much afraid that things will grow worse. Although her son completed his regular army service a year ago, she knows he might still be called into combat on reserve duty. Apart from the problems of national security, however, she describes her life nowadays as good.

SEXUALITY: PAST AND PRESENT

The first menstruation is most often remembered in negative terms by the traditional women in our study. A majority of the North African women (53%) are found in the most negative category, remembering menarche only as embarrassing, unpleasant, or even frightening. On the other hand, the great majority of the North African women remember their teenage years—for many, the early years of marriage—in positive terms only (30%), or in positive and neutral terms (44%).

For most North African women menstruation brought no special unpleasantness. There was general consensus (71%) that the best thing about menstruation was its beneficial effects on physical health. Quite a few women (30%) found nothing bad to say about menstruation; about the same proportion mentioned physical discomfort. Nearly one-quarter of the North African women described menstruation as dirty; this category of response increases with increased traditionalism—a tradition which, among both Jews and Moslems, defines the menstruating woman as ritually unclean.

The marital relationship among the North African women is, as earlier responses might lead us to expect, a harmonious one. Close to one-half of the North African women feel their husbands have treated them better than most husbands; a majority (60%) report that they have rarely or hardly ever quarreled over the years.

Harmony is also reported in the sexual relationship, though middle age has brought a decline in sexual satisfaction to both husband and wife. Looking back over the years, the North Africans describe a very satisfactory sexual relationship: dissatisfaction for husband (3%) or wife (8%) was lower among the North

Africans than any other group. By contrast, however, dissatisfaction nowadays is not at all infrequent: 23 percent of the husbands, more than any other group, and 35 percent of the wives—not an unusual proportion—are now dissatisfied. The North African women's responses differ from those of other groups, however, in that the proportions of satisfied or dissatisfied husbands and wives are more nearly equal, suggesting a relationship of mutuality—including even mutual dissatisfaction in middle age. Part of the dissatisfaction with sex in middle age which the North African women report may be, as we shall see, tied to a lingering desire—not universal, but greater in this group than in any other—for additional children.

The North African women's memories of their first pregnancies are overwhelmingly positive (87%). While stillbirth was not unknown (19%), most had no special difficulties at the time of the first birth (68%) and little or no difficulty adjusting to the first baby (70%). Speaking of subsequent pregnancies and births, the North African women were quite likely to describe their experiences as easier than other women's; few described difficulties.

These positive memories may help explain why the North African women, more often than any group except the Europeans, now say they would have wanted more children (42%), and, except for the Europeans, less often wished they had fewer children (10%)—notwithstanding families which were often very large. The reasons given for these feelings were most often nonspecific (43%)—"large families are a blessing"—although some women did mention physical (19%) or emotional (16%) factors. Notwithstanding the economic hardships the North African women had faced, relatively few (13%) claimed that economic factors had affected their family size—perhaps because these women still maintain something of the traditional values, believing that large families signify economic strength.

The North African women look back on the sexual dimension of young adulthood with satisfaction. Within a harmonious marriage, sex was mutually satisfying, and there is little recollection of problems in childbearing. There is some suggestion that middle age brings a change for the worse in sexual satisfaction; at the same time, notwithstanding very large families, many North African women wish they had more children. As we shall see, some of these themes are repeated in their attitudes toward menopause.

A majority (57%) of the North African women have ceased menstruating (of these, 6 percent as a result of surgery); another 19 percent are currently in menopause; and 23 percent still menstruate regularly. The median age at which menstruation was reported to have ceased is 46.7. The frequency of reported symptomatology is comparable to that among the Turks and the Persians.

Asked the most important thing about menopause, one-third of the North African women replied that there was nothing important about it. Just over one-fifth—fewer than any other group—mentioned changes in physical health. Almost the same number—more than any other group—mentioned social and familial implications; and some (8%) specifically mentioned the cessation of fertility. Unlike other groups, for whom the physical changes of menopause are most salient, the North Africans' spontaneous responses seem to suggest that the most important consequences of menopause are the changes it brings to the woman as mother and wife.

This suggestion is borne out by the North African women's answers when asked to describe the best thing about menopause and change of life. The modal response, given by more than one-quarter of the North African women, is that menopause and middle age bring welcome social and familial changes, such as greater respect and more independence. More than one-fifth believe menopause brings a change for the better in emotional health. Others (13%) are pleased by the cessation of fertility, or by the end of menstruation (11%); 6 percent specifically mention the release from religious limitations which comes when menstruation ends.

For the North African women, as for all other groups except the Europeans, changes in physical health are most often seen as the worst thing about menopause (43%). Less than half as many (17%) mention aging or death. And almost the same number (14 percent, almost three times the proportion in any other ethnic group) feel that some of the family changes, such as children growing up and leaving, are the worst thing about menopause.

The North African women's responses to the twenty-three closed items are consistent with earlier indications of pleasure in pregnancy and childbearing, and the strong desire for large families. Moreover, unlike the Europeans, who very often wished they had borne larger families but do not now want to become pregnant, a substantial minority of the North African women presently feel that the cessation of fertility is a loss.

Along with all women in the study, most North African women have generally positive feelings about the end of fertility, as indicated by the summary score on these five items. However, the North Africans, along with the Arab women, are less strongly positive than other groups. Between one-quarter and one-third of the North African women consistently agree that women regret they can no longer become pregnant after menopause and are sorry they have no chance for additional children.

Like other women in the study, the North Africans agree that menopause has largely deleterious consequences for physical health. However, like other transitional and traditional women, the North Africans see some compensation in the fact that the effect of menopause on emotional health is definitely positive.

The social and personal consequences of menopause and middle age, for the North African women, are mixed: most (56%) agree that at middle age women are given more respect than before, and even more (60%) disagree that middle-aged women get less respect that before. However, the feelings among the North African women are almost evenly divided between agreement and disagreement with the suggestion that middle age brings with it greater freedom, or more chance for a woman to look after herself. And there is substantial agreement (83%) that a woman begins to age suddenly during change of life.

Finally, the North African women have mixed feelings about the possible effects of menopause and middle age on the marital relationship. Many (43%) agree that women find less pleasure in sexual relations after menopause, although about one-quarter believe that a woman enjoys sexual relations more. Like the Arab women, one-third of the North African women agree that a woman might regret menopause because her husband would have wanted more children. However, most North African women disagree that a husband's interest in his wife changes at middle age, and see neither increase nor decrease.

To sum up, the sexual dimension of the North African women's lives has been generally satisfying. Their large families have been welcome; many women wish their families had been ever larger, and some, even now, are a little sorry the long period of childbearing has come to an end. The salient changes of menopause, for the North African women, are often tied to fertility and the family.

The sexual dimension can be seen in the case history of one of the North African women, who was born in Morocco in 1919. She cannot remember her father, who died when she was very young. She never went to school; she and her older brother had to go to work as soon as they were able, to support the family of seven children. She was a seamstress, and soon became well known for her work, which was a source of profit to the family.

She was a well-liked, popular girl, cheerful, and blessed with a sense of humor, which her friends enjoyed. She was betrothed young, but her husband-to-be broke off the relationship, something which hurt her very deeply.

The man she did marry, who is ten years older than herself, was someone she had known for many years. When she first knew him, her betrothal kept her from him; but when, nine years later, he asked for her hand again, she accepted it, thinking it was a sign from God that he asked twice. She remembers him when young as a vigorous, handsome man with a gentle temperament, though with the accumulated stress of the years, and of their immigration to Israel in 1952, he has lost his sunny disposition.

She remembers a time just shortly after immigration which was very hard indeed for the family. Her husband broke his leg and sat at home in a cast for an entire year. During this time, their one-year-old daughter died and their eleven-year-old daughter was hurt in a traffic accident. And, at the same time, her husband's mother died. All this time—and for some time afterward—the family lived in a shack in a transit camp, the best housing the State of Israel could provide in those days for the many penniless refugees from the Near East. Looking back on those days now, she says, "It's a miracle I survived that year. Everything went wrong for us."

Some problems lingered. After their daughter's accident, she began to do badly in school and was difficult to discipline. It was not until after the girl finished her schooling and, at her mother's insistence that she learn a trade with which she could support herself, learned from her to be a skilled seamstress, that the two grew very close.

Besides their daughter, the couple have three sons. In addition to the child who died at one year, after her last surviving child was born she had several miscarriages. She no longer menstruates, and she is pleased. She did not want any more pregnancies. Moreover, the family is Orthodox, and it is good to be finished with the burden of the ritual separation of husband and wife during the menstrual cycle. Their sexual relationship is a good one, but she feels that since menstruation stopped she has less sexual desire; together with this, her husband too seems less desirous as he ages.

In other respects her relationship with her husband is good. "In his heart, he's a good man," she says, and he loves her very much. He often does the family shopping in the market so that she won't have to carry heavy packages. He gives her all his money, and never asks for an accounting. Nowadays, though, he can sometimes be a hard man. "I have patience without end," she says of herself; she understands him when he yells at the children; his hard work—he is a construction worker—leaves him little patience for them. She knows that he actually worries very much over the children, though he doesn't show it.

Their first son is in the army. He was a sickly child, and is not in combat; nevertheless, when he didn't return home one night, the father walked out to the army base, located nearby, to look for him, afraid that somehow something had happened to him. His worries about their daughter more often show signs of conflict; the girl goes out and enjoys herself, and her father becomes very angry with her. Her mother understands her, though—"times have changed, and our home is a long way away"—and the two exchange confidences like sisters. She knows that their children need a social life and good times, and she manages to defend them from their father's quick temper, and to find ways to let him express his love. She thinks he will find it easier to indulge his grandchildren, when they come along.

PSYCHOLOGICAL WELL-BEING: BALANCING SORROW AND JOY

The pleasures of the North African women center around family and home. A majority (52%) are happy to a great extent or even more with their husbands, a larger majority (77%) with their children, and nearly all (90%) with their grandchildren. One-half also report that their work in the house is enjoyed to a great extent or more. By contrast, only one-third of those few who work outside the home find this much enjoyment in their work.

The North Africans' pleasures outweigh their worries. Only one-quarter are worried to a great extent or more about their husbands; slightly more are worried to this extent about their children. The great majority (73%) have almost no worries at all about their grandchildren. Work, in the home or out of it, is seldom a problem for the North African women.

Turning to other worries, we do find the North African women worried quite a bit or even more about their husbands' health (54%); and, like other women in this study who have borne large families, even more worried (64%) about their own health. As we might expect, a majority (64%) have financial worries; many (55%) are worried about debts. The dominant worry in this group, however, is the national security situation (86%); much of this worry is apparently related to fears for a family member in the army (82%). By contrast, relatively few North African women are very worried about growing old (23%) or death (24%).

Asked about other worries, almost one-third of the North African women expressed concerns about family matters, such as a child's marriage, or a slight sense of regret as the children leave home. Other worries were often the restatement of previous questions: finances (19%), family in the army (15%), national security (9%), or their own health (15%).

Middle age has brought with it a sense of freedom to most but not all of the North African women. Although they are a minority, the 30 percent who do not feel free to do the things they want to do are a higher proportion than in any other ethnic group. This has not changed since age forty, for most; and if there has been change, the numbers of those who now feel freer are just about equal to those who feel less free.

Perhaps the years of immigration and adaptation have taken a toll, expressed by the numbers of North African women who have felt they might break under their problems. Over half have felt this way at least sometimes— though, as the preceding case histories and the overall life satisfaction ratings (to be discussed shortly) suggest, the North African women feel, for the most part, that serious problems have been faced and are now behind them.

Most of the North African women (71%) are satisfied, to a certain extent at least, by what they have gotten out of life so far. They often begin and end the day in a good mood, rarely in a bad mood. The two-fifths who sometimes or often feel they have nothing to do may, as we have suggested earlier, be enjoying the peace of a traditional household whose tasks for the moment have been completed.

Finally, the relative optimism of the North African women is suggested by their overall life satisfaction ratings. Describing their life at present, the North Africans—like the Turks and the Persians—place themselves just barely above the midpoint (a mean response of 5.4) between the worst possible and the best possible life. What is more, life nowadays is not as good as it was at age forty (a mean response of 6.1). However, looking to the future, the North Africans anticipate substantial improvement (a mean response of 6.4). Indeed, though their overall estimate of the future is no higher than the Arabs' and is below the Europeans', the anticipated gain is greater for the North African women than for any other group, reflecting, perhaps, not so much a brighter future as higher hopes for improvement.

To sum up, the North African women's joys for the most part outweigh their sorrows—and this is certainly true in the immediate family circle. What is more, though this is a group of women who underwent a period of considerable stress when they immigrated to Israel, many have been able to put their troubles behind them and to look to the future with expectations of better things to come.

This sense of optimism is conveyed in the case history of one of the North African women, who was born in Morocco in 1917, into a traditional family. Her parents chose her husband carefully; and, though she did not meet him until the day of their marriage, when she was fifteen and he was twenty-three, she is well contented with their choice, and hopes not only to choose her daughters' husbands, but to see them settled as happily as she is.

She describes life in Israel as much freer than it was in her home in Morocco. Like most girls, she never went to school at all, although her brothers began school at the age of three. She remained at home and learned sewing and embroidery. The family was Zionist, and had always wanted to immigrate to Israel; unlike many North African Jews, who fled the rising tide of Arab nationalism, they came to Israel in 1948 of their own will, their entry made somewhat easier by the fact that they came with some property.

She began childbearing in North Africa, and, while still there, two of her children died—a son aged four, and a daughter aged nine. After her daughter's death she was deeply depressed: she stopped eating and cried frequently, and was briefly hospitalized. Nevertheless, she managed to overcome her grief fairly soon, and in the same year as her daughter's death, a son was born.

Childbirth, and nursing her infants in particular, brought her great joy; she is described by the psychiatrist as a woman with a very pleasant face, smiling eyes, and a heartwarming smile. Her face radiates warmth and tenderness, especially when she speaks of those times she was nursing infants, memories she still cherishes very much.

All her children—two sons and three daughters—were born in North Africa. Her menstruation stopped when they immigrated to Israel. She was not at all disappointed: indeed, she was even pleased. She never wanted the children, especially her sons, to notice the signs of her menstrual period. In addition, the family is devoutly Orthodox, and the ritual separation of husband and wife during menstruation required the extra work of separate beds and bed linens, work she is not sorry to see end.

Finally, she does not regret the cessation of fertility. She feels that her five living children are enough. She says it is foolish to bear children simply to throw them out onto the street; and, to rear children properly, money is needed. In her family her daughters will have dowries; moreover, she adds, children also need attention.

Her children give her a great deal of happiness. They are mischievous, she says, but they are disciplined, and their relationship with their parents is good. She doesn't want her daughters simply to be married off, but rather waits and looks to find them good husbands. One daughter was going out with a man, but when her older brother told her he didn't think it a suitable match, she broke off the relationship.

Her oldest son is married, and their relationship remains close; she gets along well with the daughter-in-law. Indeed, she remarks, if she wants to keep her relationship with her son, she has to accept her daughter-in-law, and she does welcome her into the family, though not at the expense of her own daughters. The whole family celebrates the Sabbath together; her face lights up when she describes the Sabbath preparations and how the family welcomes the Sabbath with song.

She describes her husband as a good, industrious man. He begins each day at four o'clock in the morning, going first to the synagogue and then to work. She very much wishes he didn't have to go out so early; for a man his age—he is now sixty-three—it is not easy. When he comes back from his work as a clerk, he goes again to pray; he is, she says, a learned and righteous man. He gives her his entire paycheck and never asks her for an accounting.

The psychiatrist's summary might stand for many of the North African women: a warm, cordial woman whose face shines with the goodness of her heart and the contentment she has found; a personality with a lot of life's wisdom and internal harmony. The wounds of earlier griefs have healed.

7 | The Arabs

"Things
are
as
good
as
always."

In the Arab village, continuity with the past stems from a number of factors. *
Most villages have been on the same site for at least a century. Although there
has been some migration and transfer of land, most villagers can say that their
own families lived either in the same village or in a neighboring community for as
long as can be remembered. Marital and political alliances made on the basis of
traditional kin groupings continue to be an important component of village social
structure. One consequence of the stability of village life is the persistence of the
traditional subordinate status of the woman in the male-oriented village.

Despite a strong continuity with the past, the fifty years since the end of the
Ottoman Empire have brought significant changes into Arab village life. More
and more villagers are dependent upon wages from labor in the cities or in
neighboring Jewish settlements, rather than making their living from agriculture.
Furthermore, agriculture too is increasingly influenced by the processes of
modernization. While it is still possible to see animals drawing wooden plows
through fields, it is becoming more common to see the use of combines,
threshers, and water-sprinkling systems for irrigation. The marketing of produce
is facilitated by paved roads and bus lines, linking the villages—and the villagers
themselves—to the cities.

Like the immigrant Jewish women of this study, the Moslem Arab women's
lives have been changed by the political tides of war. The establishment of the
State of Israel left the Arabs a minority, isolated by cease-fire lines from the rest
of the Arab world. Families were dispersed in the war of 1948, and while there
was some reunion after the Six Day War of 1967 with relatives on the West
Bank, the Golan, and in Gaza, reunion was not complete.

* The first section of this chapter is adapted, in part, from an ethnographic report commissioned
for this study and prepared by Walter P. Zenner.

The birthrate among Israeli Arabs is one of the highest in the world, as a consequence of the persistence of traditional values favoring large families together with a dramatic drop in maternal and infant mortality as pregnant women came under the care of the Israel public health care system. The consequent population growth in the villages has had a number of results. One is the establishment of peripheral residential settlements somewhat distant from the old village center, which often permits young couples to gain some physical and social distance from their in-laws. It is no longer necessary for a young couple to live with the husband's parents, as tradition once dictated. Large family size, together with economic means permitting separate residences, has resulted in increasing numbers of nuclear family households, as opposed to the traditional patrilocal extended family households.

These changes have affected women's lives despite the fact that male-female relations have remained more traditional than other aspects of village life. Modern medicine saves the lives of mothers and children; thus, children are rarely orphaned, while mothers rear larger numbers of surviving children and less often face the deaths of children after birth. Women now have the right to have savings accounts at banks, a right with some importance since most villages are increasingly dependent on a money economy. Women have the right to vote—although it is unlikely that a women would vote against her husband's wishes. The home is slowly modernizing; kitchen appliances, such as small gas-burners, are becoming more common, though by no means universal. Nevertheless, among the various population sectors of Israel, the village Moslem Arabs are the most traditional. And although great changes have come to the villages in the past fifty years, these changes have not been sufficiently comprehensive to bring about any major transformations in the traditional cultural climate.

The Israeli Arab family is a patriarchy, with authority vested in the men, particularly older men. Descent and inheritance are patrilineal, and inheritance by women is rare. At marriage, a bride-price *(mahr)* is generally paid for the bride by the family of the groom, representing compensation to her family for the loss of her services. Women are expected to defer to men, and to be modest. Protection of the honor of their women, even after marriage, is the duty of fathers and brothers. While the seclusion of women logically follows from the code of honor and shame, conditions of village life make adherence to such an ideal impossible.

Nevertheless, the subordinate position of women and the family concern for their honor can be seen throughout the phases of the life cycle, beginning at birth, when a daughter may enter the world as a disappointment to her parents. Sons are clearly the preferred offspring, and the birth of a daughter may not even merit an announcement. Though girls are not necessarily unloved, they take up household duties at a very early age; until the establishment of the State of Israel, and with it compulsory education for both sexes, only boys had the privilege of schooling. From before puberty throughout her adult life, a woman was expected to guard her modesty, which required particular circumspection in dealing with men other than her father, brothers, and husband. There was special concern for a woman's honor prior to marriage, or if there was any suggestion she might run away to her parents' home to protest mistreatment by her husband—a permissible act, but one which often evoked suspicion about her conduct.

Women observe a system of menstrual taboos even more elaborate than those of Orthodox Judaism. The traditions of Islam evolved, in part, from biblical Jewish tradition; the menstrual taboos prescribed in Leviticus are repeated in the Koran. Contact with a menstruating woman is forbidden, and following the conclusion of menstruation the woman must perform a ritual purification of her body: after bathing herself, she must immerse herself as many as seven times. Any bathing vessel will serve, however; no ritual bathhouse is required, as it is in Judaism.

Islamic taboos extend to a prohibition on prayer, fasting, contact with the Koran, or any other religious act; Judaic taboos are limited to a prohibition of sexual contact between husband and wife. Furthermore, sexual intercourse, under Moslem codes, does not constitute a marriage bond, as it does in Judaism. On the contrary, there is no prohibition in Islam against a man's premarital or extramarital sexual activity, so long as his partner is neither an unmarried girl nor a wife—in which case he has committed an offense against the father and brothers in the first instance, or the husband in the second instance, and he and the woman are both punishable by death. In practice, however, it is often the woman alone who is killed, often by her father or brother; this occurs occasionally even in Israel, where it is outlawed by criminal code and the father or brother knows he will be easily identified and brought to trial. The extreme harshness of this double standard for sexual activity is a dramatic example of the near-complete subordination of women to men, even today.

In addition to the religious commandments, there are customs connected with menstrual taboos which vary by locality. The regional public health officer described the customs followed by the women of our study. Women are obliged to leave their husbands' beds for the duration of menstruation and are forbidden to approach the husband in bed. During menstruation, a woman is to dress herself in old, soiled clothing, and is not to comb her hair or make herself attractive in any way, so as to avoid wakening sexual desire in men. During menstruation women are forbidden to visit mourners, to attend a funeral, or to enter a cemetery. It is also forbidden to visit a women approaching childbirth for fear of complicating the delivery, or to visit a woman who has recently given birth for fear of harming the baby or its mother's future fertility. Menstruating women are also forbidden to step across the body of a sleeping or sitting man, for fear of causing him to break out in a rash. Finally, pregnant women are forbidden to visit a bride not yet married forty days, for fear of impeding her future fertility. No special restrictions are imposed on nursing women, but lactation has potential significance in that a woman nursing another's child created "milk-ties," the equivalent of blood ties between siblings, between her own nursing child and the other child. In short, the female sex, and female sexuality, are subordinate to males and to a long tradition of elaborate ritual codes.

The sense of tradition as well as the scars of history can be seen in the case history of one of the Arab women, who was born in Palestine in 1916. She never knew her father, who died when she was very small; she was the youngest of a family of six. Like her sisters, she did not go to school; her life centered around the household and its chores.

Without asking for her consent at all, her family arranged her marriage when she was fourteen. Her marriage was part of an exchange with another family; her brother took a wife from that family, and she was given to one of their sons.

She quarreled with her husband at first, and ran away to her parents' home more than once. Since the birth of their first son, however, all has been well between them. They have five daughters and two sons, ranging in age from the oldest son, who is thirty-five, to the youngest daughter, only sixteen, who is still at home. The other children are married and live close to their parents' home. All have children; having the grandchildren nearby is "God's blessing."

All her children were born before the 1948 war. She was struck in the abdomen by a bullet during the war, and though it was removed at once, even today she still suffers from pains where she was wounded. After the war, she miscarried seven pregnancies, each time losing the baby in the sixth month. She was treated by a gynecologist during her pregnancies, who told her the miscarriages were not due to the bullet wound but to her anxieties; nevertheless, after the war she was unable to bring a pregnancy to term.

The bullet wound has clearly left emotional scars. She finds herself constantly thinking about the injury. She speaks more readily about this wound than about the scars which the forced marriage and her early quarrels may have left; she avoids questions about her husband. He is thirteen years older than she is, and has been crippled with arthritis for the past ten years; he is able, with difficulty, to walk, but he cannot work, and the family is dependent on welfare, though their married children also help them out.

Her youngest child still helps her out in the home; indeed, on some days her daughter does all the work in the house. But the girl wants to marry like her brothers and sisters have already done; and, asked how she will manage after her daughter is married, she answers, "Then God will help me," and bursts into tears. Her daughter, it seems, means more to her than household help, for she adds, "All my children will help me out"—but once her last child has married and left the home, there will be no one but herself and the husband she married so reluctantly, about whom she even now is unwilling to speak.

DEMOGRAPHIC CHARACTERISTICS

The Arab women of our study come from two adjacent villages located in the fertile coastal Plain of Sharon. Though not large, the villages have doubled in size over the past twenty years, now numbering 7,000 and 10,000. All the Arab women were born in Palestine, in these or nearby villages. Records of birth were not kept with complete accuracy at the time these women were born. On the basis of self-report, the median year of birth in this group is 1919, although 28 percent claim to have been born in 1923 or later, and 22 percent in 1914 or earlier, despite the medical records which place them within the decade of birth used as the basis for sampling.

Almost all (96%) of the Arab women are illiterate. This is not a consequence of early betrothal preventing schooling, but rather due to the prevailing cultural norm, in which education was the prerogative of boys. Indeed, the Arab women married somewhat later than the Persian and North African women: the median age at marriage for the Arab women was seventeen, and only 8 percent had married by age thirteen or earlier. This may be due in part to the bride-price, higher in Israel than in her neighboring Arab countries. Marriage was almost universal: only four women in our sample had never married.

The choice of husband was nearly always (85%) made by the family, and opposition was seldom (15%) reported by the women. This general acceptance is probably linked to the prevalence of arranged marriages in Arab culture, and to the perception of this pattern as normative. Like themselves, the Arab women's husbands were born in Palestine. For many couples the age different between husband and wife was not great: almost one-half of the Arab women married men no more than five years older than themselves. However, one-third married husbands a decade or more older than themselves, an age difference which contributes to the number (20%) widowed by the time of our study. Divorce has been rare (5%), and three-quarters of the Arab women are still married to their first husbands, while a few others have remarried.

Childbearing has taken up a major portion of the lives of the Arab women. Almost four-fifths have been pregnant seven times or more; close to three-quarters have borne seven or more live children. However, miscarriage and death in early childhood were common. Only one-half of the Arab women brought all their pregnancies to live births, and there were a few women who miscarried more than half their pregnancies. Four-fifths of the Arab women suffered the loss of at least one child after birth; indeed, one-third saw three or more of their children die. At present just over one-half of the Arab women have seven or more living children, as a consequence of the comparatively high mortality rate in early childhood. The bearing and rearing of a large family, therefore, required a very large number of pregnancies in order to compensate for the losses through miscarriage, stillbirth, and death in early childhood.

Over one-half of the Arab women still have five or more children living at home, and over one-half still have children under the age of thirteen. Thus, not only is there no drop in involvement with the maternal role, but it remains at a level which is considerably higher than for any other group in this study. And, while many have youngsters at home, four-fifths already have grandchildren. This is, of course, a consequence of the long childbearing span: more than two-thirds of the Arab women bore children over a period of thirteen years or longer.

The husbands of the Arab women, as we might expect, are better educated than their wives, but the difference is not very great. Only one-third have gone beyond the third grade, and only 10 percent went as far as high school. Their relatively low educational level is reflected by their occupations; more than one-half of them are unskilled laborers, usually agricultural, if they are regularly employed at all. Nearly one-fifth, however, are landowners, and a handful have professional employment.

The Arab women continue to reaffirm traditional values, with less shift toward modernity than in any other group. Half the Arab women continue to feel the family should choose a girl's husband, though half no longer believe things should be this way. Nearly the entire group characterize themselves as religious and observant of traditions. Finally, half the Arab women spend their free time often or almost always separately from their husbands; and those who spend their time together do so "often" rather than "almost always," indicating that the separation between men's and women's worlds has tended to persist into middle age and is not, for the Arabs, changing as rapidly as in other groups. Although the Arabs, like the immigrant Jews, have experienced the anxieties of three wars, they are the only group who have not undergone geographical mobility. Thus, while the land around them has changed dramatically in their lifetimes, within the villages change is taking place more slowly and without the discontinuity of migration.

The modal Arab woman has lived a traditional village life. Rather than departing from tradition, she has changed along with it. Born in a Palestinian village in 1919, her changes for any formal education were almost nonexistent, and she cannot read or write. When she was sixteen or seventeen, her family chose a husband for her, whom she accepted willingly. He was not likely to be more than five years older than she was and, like her, was born in a Palestinian village. She is still married to him, although some of her friends have been widowed by now. Her thirty-four years of marriage have been occupied by the bearing and rearing of children. She has been pregnant at least seven times, and, despite miscarriages, has borne at least seven children. It is likely that more than one of her children died in early childhood; but despite miscarriages, stillbirths, and deaths of small children, she is likely to have seven or more living children. As many as five may still be living at home, some of elementary-school age. Some of her children are married, too, and have given her grandchildren.

It cannot have been easy to rear this large family. Her husband, almost as uneducated as she is, has been an unskilled farm laborer, when he has had work. She is devoutly religious, but some of the customs of her traditional culture are slowly changing. She may be ready to permit her daughters to choose their husbands by themselves. And between herself and her husband the separation between the worlds of women and men is no longer as complete as it once was; both the changing times and the relative increase in freedom which middle age brings traditional women have meant that they may spend some of their leisure time with one another.

Childbearing and childrearing have taken up much of the life of one of the

Arab women, who was born in 1924 in the village where she lives today. She never learned to read or write; when she was still very young, her mother began to require her help in the home, and that is how she learned the tasks of a wife. Her family tried to arrange a marriage for her when she was fourteen, but she refused their choice. They found her a husband when she was sixteen, and she was pleased by their decision; he is about her age, born in the same village, and a cousin on her father's side. He is a farmer, and they are blessed with a regular and adequate income.

She is the mother of five sons and four daughters. She bore a total of fifteen children, but six of her children died when they were small. Her pregnancies and births were usually normal, and she continued to bear her children at home, until the birth of fraternal twins, a boy and a girl, about fifteen years ago. The girl lived, but the boy died shortly after birth. Since then she has borne her children in the hospital; her births have been more difficult, the babies were larger, and she has suffered some pain in childbirth.

Her children range in age from a son, twenty-two, who works as a carpenter, to a son, five, who is in nursery school. All nine children still live at home with her. Although her daughters attended school, she feels their primary work is housework, and they have helped her in the home since they were small.

She has begun to menstruate irregularly, and has not been pregnant for the past year and a half. Doctors have told her that at her age this is normal, and some of her women friends have told her that even though she is still menstruating, she will not become pregnant any more. She has no regrets: "My husband and I agree that we have enough children, and we don't want any more." Their marital relationship and their sexual relations were always close, and continue to be.

She would like menstruation to cease completely, but she is somewhat afraid of suffering afterward. Other women have told her that menopause can bring about pains, especially in the uterus. Her own conception of menstruation is that it releases pressure in the body; she is apprehensive that when this external bleeding stops, the menstrual blood will be pressured inward, entering the blood in her own body, and her uterus will become a shelter without an opening for the release of pressure; she thinks there is harm in this. But since none of this has yet happened to her, she says it is still only something to think about.

She is not at all afraid of old age—"There is no shame in being old." She does not think much about growing old, however; "Maybe I'll grow old, and maybe I'll die before that. It's up to God."

THE SOCIAL CONTEXT OF MIDDLE AGE

The Arab women, like the North Africans and Europeans, enjoy a stable marital relationship of mutual need. More than half the Arab women need their husbands quite a lot or even more, and very few (12%) have little or no need for

their husbands. Their perception of their husbands' needs is almost identical to
their description of their own needs: most (56%) feel their husbands need them
quite a lot or even more, and hardly any (10%) have little or no sense of being
needed. For most (53%), this need has been stable since they were forty, if not
actually increasing (31%); and the great majority of the Arab women (82%) are
satisfied by things as they are.

A range of cultural values is reflected, however, by a comparison of these
women's descriptions of their husbands' needs. The European women typically
mentioned love and affection; the North African women replied "as a wife."
The modal response among the Arab women is that their husbands need them
for housekeeping (41%)—a response similar to that of the Persian women,
although the similarity ends here. Love and affection are mentioned by one-
quarter of the Arab women—more than any group except the Europeans—and
this, as we shall see, is not the only indication that the traditional marriage
involves more than just the traditional division of labor.

Despite relatively large numbers of children at home, many still of school
age, the Arab women report less often (38%) that they are very, very much
needed by their children than do the North Africans, Persians, and Turks. What
is more, the Arab women more often (34%) say that they are now needed less by
their children than do the Persians or Turks. And, like most of the women in the
study, they are not at all sorry (62%) that their children are becoming independent.

The explanation for the Arab women's more tempered sense of their
children's needs, by comparison to other women in this study with large numbers
of children at home, may lie in a combination of cultural factors. The modal
Arab woman, unlike women in other groups, is needed by her children—as by
her husband—for homemaking chores (43%). As small children grow,
household duties diminish somewhat; moreover, in the large, traditional family,
these duties are shared by mother and daughters. In this respect as well as others,
we find indications that the Arab women continue to reap those benefits afforded
by a traditional culture. There is certainly no suggestion that the Arab women
feel their efforts have gone unnoticed by their children: two-thirds feel their
children appreciate them quite a lot or even more, and almost the same number
reject the suggestion that children nowadays do not pay much attention to their
parents.

Almost four-fifths of the Arab women are grandmothers, and most see their
grandchildren daily. Many (44%) report that they cook or sew or knit for their
grandchildren; however, a substantial number—29 percent, a proportion much
greater than in any other group—answer "nothing in particular." This response,
we suspect, is likely to reflect the habit of close, regular contact which is part of
traditional culture. This notion finds some support in the relatively large
number—about four-fifths of those who had grandchildren by age forty—who
report no change in their contact with their grandchildren since then. Most Arab
women (72%) are satisfied by their contact with their grandchildren, and if there

is any discontent, it is more likely to be the feeling that they demand too much than the reverse.

While we might suppose that the Arab women would spend much of their day in homemaking, this is not what they report. Less than one-third tell us that they spend much or most of the day in homemaking—fewer than any other group—and most spend not so much (42%) or only a very small part of the day (27%) in homemaking. For many (45%) this has not changed since they were forty; quite a few (37%), though not as many as in other groups, report that they now give less time to homemaking. Most of the Arab women (65%) are satisfied by the time they spend in homemaking.

This description of a woman's workday in a traditional home is not what we might have expected from women who still have small children at home. There are several possible reasons for their responses, and all may be partial explanations. First, it may be that some of the routines of household management are taken for granted, and hence the time consumed is underestimated. Second, there are indications that household work is frequently shared with daughters. Finally, as we shall see, more than one-third of the Arab women work outside the home, necessarily reducing the time spent in housework, and perhaps diminishing its salience as well.

Despite our ethnographic report that Moslem Arab villages typically have extensive kin networks, only a minority (22%) of the Arab women told us that any relatives need them. We are tempted, as we have speculated in describing their workday, to wonder whether kin contact is so natural a part of the daily routine that it is not salient to them. Furthermore, the Arab women may be interpreting *need* somewhat differently from women in other groups, who typically described relatives' needs for affective ties. The modal response of the Arab woman who feels she is needed to any extent by a family member is that the need is instrumental: household help or the care of a relative's children or tending an inlaw's needs (38%). While affective ties are mentioned (29%), they are not the dominant response, as is the case in other groups. We are led to surmise that in the absence of extraordinary efforts on behalf of a relative, many Arab women do not feel themselves to be needed, notwithstanding fairly frequent contact with their families. For most, the needs of their relatives have been stable since the women were aged forty, whether they were needed then or not; and the great majority (85 percent, more than any other group) are satisfied with things as they are. This widespread satisfaction may be additional indirect evidence that satisfying contact with family members may be more frequent than the Arab women's reports of relatives' needs would indicate.

Contact with friends and neighbors—who are often distant kin, though the family tie may not be the salient one—is somewhat more frequent for Arab women than for women in other groups, as we might expect of village women. Nearly three-fifths of the Arab women see their friends and neighbors several times a week or even more often. For about one-half, this has not changed since they were forty; but if there has been change, decreased contact is about twice as common as increased contact. More often than any other group, the Arabs are satisfied with things as they are (68%); but if there is any desire for change, it is most often a desire for more frequent contact (27%).

A substantial minority of the Arab women (35%) work outside the home, typically helping out in the fields in some capacity. However, although most of those who do work say they enjoy their work, few who do not work wish that they did. Although the traditional woman often has a share in the economy of the household, the idea of paid work as a source of personal reward is found in modern cultures, where greater leisure permits the question of self-fulfillment through work to find expression. The scarcity of leisure and of opportunity probably also explain the Arab women's lack of involvement in volunteer activities.

To sum up, the center of the Arab woman's social world is home, husband, and children. Although she defines her roles as wife and mother in terms of the household duties which these role bring, rather than in terms of comradeship and advice, she is contented with her husband's and children's needs. Her social boundaries, however, are somewhat wider than for many women in the transitional Turkish, Persian, and North African groups; she is more likely to work, perhaps helping her husband in the field; and her daily routine is likely to include quite a bit of time with friends and neighbors as well as frequent contact with grandchildren.

Despite the satisfactions available to traditional women, this is a social context in which their subordinate status leaves them disadvantaged, as we can see in the case history of one of the Arab women, who was born in this village in 1919. She was the youngest of five children. Her father died suddenly when she was only a year old, and shortly afterward, "My mother's heart burst with grief and she died too." She was reared by her father's sister and her husband. They chose her husband for her when she was fifteen, a man eight years older than herself who was a farmer. The marriage was a happy one, with a close relationship in all ways, including their sexual relationship; she very much desired him, and they were satisfied together.

She bore six children; two died when they were small, and four survive, married, with grandchildren. But her husband left her suddenly after only ten years of marriage, when the children were small; he traveled to Cyprus and took a second wife, who bore him a new family. He continued to contribute to the support of his first family, and to visit her; their two youngest children she bore him "out of love," after he had left her to marry a second wife, "but—he never came back to me."

Her economic burdens were somewhat eased by some inherited land; she managed most of the support of her children, through their youth, as her problem. But the family scraped along until the children grew up, and now they contribute a little to her support.

She has managed throughout her life to survive on the basis of devout faith. She is Orthodox and feels that everything comes from a higher power, which all her life has been her aid, support, and comfort in life's crises.

SEXUALITY: PAST AND PRESENT

Cultural customs of reticence in providing Arab girls with sexual information seems to make the first menstruation an unpleasant experience, as most (72%) of the Arab women remember it today. Indeed, the proportion of women who remember the first menstruation only in negative terms rises steadily as modernity decreases, perhaps as a consequence of a greater unwillingness to prepare girls for menstruation in more traditional cultures.

No comparable cultural differences are found in the women's memories of their teenage years, despite the fact that for some these years were the period of adolescence and for others the beginning of adulthood. Women in all groups, as we have seen, remember their youth in favorable terms; for the Arab women, more often than for any other group, these memories are in positive terms only (49%).

Despite an unpleasant first memory of menstruation, most Arab women (67%) reported no unpleasantness whatsoever associated with menstruation throughout their adult lives. Their frequent pregnancies, however, may be the reason these women report menstrual irregularity more often than any other group. Nevertheless, irregularity was the exception (12%) and regularity the rule (79%).

Like women in the transitional groups, most Arab women (68%) feel that menstruation benefits physical health; and quite a few (14 percent, more than twice the proportion in any other group) specifically state that menstruation cleanses the body. Asked the worst thing about menstruation, about two-fifths of the Arab women, a proportion almost constant across our five groups, describe physical discomfort. The second major response is that menstruation is dirty (27%); the proportion of women giving this response, as we have seen, increases with successively more traditional groups of women—for whom tradition defines menstruation as ritual uncleanness. The social rituals attached to this state of ritual uncleanness, it should be recalled, are most extensive for the Arab women. Nevertheless, one-fifth of the Arab women found nothing at all bad to say about menstruation.

As we have seen, the Arab women define female roles, marriage and motherhood, in terms of traditional homemaking tasks. While we would assume this affects the content of the marital and maternal ties, there is no indication in the Arab women's responses that it diminishes the perception of satisfaction. Nearly one-half of the Arab women say their husbands treat them better than most husbands, and quarreling is less frequent among the Arabs than among any other ethnic group (63 percent quarrel seldom or hardly ever), though this may reflect factors other than marital harmony, such as the general tendency toward a separation of the worlds of women and men and the subordinate status of women.

Evidence that a measure of interpersonal harmony is reflected by the women's descriptions of the marital relationship, however, might be seen in the reports of sexual satisfaction. The sexual relationship is seen as satisfactory to both husbands and wives, though, as we have seen in other groups, some Arab women report a decline in sexual satisfaction in middle age. This decline is slight, however, and not much greater among women (17 percent currently dissatisfied, as opposed to 11 percent dissatisfied over the years) than among their husbands (11 percent currently dissatisfied, as opposed to 9 percent dissatisfied over the years). At the other extreme, there is a slight rise in the proportion of reports of "very satisfied" now, as compared to satisfaction over the years (from 30 percent to 31 percent for husbands; from 22 percent to 26 percent for wives); in all other groups, the proportion reporting either themselves or their husbands to be "very satisfied" consistently declines in middle age. It would appear that for the Arab women the loss of fertility, and, perhaps, freedom from the elaborate code of menstrual taboos, offset the biological decline in sexuality which is thought to accompany aging. As we shall see, there is some direct evidence for this in the Arab women's attitudes toward menopause.

The first pregnancy, as the Arab women remember it now, was an unequivocally (50%) or largely (32%) happy experience. The first birth brought no special difficulty for most (68%); for some, however, it ended in stillbirth (10%)—a small proportion, but one which rises consistently with increased traditionalism. Many Arab women (57%) reported no difficulty at all in adjusting to the care of the first baby. And, at the other extreme, the number reporting quite a bit of difficulty in adjustment (9%) was smaller than in other ethnic groups, perhaps as a consequence of the greater likelihood that these women had already, as daughters, shared in the care of small babies; cultural expectations may also have helped smooth the transition to motherhood.

Cultural expectations may also have had some part in shaping the Arab women's perceptions of subsequent pregnancies and births; like the Persians and North Africans, one-quarter of the Arab women remembered pregnancies and births as easier than most women's, despite miscarriages and stillbirths in these groups at rates which would be considered quite high by the European women. The perception of ease among the Arab women, therefore, may reflect a relative lack of anxiety about childbirth in a culture where birth is frequent, along with some readiness to accept miscarriage or stillbirth as an expectable hazard of pregnancy. It was very uncommon (6%) for the Arab women to describe serious problems in adjusting to the care of subsequent babies; generally, there were no special problems (34%) or everything went smoothly (49%).

Notwithstanding the relatively pleasant memories of pregnancies and births, the proportion of women who now wish they had had fewer children (22%) exceeds the proportion wishing they had had more (19%). This pattern of response is not found in any other ethnic group; in all other groups, the number of women who wish they had more children is greater than the number who wish they had fewer children. On the other hand, the Arab women are the only group who are for the most part (59%) satisfied by the number of children they have borne. A large majority of the European women, and substantial minorities of the Turks, Persians, and North Africans, now wish their families were larger. For the Arab women, then, "femininity," if this is defined as fertility potential, is a potentiality which has been fully realized, to the satisfaction of most. We shall now see whether this satisfaction is reflected in their perceptions of menopause.

Most of the Arab women have ceased menstruating (61 percent; of these, 7 percent as a result of surgery); another 9 percent are now in menopause, while 30 percent still menstruate regularly. The median age at which menstruation was reported to have ceased completely is 45.3, earliest of all the ethnic groups. Like the European women, the Arab women report relatively fewer menopausal symptoms than women from the Turkish, Persian, or North African groups.

The relatively low salience of menopausal symptomatology seems to be reflected by the Arab women's responses to the question, "What is the most important thing for you about change of life?" The Arabs, like the North Africans, mention the physical symptoms of menopause relatively less often (29%) than other groups. However, the Arab women note the cessation of menstruation as a salient change more than twice as often as any other group (20%), perhaps as a consequence of the extensive observance of menstrual taboos. This may contribute to the frequency with which social and familial changes are mentioned (19%), as well. The cessation of fertility is noted more often by the Arabs (10%) than by any other ethnic group—and, as we shall see, it is usually, but not always, welcomed.

This is seen in the Arab women's responses when asked to describe the best thing about menopause. The cessation of fertility was most frequently mentioned (25%), twice as often as in any other ethnic group. The cessation of menstruation was mentioned almost as frequently (22%), as were social and familial changes, such as raised social status. For the Arab women, then, the "best" thing about menopause is often also the "most important"—suggesting that the changes of menopause are generally viewed favorably.

The worst thing about menopause for most Arab women, as for the Turks, Persians, and North Africans, is its effects on physical health (47%); some see menopause as a sign of aging and death (19%). Not very many Arab women see the cessation of fertility as the worst thing about menopause (8%), but this proportion is twice as high as in any other group. Finally, some (12%) see nothing bad about menopause.

The responses of the Arab women to the twenty-three closed items bear out the sugestions in their spontaneous responses that the salient changes of menopause, such as the loss of fertility and changes in social status, are generally welcomed. The summary score on the five items reflecting attitudes toward the loss of fertility shows most Arab women (57%) to be in the two most positive categories. However, though their feelings are clearly positive, the Arabs as a group are less emphatically positive than women in other groups; for example, two-fifths disagree that a woman is pleased that there are no chances for additional children after menopause. As we shall see, part of the women's attitudes toward the cessation of fertility may be shaped by their perception of their husband's desires for additional children.

Arab women do not agree as strongly as women in other groups that menopause has deleterious consequences for physical health. Indeed, the summary score indicates that one-third of the Arab women believe that menopause brings about an improvement in physical health; in particular, the Arab women often believe that a woman has a feeling of better health and more abundant strength after menstruation has stopped (42%) and is pleased to be finished with the unpleasantness of menstruation (72%).

With increased traditionalism, the women in this study in increasing numbers agree that menopause benefits emotional health. A majority of the Arab women, more than any other group, agree that women feel more tranquil after menopause (55%), and reject the suggestions that after menopause a woman becomes more nervous and moody (66 percent disagree) or that as a result of menopause a woman might go crazy (90 percent disagree).

Social and personal changes at menopause and middle age are, with increased traditionalism, increasingly perceived as positive. Three-quarters of the Arab women, more than any other group, see the net balance of these changes, as measured by the summary score on these items, to be positive. In particular, Arab women believe that in middle age a woman is given more respect that before (87%).

Two-thirds of the Arab women feel that if there is change in the marital relationship in middle age, it is for the better. A majority (59%) feel that a husband is more interested in his wife at middle age than before. And, like the European women, almost one-half of the Arab women agree that after menopause a woman enjoys sexual relations more. The single negative element is the women's feelings of possible regret after menopause because their husbands would have wanted more children (37 percent agree, and of these, 26 percent definitely agree—a figure more than twice as large as the proportion in any other ethnic group).

To sum up, the sexual dimension, past and present, has been gratifying to the Arab women. The marital relationship has been a harmonious one, and sexuality has been satisfying, with little decline in satisfaction—perhaps, for some, an increase—with menopause. Menopause brings the long childbearing period to an end, and the loss of fertility is generally welcomed by the Arab women, who are satisfied by the number of children they have borne, though some feel their husbands might have some regrets. The physical changes of menopause are not seen as particularly troublesome, and middle age brings with it increased respect for these traditional women.

Some of these themes can be seen in the case history of one of the Arab women, born in the village in 1915. She was a only child; her mother died when she was five years old, and her father died just four years later. She was reared by her uncle and aunt. They chose a husband for her when she was nineteen, a man three years younger than herself. The relationship between them has always been good: "First of all, he's my cousin; second, we agree in everything." The sexual relationship is also close. She bore eight children, of whom four died in early childhood. She remembers her pregnancies and births as easy, and she enjoyed rearing her children.

Menstruation stopped four years ago. Menopause brought no changes, either in her health or in her relationship with her husband. Asked whether she would prefer menstruation to continue, she smiled and replied: "This is in my hands? When it was, it was good; when it stopped, it had to stop, and that's that—that's nature's way."

PSYCHOLOGICAL WELL-BEING: BALANCING SORROW AND JOY

The Arab women find their pleasures in the home, with their husbands, children, and grandchildren, and pleasures outweigh worries in their family relationships. Three-quarters of the Arab women are happy to a great or very great extent with their husbands—more than any other ethnic group—and only one-third report a comparably high level of worry about their husbands. The proportion of women who enjoy their children is just as high, and worries are even more uncommon (22%). Grandchildren are even more often enjoyed to a great extent or more (86%), and worries are still more uncommon (18%); however, perhaps the close contact of village life means that grandchildren are more often part of the family than a special treat—in turn subduing the Arab women's pleasure in their grandchildren just slightly, and making worries just slightly more frequent, than among women in other ethnic groups.

Housework is a source of pleasure to most Arab women (57 percent enjoy their housework to a great extent or even more), and rarely a source of worry (16%). Work outside the home, for those who do work, is almost equally enjoyed (53%) and hardly more often a source of worry (17%) than housework. It is worth noting that the frequency with which work is perceived as rewarding has some relationship to the proportion of women working in any particular group. It is only among the Europeans and Arabs that sizeable minorities work, and it is only in these groups that a majority of those women working outside the home view their work as quite enjoyable.

Turning to other worries, we find the Arab women, like other women who have borne large families, more often are quite or especially worried about their own health (62%) than about their husbands' health (48%). Health may be the underlying factor which explains the relative frequency of Arab women describing themselves as especially worried about growing old (24 percent, three times the proportion in any other ethnic group; an additional 17 percent are quite worried). Worries about death, in any connection, are not so common (30 percent quite or especially worried). Finances are a matter of some concern to every group except the Europeans; however, the Arab women, like the Turkish women, are somewhat less often worried about finances (48%) or debts (41%) than the Persians or North Africans, perhaps because the expenses of a traditional household are more easily managed in a traditional setting. Finally, like all Israelis, most Arab women are quite or especially worried (65%) about security conditions in Israel. Although the Arab women's level of concern is somewhat lower than that expressed by the Jewish women, whose children are drafted into the Israel Defense Forces, national security is nevertheless the most common of worries, for the Arabs as well as for the Jews.

Asked if they had any other worries, the Arab women most frequently mention family matters, such as a child's marriage or an in-law problem (39%). Not only is this the most frequent response among the Arabs, but it was more often given by the Arabs than by any other group. Their own health is the second most frequent source of concern (27%), and troubles the Arab women almost twice as often as women in other groups. These seem to be the worries of the traditional lifestyle—like its pleasures, centered around the home and family, and perhaps the consequences of having borne so many children.

Like other women in our study, the Arabs feel free to do the things that attract them (57 percent feel very free), and for the great majority (70%), this has not changed since age forty. Notwithstanding a sense of personal freedom, the Arabs do not perceive their lives as free of troubles: 44 percent have felt, sometimes at least, that their problems are likely to break them. On the other hand, the Arab women are more often quite or very satisfied (40%) by what they have gotten out of life so far than are women in other ethnic groups.

A question we had intended to elicit possible self-consciousness about aging among women in the more modern, youth-oriented groups, asks for the extent of satisfaction with one's personal appearance. For the most part women in other groups expressed neither satisfaction nor concern. The Arab women, however, whose long years of physical stress in repeated childbirths are written on their faces, quite often (41%) told us that their personal appearance gave them a great deal of satisfaction. As one of the Arab women remarked, "There is no shame in being old"—a sentiment shared, evidently, by many.

As we have indicated, the proportion of women who feel that they sometimes or very often have nothing to do rises steadily with increased traditionalism: 43 percent of the Arab women report feeling this way, 20 percent very often. Though we had intended this question to measure a possible sense of emptiness, the consistency of these findings leads us to surmise that, for the traditional woman, at least, the feeling of nothing to do means that the tasks of the household are, for the time being at least, completed.

The Arab women more often than not begin their long day in a bad mood (28%); but, by the time the day is over, good moods (38%) are twice as frequent as bad moods (17%). This suggestion of contentment is borne out by the ratings of the Arab women as they evaluate their lives on the ladder ranging from the worst possible life to the best possible life. They see their present lives in more positive terms than any other group (a mean response of 6.5); what is more, unlike the Turks and North Africans, they do not feel the quality of life has declined since they were age forty (a mean response of 6.2). And nearly all the Arab women expect life to continue to be as satisfying as it is right now, as they try to anticipate the future (a mean response of 6.4). Thus, while the Arab women do not see their lives changing for the better over the next five years, they expect no decline in their present relatively high level of contentment.

Satisfaction is the theme underlying the case history of one of the Arab women, despite a life which has seen some adversity. She was born in this village in 1917, into a family of seven children. Like her sisters, she stayed home to help her mother with the housework, until her marriage at the age of fifteen, to a husband twelve years older than herself.

Her husband has never worked a day in his life. At one time they had some income from tenant farmers; they have lived on welfare and their relatives' support, and nowadays their sons help to support them. Although recently he has not been so healthy, most of his life he was healthy, and simply never had any desire to work. She never worked outside the home either, although she does all the work in the home, with her daughters' help. She has never minded his unwillingness to work; she says he just never did want to work, and that's the way he is. Their marriage was always a good one, and now also their life together is fine.

They have nine children, of whom three daughters and four sons are now married. Two of their sons died while they were small babies. Two children still live at home; their married sons and daughters-in-law also live at home, or in homes built just beside their parents' home. "My daughters live far away"—beside their husbands' parents' homes—but they visit often, almost daily. The relationship she enjoys with her daughters-in-law is "as sweet as honey," and things between her and her sons-in-law also are fine. She very much enjoys her grandchildren.

She reached menopause three years ago, with no physical discomfort at all. She was very pleased with menopause, because she didn't want any more children; she says, "I have enough." She is glad to be finished with pregnancy and the problems of little children. Her husband agrees with her, and "between us things are as good as always."

8 | The Age of Transition

Researchers who stray too far from the focus of their work are irresponsible, but researchers who ignore the broader implications of their work are no less irresponsible. In this chapter we shall try to avoid either of these two extremes, speculating on the implications of our study within the bounds of good sense, recognizing that we are obliged to address the broader issues of women's lives in a modernizing world, acknowledging in advance that our research is suggestive but far from definitive. If you must hang, choose a tall tree, advises the Talmud; in this chapter we hope to creep cautiously out on one or two limbs.

We shall commence by restating the most important lessons we learned from our study: the strengths and weaknesses of our original hypotheses; middle age as neither loss nor liberation, but transition; the centrality of cultural stability; the significance of the fit between personal aspirations and socially accessible roles; the overwhelming consensus in welcoming the cessation of fertility; the relation of culture to stress. We will go on to review some of the struggles which accompanied our learning. And finally, we shall conclude by suggesting some of the larger lessons we have learned.

At the Israel Institute of Applied Social Research, our study was known by its Hebrew identification: *Gil Hama'avar.* In everyday Hebrew this phrase can refer specifically to menopause; it can also signify middle age, in women or in men. *Menopause:* the cessation of menstruation and of fertility. *Middle age:* no longer young. The literal meaning of *gil hama'avar,* however, is "the age of transition," a meaning we came to appreciate more fully as our study progressed into the final phases of analysis and interpretation. Either of the common translations seemed an incomplete representation of our findings, in which change, more often than loss, was a dominant theme for women in all five subcultures.

Our first glimpse of this understanding came in the pilot study, which led us to begin to think in terms of a net balance of gains and losses and helped us design a questionnaire which opened the way to our first major lesson. This lesson we would now phrase—and it is applicable to all stages of the life cycle, from early infancy through old age—as neither loss nor liberation, but *transition.*

Our study began with competing hypotheses about the relationship between women's responses to the changes of middle age and the degree of modernity characteristic of their ethnic groups. Antonovsky and Maoz anticipated that the traditional woman would welcome the changes of menopause and middle age, which bring an end to childbearing and menstrual taboos, the raised social status of matriarch, and the powerful and meaningful roles of mother-in-law and grandmother. The modern woman, on the other hand, would resist and regret these changes, which signify the loss of youth in a youth-oriented culture and a lost childbearing potential which had never been fully used. These differences, they anticipated, would be expressed as an inverse linear relationship between psychological well-being and the degree of modernity, with the more traditional women the most contented at middle age. Looking back with the wisdom of hindsight, they now wonder whether their scientific hypothesis may have been grounded not only in the dominant literature of psychoanalysis and the observation at a distance of traditional culture, but also in their own identity: they were middle-aged males who were closely familiar with modern women and were living in the cultural climate of the mid-1960s.

Datan rejected this view—influenced by the work of Bernice Neugarten and, it must be admitted, having a personal stake in the outcome of the study herself—and predicted that the modern woman would be best prepared to cope with the changes of menopause and middle age, having coped actively with changes earlier in the life cycle and bringing to her middle age a broader range of coping skills in a predominantly modern culture which, at least in principle, prized these skills. Datan regarded the loss of fertility as inconsequential to the modern woman, who had ceased childbearing years before; it was the traditional woman, she suggested, who would regret her lost fertility, since so much of her identity was bound up with childbearing, leaving her with little besides losses for her later years. Datan expected these differences to be expressed as a direct linear relationship between psychological well-being and the degree of modernity, with the most modern women the happiest in middle age.

If it was our fortune to commence our research with the aid of clear, conflicting hypotheses, it was our exceptional good luck to find our questions answered. Our hypotheses as well as our unstated expectations found answers. As it turned out, each hypothesis was half right. The survey findings yielded a curvilinear relationship between the degree of modernity and self-reported psychological well-being. That is to say, the balance of *naches* and *tsoris,* of joy and sorrow, was most positive for the Central Europeans and the Arabs—the most modern and the most traditional women in our study. Psychological well-being was lowest among the Persian women, who represent the midpoint on our continuum between tradition and modernity. The Turks, midway to modernity, and the North Africans, still close to tradition, were intermediate between the relatively high well-being of the European and Arab women, and the relatively low well-being of the Persians.

Datan, then, had been right—but only about the modern women. Antonovsky and Maoz had also been right—but only about the most traditional women. With the wisdom of hindsight, we learned our second major lesson: the stability of the cultural context, rather than its specific content, may facilitate adaptation to life cycle change. Our European and Arab sub-cultures have the highest measure of cultural stability: the immigrant European women came to a country where the dominant cultural values were European, while the Moslem Arab villagers, living in a stable traditional setting, saw change gradually penetrate their lives. The transitional groups, however—the Turks, Persians, and North Africans—had been socialized into traditional settings and were then transplanted into a modern culture where traditional cues no longer served them. At the same time, the freedoms of modernity were not open to them: they saw no choices for themselves among a plurality of roles, seeing only the broadened horizons open to other women. Self-reported psychological well-being was lowest among the Persians, the group which, by external indicators, such as the degree of traditionalism in the life history and the modernity of the present life context, would appear to have experienced the greatest measure of discontinuity. The Turks, born into a modernizing culture and immigrants to modern Tel Aviv, and the North Africans, born into traditional families and immigrants to towns in which they were the dominant group, experienced less abrupt transitions than the Persian women, born to traditional families and immigrants to modern Tel Aviv.

We found that the content of women's responses to menopause and middle age is shaped by the cultures in which they grew up: the balance of gains and losses seen by women is specific to each culture, a product of earlier life experiences and the resulting resources a woman brings to middle age, as well as the dominant values in her culture. Women in each of the five subcultures of our study viewed menopause as a combination of gains and losses, but this combination differed by subculture. The Europeans, for example, saw a possible decline in emotional health; the Turks, Persians, and North Africans were concerned over a decline in physical health; and the Arabs' responses included pleasure at an end to ritual uncleanliness.

Cultural stability, then, shapes the likelihood of personal adaptation; cultural context, the specific responses to specific concerns. However, the cultural context also specifies the extent to which the social structure makes provision for the fulfillment of the cultural expectations. The modern European woman's psychological well-being may be threatened if her expectations of enhanced companionship with her husband or of a return to work or of voluntary activities are frustrated by the options her social reality makes available to her. The Arab women—and we cite a pattern increasingly frequent since our study—may no longer adapt as well as in the past when her sons marry and, instead of moving into the household with daughters-in-law and grandchildren, move out of the village into town. Successful adaptation requires a fit between the specific cultural expectations and the structural realities. Not all European or Arab women in our study were able to find an ecological niche.

Differences among women in five such different groups were not surprising. What was surprising, however, was the finding that women in all groups welcomed the cessation of fertility, despite large variation in conception control and fertility history, ranging from the Europeans at one extreme, who typically bore one or two children and prevented or aborted unplanned pregnancies, to the Arabs at the other extreme, some of whom were continuously pregnant or lactating between menarche and menopause. That this response is paced by the life cycle and not shaped by prior events in the psychosexual history is suggested by the Europeans' attitudes toward their actual and ideal family size: two-thirds of the European women reported that they would have wanted larger families, but that economic or political circumstances—this cohort bore children at the time of the establishment of the State of Israel, the War of Independence, and a period of economic austerity—prevented larger families. Notwithstanding the desire to have borne more children, often expressed strongly and poignantly, the European women—like women in all other groups—no longer wished to be capable of pregnancy. We have interpreted this finding as suggestive of a developmental change in adulthood, linked—like many earlier developmental changes—to a maturational change.

Finally, our multidisciplinary approach to the question of women's responses to the changes at middle age permitted us to answer the question which originally stimulated the broader study: Is the higher rate of hospitalization of European women for involutional psychosis a consequence of differential rates of stress in different cultures, different modes of expression of stress, or differential diagnosis? From the survey, the medical examination, and the follow-up psychiatric interviews, we were able to provide tentative answers.

There was no support for our first hypothesis, that cultural patterns produced greater stress in more modern cultures, manifest at the extreme as involutional depression. On the contrary, as has been shown, self-reported well-being was greatest at the two poles of the traditionalism-modernity continuum. There was some support for the second hypothesis. That is, there was a greater incidence of psychosomatic complaints on survey responses among the Persian and North African women, while the follow-up psychiatric interviews showed "psychological" symptomatology among the European women and "somatic" symptoms among the women in other groups. The third hypothesis, that involutional psychosis is diagnosed among European but not Near Eastern women, found some support through our follow-up diagnosis of depression among Near Eastern women. The tendency to express stress in psychic symptoms among Europeans and in somatic symptoms among Near Easterners would probably facilitate a diagnosis of depression among Europeans and impede such a diagnosis among Near Eastern women, unless psychiatrists were particularly alerted to consider depression in these ethnic groups. In general, however, our broad-scale study of normal women showed involutional depression to be an extremely infrequent response in any culture. Psychiatrists continue to question the diagnostic label, "involutional psychosis." Whatever their answer, we have no evidence that extreme maladaptation is any more frequent in middle age than other maladaptive responses in other periods of the life cycle.

What, then, have we—the writers and readers of this book, who are far removed from the traditional, transitional, even the modern worlds of the women of our study—learned?

The principal finding of our study is simple. We completed a study of middle-age women in five Israeli sub-cultures, only to discover what Ecclesiastes had said long ago: that to every thing there is a season, a time to sow, and a time to reap. We found that women from cultures selected for their differences responded differently to the changes of middle age—not remarkable, but satisfying findings in the social sciences, where expected differences are not always found and, when found, are sometimes different from what was expected. Nevertheless, our surprising finding was one of similarity: menopause and the loss of fertility did not signify a "closing of the gates"—regardless of a woman's childbearing history. On the contrary, whether a woman had planned and restricted childbearing to only one or two children, or had been bearing children over most of her fertile years, the response to the cessation of fertility was positive.

The significance of this finding, however, is not that it echoes the words of Ecclesiastes, but that the words of Ecclesiastes have gone so long unheeded. The psychoanalytic and psychiatric literature is anchored in themes of loss rather than of change and transition. Indeed, we were no exception; our own expectations about women's responses to menopause were based on culturally shaped differences in the family life cycle, leading in turn to differences in responses to the loss of fertility.

The direction of these differences was a question over which we had argued at length in the early phases of the study. This, then, was the first issue to which we turned our attention when our survey responses had been transformed into computer printout. We discovered, of course, that neither the hypothesis of a positive response varying directly with the degree of modernity, nor its converse, the hypothesis that positive response would vary inversely with modernity, was borne out. Nor did we have a scattering of positive and negative responses across groups, to be traced—if only we had found them—to individual differences in personality, social context, or childbearing history.

Instead, our finding was that women in all cultures responded positively to questions about the loss of fertility at menopause—and our own first response was to suspect computer error, or a failure of the survey technique. Only when we found expectable cultural differences in response to other questions—among them other questions related to menopause—convincing us that neither our computer nor our subjects were fooling us—then and only then did we begin to consider what near-unanimity among nearly twelve hundred women from five very different ethnic groups might signify.

Our interpretation of this finding—that there is a natural rhythm to the seasons of the life cycle—is little more than a restatement of ancient wisdom. The value of our discovery—or rediscovery—is that times have changed greatly since traditional folkways provided a stable culture against which the natural rhythms of the life cycle were highlighted; if traditional wisdom retains its force, it may testify to developmental patterns which transcend culture and history.

The Moslem Arab and North African Jewish women in our study may be among the last generations in Israel to represent a traditional family lifestyle. Folk wisdom guided these largely illiterate women, but their daughters have completed at least eight years of school, often more; the women in our study bore children over most of their fertile years, while their daughters plan families of two or three children. The Turkish women in our study may have come from traditional families similar to those of the Arabs and North Africans, but they, like the daughters of the more traditional women, have grown up in school, and along with literacy came a larger vision of life and fewer children. Yet the Turks feel no regret in middle age over lost fertility, just as the Europeans, for whom these changes are not recent, do not. Times change—in our study we can almost feel the changing times—but the rhythm of the life cycle does not.

The significance of these women's responses reaches beyond the arena of the behavioral sciences into the politics of sexuality and family life. At this writing, abortion is a controversial issue in American politics, while some of the opponents of the Equal Rights Amendment to the American Constitution fear this amendment will threaten family stability. Yet the declaration of the State of Israel guarantees equal rights to both sexes—as well it might, since the three great religious traditions of which the population is comprised do not—and there is no evidence at all to suggest a consequent breakdown of family stability. Most of the European women in our study have aborted at least one unplanned pregnancy, as have many women in other ethnic groups; we have no evidence that abortions in the context of an accepting culture leave emotional scars. On the contrary, there is evidence in our study that bearing too many children with too few resources, whether economic or emotional, can erode both emotional and physical health.

Our study of middle-aged women at a developmental period of transition, against an historical background of transition, permits us a further suggestion. We speculate, remembering that psychological well-being is highest for the Europeans, who are closely followed by the Arabs—two cultures marked by relative stability—and lowest for the Persians, for whom transition is greatest—that the process of transition is costly and painful. This is a speculation with unexpected implications. As we look across the five sub-cultures in our study, it almost seems that we can watch the process of modernization, and with it the changing roles of women. Increased literacy, diminished dependence on traditional rituals, an increased separation between the biological life cycle and the social life cycle, fewer children, the acquisition of political and social rights—these differences, conspicuous in a comparative historical and demographic overview of the five ethnic groups, converge around a common theme. This theme is the liberation of women from the constraints of traditional roles.

Yet our study has taught us that liberation, with its attendant consequences of autonomy and choice, is not a simple progression toward new freedom and prerogatives. On the contrary, liberation, as we see it in a comparative overview of the five sub-cultures of our study, is the exchange of one set of prerogatives for another. It is certainly true that the prerogatives of the modern woman are broader and her constraints fewer; but it is also true that freedom of choice can be accompanied by uncertainty and doubt. The relative certainty of the traditional woman, moreover, seems to us to be bought at the price of ritual constraints; we may fail to see, as outsiders looking into an earlier chapter of our own cultural history, that the traditional woman has confidence in her tradition and rituals. The significance of her confidence will become clear in an examination of our own early assumptions as researchers preparing to explore this area.

Our competing hypotheses about the effects of traditional culture on women's responses to menopause grew out of a shared premise that the traditional woman is fatalistic and passive, while the modern woman copes actively with the changes of the life cycle. Since menopause is an inevitable and universal maturational change, Antonovsky and Maoz reasoned, acceptance is the adaptive response, and is most likely to be seen among women of traditional cultures. Datan rejected the exclusive focus on menopause and reasoned that the family life cycle changes of middle age, such as the departure of children from the home, could best be faced by the active, modern woman, who shapes her life to suit her needs.

Our pilot interviews suggested that we had mistaken tradition for passivity. These findings, together with our survey responses, which showed psychological well-being to be nearly as high for women in the most traditional culture as for women at the modern extreme, encouraged us to rethink the significance of traditional culture.

Our error in equating tradition with passivity was apparent in the responses of one of the Arab women in our pilot study. When we asked whether menopause was a matter of concern to her, she replied that it was, and went on to describe the measures she had taken in response to her concern: free hormone shots at Kupat Holim, the Israel national health service clinic; visits to a gynecologist in Tulkarm, a village just over the Israeli border in what was then the newly opened West Bank, for the sake of the excursion; and finally, the advice of a faith healer. In other words, she employed the full range of medical, political, and spiritual resources, from socialized medicine to magic and witchcraft, in the service of her concern. Through her response, we were helped to remember that what our culture identifies as magic and witchcraft are simply ritual practices which we now know to be ineffective, while scientific measures are those which, as far as we can tell, *do* work—or at least have not yet been proven ineffective.

Magic and witchcraft evolved as means of control over the environment, and we err when we dismiss ritual practices as ineffective and their practitioners as passive. We are equally in error if we identify modernity with active coping. "I don't want menstruation to stop," one of the European women in our pilot study told us, "It stopped in Auschwitz." The machinery of modernity can immobilize the human spirit at least as effectively as any network of ritual and tradition.

Our pilot study also reminded us of the position of women in the traditional family. While formally subordinate in status and power, the traditional woman, like the "woman of valor" described in Proverbs, occupies a pivotal place in the household economy. Thus, while she is formally subordinate, the traditional woman need not necessarily be functionally subordinate. The Arab woman we have quoted was candid about the marital concerns which come with menopause in a traditional culture; she told us she was worried her husband might do as a neighbor had done and marry a younger second wife, over the border in a West Bank town where polygyny, outlawed in Israel, was still practiced. We asked how she dealt with her concerns over her own husband. "Oh, I just keep him at home—I don't let him go to Tel Aviv"—not quite the passive answer we might have expected.

Of course the traditional subordination of the Moslem Arab women cannot be overlooked. Polygyny is legal just over the border, not many miles away from the Israeli villages where our studies were carried out. However, it would also be a mistake to ignore comparable phenomena in modern cultures: a monogamous businessman's affair with his secretary cannot be said to represent progress toward the liberation of women. The secure, pivotal position of the traditional woman makes her vital to the traditional household economy. With transition toward modernity and urbanization, the traditional woman's centrality and security are eroded, as are her stable expectations for a known future.

In place of traditional stability, transition brings change, and with change comes the unknown. The transitional women in our study face the unknown with apprehension—"Don't take me out of my kitchen," says a Persian woman—and look to their broadened potentials, incompletely fulfilled, with regret—"I tasted nothing of life," sighs a Turk. We have speculated that the transitional women, socialized in a traditional culture and then transported to a modern setting where their traditional cues no longer serve them, experience the greatest measure of stress arising from discontinuity.

But in a larger sense we are all in transition. No one in middle age today was reared prepared for today's social climate. Indeed, this is particularly and poignantly apparent for many "modern" middle-aged women. Reared to become wives and mothers, often at the expense of careers, they may be entering the labor force today, when affirmative action programs mandate the hiring of qualified women in preference to men—programs which create new horizons for younger women, but highlight the constricted horizons of older women, whose decisions earlier in the life cycle are likely to leave them at a disadvantage in today's social context.

Yet liberation from traditional role constraints may not inevitably create an easier old age, but rather a different old age. Today's young women may postpone childbearing for a career, and in doing so face the risks of diminished fertility and increasing likelihood of complications during pregnancy and birth—and perhaps some may face a middle age with regret over children not born earlier in the life cycle, while their more traditional counterparts contend with their troublesome grown children.

Many of these observations apply to men as well as to women. But the constraints of biology are more rigorous for women; risk in childbirth is never absent, and it becomes a matter of some concern toward the end of the thirties, while their fertility ends about a decade later. Men do not face the risks of pregnancy and childbirth—a trite statement with nontrivial implications. Moreover, men may remain fertile until the end of life. Thus the outer bounds of egalitarianism and liberation are biological as well as social.

Women seeking both the rewards of family, which we associate with tradition, and the prerogatives of paid work, often considered the prize of modernity, are likely to have to juggle, if not struggle, with the interaction of reproductive biology and the social context. It is clear that our world is moving away from tradition and toward modernity, whatever the particulars of our definitions. The traditional women in our study are a remembrance of the past; even the modern women in our study, housewives more often than not, would not seem modern in the company of a group of young career women. But an overview of our five sub-cultures permits us to anticipate the new directions of modernity—and perhaps to comment on the durability of tradition as well.

Our study suggests that it would be a mistake to assume that certain traditional values are no more lasting than the rituals and folkways of the traditional lifestyle. Women in all five sub-cultures value the companionship of a good marriage and cherish their children, while seeking personal autonomy and the satisfaction of a job well done. Looking across the panorama of social change represented by these five groups, it seems to us that those themes common across cultures may well transcend tradition and modernization, and represent enduring human values, which Freud summed up as the mark of the healthy adult: love and work. Perhaps we might close by suggesting that the task for future generations of women and men is a liberating translation of the best of human tradition.

Appendix 1

Method

Review
of
Study
Procedures

Our study was carried out in four phases: a pilot investigation of 55 women of European, Near Eastern, and Israel-born Moslem Arab women; a broad-scale survey of 1,148 women from five Israeli sub-cultures (Jewish immigrants from Central Europe, Turkey, Persia, and North Africa, and Israel-born Moslem Arab women); a follow-up medical examination, to which all survey respondents were invited (of them, 697 women agreed to come); and finally, a follow-up phase of psychiatric interviews with 160 women representing selected sub-groups from each of the five ethnic groups.

Findings from the pilot investigation and the medical examinations have been reported in earlier publications (see the Bibliography). In this book we discussed the responses of the 1,148 women who were our survey respondents. These responses, and the cultural patterns which they indicate, have been illustrated through the use of selected case histories chosen from the 160 psychiatric interviews conducted in the fourth phase of the study.

THE SAMPLES

The five ethnic groups were chosen to represent the broadest possible range between the urban modern woman and the rural traditional woman. To maximize ethnic homogeneity, each ethnic sample was drawn from a residential region in which that ethnic group was highly concentrated. Central Europeans were drawn from a largely middle-class city near Tel Aviv; Persians and Turks were drawn from two predominantly lower-income administrative divisions of Tel Aviv; North Africans were drawn from two towns in the foothills of the Judaean Mountains; and Arabs were drawn from two large villages in the Little Triangle, an area in the central plain of Israel settled predominantly by Arabs. Areas of high concentration of these ethnic groups tended also to be homogeneous socioeconomically, since many factors indicative of traditionalism or modernity, such as level of education or number of children, also affected socioeconomic status.

The Jewish populations were taken from the lists of the Population Registry. A list was obtained for each region containing the names and addresses of all women in the appropriate ethnic group born between the years 1914 and 1923, and thus aged forty-five

117

through fifty-four in 1969, the year in which interviewing was conducted. These lists were handled separately for each ethnic group. Names on the lists were then ordered, using a table of random numbers.

The total number of Europeans eligible for interviewing was 766; the total of eligible Persians and Turks was 805. These numbers were reduced to sampling pools of approximately 600 Europeans and 600 Persians and Turks combined.[1] The original North African population in Ramla and Lod totaled 605 and was not reduced. The goal was 300 interviews in each group, with an estimated nonresponse rate of 50 percent. Subject numbers were assigned within each ethnic group beginning with the first, randomly selected list of names, and proceeding through the lists as they had been randomly ordered. Interviewing began with subject number one and proceeded in numerical order.

The Arab sample consisted of all 360 women in the two villages selected for sampling, who were listed in the regional health center files as having been born between 1914 and 1923. This age group included women whose births were never recorded; consequently, when the Arab population was registered in 1948, the ages recorded in the Population Registry were based on estimates made by census officials. More accurate estimates were later made by the staff at the regional health center, to whom guidelines such as the recorded birthdates of children were available; these latter records were used in preference to Population Registry files. Nonetheless, interviewers discovered cases of young mothers of twenty-five and grandmothers of seventy-five who had been selected for interviewing on the basis of inaccurate records. Although great efforts were made to select women in the appropriate age range, and although known instances of error were eliminated from the research sample, it is nevertheless almost certain that the Arab sample showed greater variation in age than other groups.

On the basis of age records, the age distribution in each sample was similar. Furthermore, comparing the age distribution in the sampling pool, the interview sample, and the medical sample revealed no systematic or substantial sampling bias in any ethnic group. Slight but not significant differences exist between ethnic groups—the Turks are oldest and the Europeans youngest—but within a possible age range between forty-five and fifty-four the groups are on the whole comparable in age distribution.

FIELDWORK

The interviewers for the Jewish groups were mature women, most of them married with children, recruited from the interview staff of the Israel Institute of Applied Social Research. They underwent intensive training sessions at the outset, and in addition, their work was under constant review by the fieldwork supervisor and by the senior research assistant. A majority of those who began continued as interviewers until the very end.

The interviewing staff included women who spoke Moghrabi (the Arabic of North Africa), Persian, Spanish, French, and Yiddish, as well as Hebrew, which was spoken fluently by all the interviewers. While the intention had been to conduct all interviewing among the Jewish groups in Hebrew, this proved impossible. In every ethnic group there were cases in which some translating had to be done on the spot by the interviewer, sometimes into a third language which was not the native tongue of either interviewer or respondent. Such cases were later reviewed to ensure that no distortion had ensued.

[1] Persians and Turks are combined as a single category in the Population Registry. They were sampled together from a single region and later separated in analysis.

Approximately one-third of the Persians and one-half the North Africans were interviewed in their native languages by interviewers of Persian or North African origin; these interviewers had additional training and supervision. Interviewing among the Jewish groups began in the North African community in December, 1968, moved to the Persians and Turks, and finally concluded with the Europeans, where interviewing was completed in June, 1969.

Interviewing among the Arab women was done by Israel-born Moslem Arab high-school teachers who spoke fluent Hebrew in addition to Arabic. Training sessions were conducted in Hebrew by the senior research assistant, and the accuracy of the translation prepared by the Institute was checked by the fieldwork supervisor with the interviewers, who altered some terms to conform to village usage. The original Hebrew answer sheets were used; precoded answers had only to be circled, and responses to open questions were recorded in Hebrew translation, with the exception of idiomatic expressions, which were recorded in Arabic and subsequently translated. Interviewing in the Arab villages was carried out from June to August, 1969.

Initial contact with all respondents was made by mail. Shortly before a woman was scheduled to be interviewed, a letter explaining the general purposes of the study was sent to her. In addition, among North Africans, a public health nurse from the local center acted as a liaison, going to the homes of women to urge their participation. Similarly, in the Arab villages the regional health officer contacted the men of the families to request permission for their wives' participation.

Among the Jewish groups, an interviewer went to the home of the respondent. At the conclusion of the interview the woman was asked to come for a general medical examination. If the woman agreed, an appointment was made for her. It was anticipated that privacy would be difficult to obtain in Arab homes—as had been the case among North Africans—and the public health center permitted us to invite respondents to the center for interviewing as well as for subsequent medical examinations.

Table 2 summarizes the outcome of fieldwork. Records of reasons for nonresponse among the Arab women were not kept, since almost all women whose husbands had initially agreed did come to the interview. The rate of nonresponse was just over one-third in each Jewish group, and about one-fifth among the Arabs. Among the Jewish groups, the reasons for nonresponse varied by ethnic group. The most frequent reason for

Table 2. Outcome of Fieldwork.

	Number of Europeans	Number of Turks and Persians		Number of North Africans	Number of Arabs
Total eligible attempted contacts	452	520 [a]		362	360
Completed interviews	287	176	160	239	286
Completed medical examinations	154	91	101	154	197
Nonresponse	165	184 [a]		165	
Reason for nonresponse:					
Failure to locate respondent	135	112 [a]		55	
Refusal	5	26 [a]		51	
Other (includes: abroad, ill, no contact after three visits)	25	46 [a]		59	

[a] Sampling pool of Persians and Turks combined.

nonresponse among the North Africans was a failure to locate the respondent; this accounted for all but 18 percent of the cases of nonresponse. Refusal was rare (3%) among North Africans, infrequent (14%) among Persians and Turks, but common (31%) among Europeans. In other words, the most traditional women were the most cooperative, the most modern women least cooperative. The same pattern was seen in the proportions of women interviewed who subsequently came to the medical examination. A greater proportion of Arabs, North Africans, and Persians came for medical examinations as compared to Turks and Europeans. It is true that fieldwork was coordinated through the local public health services in the Arab and North African communities, and this probably stimulated greater receptiveness to the medical examination in these groups. However, this would not explain the differing responses among Persians and Turks, where fieldwork procedures were identical and conducted simultaneously. Informal reports by the interviewers indicated that the Persians—like the North Africans—perceived the medical examination as a favor done for them by the research team, while the Turks often replied that they did not need our medical services because they already belonged to Kupat Holim (the national health service).

THE INTERVIEW SCHEDULE

The interview schedule for the survey, the second and major phase of the study, was constructed on the basis of guidelines derived from a review of relevant literature and from the findings of the pilot study. The interview schedule consisted of 168 items, all but 11 precoded, covering aspects of middle life including climacterium, social roles, personality, and psychological well-being, and aspects of the life history including reported responses to earlier psychosexual events. The items used in summary scales are reproduced in the section describing the construction of indices. The interview schedule is reproduced in full in appendix 2.

A pretest of the interview schedule was carried out with middle-aged women of European and Near Eastern origin, and revisions based on the result of the pretest were incorporated into the final draft. The interview schedule was translated from Hebrew into the local Arabic spoken in the rural Triangle region where the sample was to be drawn; the Arabic was then retranslated independently into Hebrew, and after clarification the final version was prepared. The time taken to complete an interview was, on the average, one and one-half hours; this did not vary by ethnic group.

THE MEDICAL EXAMINATION

The medical examination included a pregnancy history and a general history recorded by a nurse, a general medical examination, and for a sub-sample, a hormone measurement. Overall evaluations of physical and emotional health, and of any impairment of functioning, were made by the physicians. Any pathological condition discovered in the examination was reported to the woman's regular physician. The total of 697 medical examinations were performed by seven physicians, of whom three examined Jewish women only, three—from the staff of the regional health center—examined Arab women only, and one examined both Jews and Arabs.

THE PSYCHIATRIC INTERVIEW

At the conclusion of the survey, follow-up psychiatric interviews were conducted with selected sub-groups of women in each ethnic group. Women who, on the basis of the survey interview, had been classified as well adjusted or poorly adjusted were selected. These judgements were based on a combination of self-reported coping and personality measures, and self-reported menopausal symptomatology. Rankings on adjustment were made separately for each ethnic group, taking the high and low extreme responses on each item. A woman was judged well adjusted if she had low symptomatology and high coping and mood responses. The psychiatrists who conducted the interviews received no indication as to which women had been judged well adjusted or poorly adjusted on the basis of the survey ratings. The psychiatrists conducted unstructured interviews, and on the basis of these interviews they made a diagnosis of presence or absence of pathology. These diagnoses were reviewed by the project codirector, who is a psychiatrist, and very few disagreements appeared.

Table 3 compares the survey-based classifications of adjustments with the psychiatric diagnoses. The outcome of this comparison provides some validation of the survey data, for there is a strong tendency toward agreement between the survey-based classification, based on self-report in response to structured interview items, and the probing psychiatric examination. In addition, it can be seen that agreement is strongest for the Arabs, a group unaccustomed to being interviewed, where difficulties in communication might have been expected. When it is considered that the survey-based and psychiatric-based ratings are not made on the same, but only on presumably related bases—self-report and professional diagnosis—the measure of agreement is an encouraging indication of successful communication between survey interviewer and respondent.

Table 3. Comparison of Survey-Based Ratings of Adjustment and Psychiatric Diagnosis by Ethnic Group.

ETHNIC GROUP	PSYCHIATRIC DIAGNOSIS	SURVEY-BASED RATINGS	
		Well adjusted	Poorly adjusted
Europeans	No Pathology	20	8
	Pathology present	4	10
Turks	No pathology	5	0
	Pathology present	2	8
Persians	No pathology	6	3
	Pathology present	3	6
North Africans	No pathology	10	7
	Pathology present	4	8
Arabs	No pathology	13	2
	Pathology present	5	17

CONSTRUCTION OF INDICES

This study entailed the use of indices of modernity, responses to earlier psychosexual events, and responses to climacterium. These indices were derived from items on the interview schedule.

Index of modernity

Four items were used in constructing the index of modernity. These items, and the categories of responses, are as follows:

Item	Response		
	Traditional	Transitional	Modern
How many living children do you have?	8 or more	4 or 3	1 to 3
Who, mainly, determined your choice of husbands?	Family		Myself
Are you able to read (any language at all)?	No		Yes
Do you observe Orthodox religious tradition?	Yes		No

These items formed a six-point Guttman scale with a coefficient of reproducibility of .90. The scale typologies are as follows:

    I. (Traditional) 8 or more children, spouse chosen by family, religious, illiterate
    II. (Traditional) 4 through 7 children, spouse chosen by family, religious, illiterate
    III. (Transitional) 4 through 7 children, spouse chosen by girl, religious, illiterate
    IV. (Transitional) 4 through 7 children, spouse chosen by girl, religious, literate
    V. (Modern) 1 through 3 children, spouse chosen by girl, religious, literate
    VI. (Modern) 1 through 3 children, spouse chosen by girl, nonreligious, literate

Psychosexual indices

The interview schedule included items which dealt with responses to earlier psychosexual events: (1) menstruation; (2) marital relationship (interpersonal and sexual); (3) first childbearing; and (4) subsequent childbearing. Items measuring positive or negative response were used in the construction of indices for each of these four psychosexual events.

Menstruation. A list of the items used in constructing an index of response to menstruation follows. Responses to each item were scored as positive or negative on the basis of the frequency distribution for the entire sample on that item. A response at or above the median was scored 2, positive; a response below the median was scored 1, negative.

    Menarche. Please, try to remember the very first time you menstruated. Of the following words, which are the two which are closest to your feelings then? Happiness, Fear, Unpleasantness, Pride, Natural, Shame. (Scoring based on proportion of positive, neutral, or negative words.)

Menstrual history. (A) When you were a young girl, and until the time you married, to what extent was menstruation unpleasant? (B) And how did you feel from the time you married until about age forty? (C) And what about menstruation during your forties? (Scoring based on extent of unpleasantness reported throughout menstrual history.)

Menstrual regularity. Did you generally menstruate regularly once every month, more often than once a month, or every few months (other than during periods of childbearing and lactation)? (Report of regularity scored positive; of irregularity scored negative.)

These three items formed a four-point Guttman scale with a coefficient of reproducibility of .91. The scale typologies are as follows:

I. *(Negative)* Menarche recalled negatively, menstruation unpleasant, menstruation irregular.
II. Menarche recalled negatively, menstruation unpleasant, menstruation regular.
III. Menarche recalled negatively, menstruation not unpleasant, menstruation regular.
IV. *(Positive)* Menarche recalled positively, menstruation not unpleasant, menstruation regular.

Marital History. A list of the items used in constructing an index of marital history follows. Positive or negative scores for items dealing with interpersonal aspects of the marital history were determined by the median for the entire sample. For the sexual relationship, the score was the original response; a high numerical score was positive, and a low score was negative.

Quarreling. In every family, even the best, there are quarrels between husband and wife. The difference is that in one family there is more quarreling and in another less. How is this with you? (Frequent quarreling scored negative; infrequent quarreling scored positive.)

Husband's treatment of wife. Compared to other husbands of women you know, how did your husband treat you over the years? (Worse, no worse, and no better than others, scored negative; better, scored positive.)

Husband's sexual satisfaction. As you know, there are many couples who don't get along in sexual relations, although in other areas they get along very well. How was this for the two of you over the years—was your husband very satisfied, satisfied, or not satisfied by sexual relations over the years? (Very satisfied, scored 3; satisfied, scored 2; not satisfied, scored 1.)

Wife's sexual satisfaction. And what about you? Over the years, were you very satisfied, satisfied, or not satisfied? (Scored as for husband.)

These four items formed a seven-point Guttman scale with a coefficient of reproducibility of .90. The scale typologies are as follows:

I. *(Negative)* Frequent quarreling; husband treats wife worse, or no better, than other husbands; husband sexually dissatisfied; wife sexually dissatisfied.
II. Frequent quarreling; husband treats wife worse, or no better, than other husbands; husband sexually satisfied; wife sexually dissatisfied.

III. Frequent quarreling; husband treats wife worse, or no better, than other husbands; husband sexually satisfied; wife sexually satisfied.

IV. Infrequent quarreling; husband treats wife worse, or no better, than other husbands; husband sexually satisfied; wife sexually satisfied.

V. Infrequent quarreling; husband treats wife better than other husbands; husband sexually satisfied; wife sexually satisfied.

VI. Infrequent quarreling; husband treats wife better than other husbands; husband sexually very satisfied; wife sexually satisfied.

VII. *(Positive)* Infrequent quarreling; husband treats wife better than other husbands; husband sexually satisfied; wife sexually very satisfied.

First Childbearing. The items which comprised the indices of first and subsequent childbearing, which appear in the following list, dealt with ease or difficulty in pregnancy, in childbirth, and in the first months of the child's life. In constructing the index of first childbearing, responses were dichotomized on the basis of frequency distributions into negative and positive, reflecting difficulty or a lack of it. These items were:

First pregnancy. Please, think back to the first time you were pregnant. How did you feel during the pregnancy? Did you feel: Worried? (Yes or no answer obtained for each question.) Pleased? Ill? Fear? Proud? Happy? (Score based on balance between positive and negative feelings.)

First childbirth. And what about the first birth? Did you have problems at the time of the birth? What were they? (Any expression of difficulty scored negative. If none, scored positive.)

First postpartum period. After the first birth, it is sometimes hard for women to adjust to becoming mothers who must take care of the new baby. For you, was this very hard to adjust to . . . or not at all hard? (Any expression of difficulty scored negative. If none, scored positive.)

These three items formed a four-point Guttman scale with a coefficient of reproducibility of .88. The scale typologies are as follows:

I. *(Negative)* Difficult pregnancy, difficult birth, difficult postpartum period.

II. Difficult pregnancy, no difficulty at birth, difficult postpartum period.

III. Difficult pregnancy, no difficulty at birth, no difficulty postpartum.

IV. *(Positive)* No difficulty in pregnancy, no difficulty at birth, no difficulty postpartum.

Subsequent Childbearing. Responses to items dealing with subsequent childbearing showed somewhat greater spread, and it was possible to trichotomize the answers to questions on subsequent pregnancy and childbirth; subsequent postpartum period was again dichotomized. These items were:

Subsequent pregnancies. What about pregnancies after the first—how was it, generally, compared to most women you know? During pregnancy, did you have: Almost always exceptional difficulties . . . usually about the same as for most women, or usually easier pregnancies than other women? (Difficulty, scored 1; about the same, scored 2; easier, scored 3.)

Subsequent childbirths. And what about births after the first—how was this for you, in general, compared to most women you know? Was childbirth almost always exceptionally difficult, about the same as for other women, or generally easier than for other women? (Scored as for subsequent pregnancies.)

Subsequent postpartum periods. During the first three months, with babies after the first, did you usually have serious problems . . . no special problems, or did every thing go smoothly? ("Everything went smoothly," scored 2; and any other response, scored 1.)

These three items formed a six-point Guttman scale with a coefficient or reproducibility of .91. The scale typologies are as follows:

   I. *(Negative)* Difficult pregnancies, difficult births, difficulties postpartum.
  II. Difficult pregnancies, births about the same as other women, difficulties postpartum.
 III. Pregnancies and births about the same as other women, difficulties postpartum.
  IV. *(Neutral)* Pregnancies, births, postpartum about the same as other women.
   V. Pregnancies about the same as other women, births easier than other women, no difficulty postpartum.
  VI. *(Positive)* Pregnancies and births easier than other women, no difficulties postpartum.

Climacteric Indices

Two sets of items were used in the construction of the six indices of response to climacterium: the list of symptoms replicated from an earlier study (Neugarten *et al.,* 1965) and a series of attitudinal items which were derived from the pilot study interviews.

The symptomatology score was based on the number of symptoms reported by a woman, together with the frequency she reported experiencing the symptom. For each of twenty-five symptoms (for example, hot flushes, headaches, pounding of the heart, feeling of anxiety, breast pains, dizziness, cold sweats, weight gain, trouble sleeping; the complete list appears as items I:53–II:9 in appendix 2), women were asked whether they had experienced the symptom often, sometimes, or never in the past year. In order to make a high numerical symptomatology score reflect positive response, and a low score, negative (so that the direction of high and low would be the same as for other scores), scoring was as follows: a symptom reported as frequent was scored as one point; a symptom reported as sometimes was scored two points; and a symptom reported as never in the past year was scored three points. The symptomatology score was the total number of points, ranging from a possible twenty-five—which meant that every symptom on the list was experienced frequently—to a possible seventy-five, or no symptoms. The actual range of response was concentrated between fifty and sixty.

Attitudes toward climacterium were assessed by means of a series of twenty-three items (III:8–30, appendix 2). These items were single statements, each expressing a positive or a negative view about one of five aspects of change at climacterium: (1) cessation of fertility; (2) physical health; (3) emotional health; (4) changes in status; and (5) changes in the marital relationship. Respondents were asked whether they agreed or disagreed with each statement.

The specific items from which the five scores were constructed follow; they are grouped according to scores and not in the order in which they appeared in the question-naire (see appendix 2, III:8–30, for the interview format).[1]

1. Cessation of fertility

A woman is pleased that after menopause she cannot become pregnant.

A woman is sorry she has no chance for additional children after menopause.

A woman is sorry that after menopause she can no longer become pregnant.

A woman is pleased that after menopause she no longer needs to suffer the pains and complications of pregnancy and birth.

A woman is pleased there are no chances for additional children after menopause.

2. Physical health

A woman has a feeling of better health and more abundant strength after menstuation has stopped.

At change of life, a woman begins to suffer from weakness and disease.

So long as she is still menstruating, a woman's body is released every month from pressure and harmful materials.

A woman in change of life has more strength than before.

A woman in change of life is pleased to be finished with the unpleasantness of menstruation.

3. Emotional health

As a result of menopause, a woman becomes more nervous and moody.

After menopause a woman feels more peaceful and tranquil.

As a result of menopause a woman is likely to go crazy.

4. Changes in status

At middle age a woman is given less respect than before.

At middle age a woman is given more respect than before.

At middle age a woman feels freer to do the things that attract her than she did formerly.

At middle age a woman has more chance than before to take good care of herself and her appearance.

A woman begins to age suddenly during change of life.

5. Changes in the marital relationship

A husband is more interested in his wife at middle age than he was before.

A husband is less interested in his wife at middle age than he was before.

After menopause, a woman enjoys sexual relations less.

After menopause, a woman is sorry because her husband would have wanted more children.

After menopause, a woman enjoys sexual relations more.

In constructing the five scores, agreement with a positive statement or disagreement with a negative statement was considered a *positive* response, and disagreement with a positive statement or agreement with a negative statement was considered a *negative*

---

[1] There were frequent cases of repetition and possible response set, where one item stated that, for example, there was regret over the cessation of fertility, while a later item stated that the cessation of fertility was welcome, as can be seen in the original interview schedule; however, when repetition and contradiction were noticed by respondents, the interviewers reminded them that these were various views held by different women, and that we were interested to hear whether they themselves happened to agree or disagree with that particular statement.

response. It was sometimes true, however, that a respondent did not answer the entire set of twenty-three items, frequently remarking in such a case, "I don't know." The construction of positive and negative scores was based, therefore, on a combination of the proportion of positive to negative responses together with the number of items which were answered. Thus, for example, three positive and no negative responses was scored "extremely positive," while one positive and no negative responses—indicating no answer to a majority of the items—was scored "slightly positive." Each of the five scores ranged from a low of one (extremely negative: three or more negative responses, no positive responses), through four (balanced or ambivalent: equal numbers of positive and negative responses), to a high of seven (extremely positive: three or more positive responses, no negative responses).

TREATMENT OF DATA

The data which were taken from the survey instruments have undergone, for the most part, gentle handling. Our comparative portraits of women in five ethnic groups (chapters 3 through 7) are based on percentages, medians, and similar descriptive statistics. The differences between the groups, when they emerge, are so striking that no test of significance is adequate—nor is a statistical test of significance an appropriate measure of differences between cultures which have been selected for their differences. The test of significant differences among these cultures lies in our interpretation of our findings.

There is, however, one realm in which more robust statistical inquiry is appropriate. Although our five ethnic groups were chosen to represent points along a continuum ranging from tradition to modernity, it is possible to ask whether the degree of modernity—independent of ethnic origin—is an appropriate descriptive variable. A two-way multivariate analysis of variance, using ethnic identity and index of modernity as the independent variables, and the four psychosexual and six climacteric indices as the dependent variables, was performed (Datan, 1971).

Analysis of variance indicated that ethnic identity not only was a better predictor of psychosexual and climacteric responses, but that in fact it was a better measure of modernity than was the index of modernity. The index was derived from four survey items—number of living children, spouse chosen by family or by woman, level of education, and degree of religiosity—which covaried with modernity, as chapter 2 has shown. However, although these items did reflect modernity, they evidently were not sufficient to measure modernity. Indeed, such questions as the number of children or the choice of spouse might yield responses such as few children and choice by the woman in an apparently traditional culture—and may reflect infertility or a lack of family around the woman. In any such instance, the "modern" score not only misrepresents the woman's values but also obscures the conflict between these values and her own departure from them.

This finding, that ethnic identity is a better measure of modernity than our "index of modernity," is of particular significance in discussing group differences among the transitional cultures—the Turks, Persians, and North Africans. Although a certain amount of heterogeneity on the index of modernity was found in each of these groups, analysis of variance suggests that ethnicity is a better predictor of response than is the index of modernity. Thus, for example, a modern Persian is more likely to be similar to a traditional Persian than to a modern Turk or a modern North African. In describing differences between groups, then, ethnicity was used as the variable of classification, and the five ethnic groups are viewed as representing varying degrees of traditionalism or modernity.

Appendix 2

Findings

The
Survey
Instrument
and
Tabled
Responses

BEILINSON MEDICAL CENTER
TEL AVIV UNIVERSITY SCHOOL OF MEDICINE
THE ISRAEL INSTITUTE OF APPLIED SOCIAL RESEARCH, JERUSALEM
SOCIOCULTURAL PATTERNS AND THE INVOLUTIONAL CRISIS

DECK I

1–4: Respondent serial number

  Col. 1: Residential area of respondent

  Code 0 *(N=239)* Ramle, Lod (born in North Africa)
       1 *(N=160)* Tel Aviv (born in Iran)
       2 *(N=287)* Ramat Gan (born in Central Europe)
       3 *(N=286)* Taybe, Tireh (Israeli Arab)
       4 *(N=176)* Tel Aviv (born in Turkey)

5. Are you married, widowed, divorced, or single? [1]

Europeans	Turks	Persians	North Africans	Moslem Arabs	
90	88	88	83	77	1 - married
5	9	10	13	18	2 - widowed
3	1	2	5	4	3 - divorced
2	2	1	0	1	4 - single (skip to q. 39)

[1] Unless otherwise indicated, tables present percentage of response by ethnic group.

129

6. (Ask also widows and divorcees)
   A. How many living daughters do you have?
   B. How many living sons do you have?
   (Record total number and code below)

Europeans	Turks	Persians	North Africans	Moslem Arabs	
24	7	1	6	2	1 - one child
49	21	6	6	3	2 - 2 children
18	25	7	6	6	3 - 3 children
2	24	15	8	10	4 - 4 children
0	8	17	16	11	5 - 5 children
0	1	13	9	15	6 - 6 children
0	2	12	9	11	7 - 7 children
0	3	26	34	39	8 - 8 children
7	9	3	6	3	9 - no children (skip to q. 30)
					0 - (single)[2]

(N.B.: Include: Adopted children from a former husband, children from husband's former marriage if they live (or lived) with the woman.

If there are only children of this kind, and none of her own children, skip to q. 16.

If there are no children at all, skip to q. 30.)

7. (Ratio of boys to girls: office coding)

Europeans	Turks	Persians	North Africans	Moslem Arabs	
11	12	5	4	3	1 - all boys (more than one child)
8	27	42	31	40	2 - a majority of boys
29	20	20	16	19	3 - half boys, half girls
8	22	30	41	33	4 - a majority of girls
17	12	2	1	2	5 - all girls (more than one child)
13	4	1	3	2	6 - one boy
14	3	1	4	0	7 - one girl
					0 - no children

[2] Unless otherwise specified, code 0 always includes no answer, don't know, does not apply, and so on.

8. Please, think back to the first time you were pregnant. Did the pregnancy come to term? (If child was born alive:) How did you feel *during the pregnancy?* Did you feel (obtain answer to each question):

	Yes	No
A. worried	‎———‎	‎———‎
B. pleased	‎———‎	‎———‎
C. ill	‎———‎	‎———‎
D. fear	‎———‎	‎———‎
E. proud	‎———‎	‎———‎
F. happy	‎———‎	‎———‎

> *Office coding*
> Positive items: pleased, proud, happy
> Negative items: worried, ill, fear

Europeans	Turks	Persians	North Africans	Moslem Arabs	
12	5	3	3	4	1 - (abortion or stillbirth)
42	53	46	62	50	2 - only positive items checked "yes"
29	25	30	25	32	3 - more positive items than negative items checked "yes"
9	10	11	6	8	4 - equal number of positive and negative items
4	2	6	4	3	5 - more negative items than positive items checked "yes"
4	5	5	0	3	6 - only negative items checked "yes"
					0 - never pregnant, etc.

(N.B.: Coded only when at least 4 items were answered.)

9. And what about the first *birth?* Did you have problems at the time of the birth? (If yes) What were they?

Europeans	Turks	Persians	North Africans	Moslem Arabs	
2	5	7	9	10	1 - stillbirth, child dead after birth (skip to q. 11)
7	5	3	2	6	2 - serious problems (Caesarean, premature birth)
25	23	32	21	16	3 - difficulties (prolonged or painful labor)
66	67	58	68	68	4 - no special difficulties
					0 - (never pregnant, etc.)

10. (Explain the form of a closed question)
    After the first birth, it is sometimes hard for women to adjust to becoming mothers who must take care of the new baby. For you, was this:
    (Read aloud)

Europeans	Turks	Persians	North Africans	Moslem Arabs	
6	6	11	5	1	1 - very hard to adjust to
9	10	15	10	8	2 - quite hard
9	14	12	14	18	3 - not so hard
14	13	11	10	16	4 - a bit hard
62	57	51	60	57	5 - not at all hard
					0 - (never pregnant, etc.)

(If only one child, code 5 in q. 11 and skip to q. 14)

11. What about *pregnancies* after the first—how was it, generally, compared to most women you know? During pregnancy, did you have:
    (Read aloud)

Europeans	Turks	Persians	North Africans	Moslem Arabs	
3	6	2	1	2	1 - almost always exceptional difficulties
14	15	18	13	14	2 - usually harder than other women's pregnancies
47	57	55	54	56	3 - usually about the same as for most women
18	18	25	29	28	4 - usually easier pregnancies than for other women
18	3	0	3	1	5 - pregnant only once; skip to q. 14
					0 - (never pregnant, etc.)

12. And what about births after the first—how was this for you, in general, compared to most women you know? Was childbirth:
    (Read aloud)

Europeans	Turks	Persians	North Africans	Moslem Arabs	
2	5	4	3	3	1 - almost always exceptionally difficult
9	12	15	9	12	2 - generally harder than for other women
57	59	60	57	60	3 - about the same as for other women
32	23	21	31	25	4 - generally easier than for other women
					0 - (pregnant only once, etc.)

13. During the *first three months,* with babies after the first, did you usually have:
    (Read aloud)

Europeans	Turks	Persians	North Africans	Moslem Arabs	
9	6	7	4	6	1 - serious problems
11	17	15	16	12	2 - problems, but not serious
27	31	34	31	34	3 - no special problems
52	47	44	48	49	4 - everything went smoothly

14. On the basis of your experience, if you were a young woman starting a family, would you want more children than you had, fewer, or the same number that you have?

Europeans	Turks	Persians	North Africans	Moslem Arabs	
68	38	35	42	19	1 - would want to have more children
3	15	26	10	22	2 - would want to have fewer children
28	47	39	48	59	3 - would want the same number
					0 - (no children; single)

15. Is this a general feeling, or do you have some special reason? (If yes) What is the reason? (Record verbatim)
    Office coding

Europeans	Turks	Persians	North Africans	Moslem Arabs	
16	24	26	19	19	1 - physical factors: energy; strength; hard to raise or care for children (excluding economic aspect); pregnancy or childbirth difficulties; good or bad for health
31	21	12	16	28	2 - emotional factors: love; patience; attention; worry positive or negative emotionally; satisfaction or lack thereof

15. *(continued)*

Europeans	Turks	Persians	North Africans	Moslem Arabs	
1	1	4	6	0	3 - husband: any reason expressing husband's wishes
2	1	1	2	0	4 - national: any reason expressing needs of the society
1	0	1	0	0	5 - effect on roles of respondent other than as a mother: private life; "no time for children."
24	30	27	13	7	6 - economic factors
25	23	30	43	46	7 - nonspecific reason: it's difficult; it's good; I have enough; I want a large (small) family, etc.
					0 - no special reason, no children, etc.

(N.B.: If more than one type of reason is given, only the first one mentioned is coded, unless one of the others is explicitly stated to be most important.)

16. How many of your children live at home with you?

Europeans	Turks	Persians	North Africans	Moslem Arabs	
45	22	15	14	9	1 - one child
29	28	14	12	11	2 - 2 children
7	22	22	13	12	3 - 3 children
0	8	14	18	13	4 - 4 children
0	3	9	14	15	5 - 5 children
0	0	11	6	13	6 - 6 children
0	0	5	8	11	7 - 7 children
0	0	4	8	14	8 - 8 children or more. How many?
19	17	5	9	3	9 - no children now living at home
					0 - (no children)

17. How old is your youngest boy or girl? Aged _____.
    (Record and code)
    (N.B.: If only one child, code and skip to q. 19.)

Europeans	Turks	Persians	North Africans	Moslem Arabs	
0	1	3	2	6	1 - less than 3 years
0	1	7	7	12	2 - 3–5 years
16	28	37	48	38	3 - 6–13 years
30	35	31	17	21	4 - 14–17 years
54	37	22	26	24	5 - 18 years or more
					0 - (no children, etc.)

18. How old is your oldest boy or girl? Aged _____.
    (Actual childbearing span: difference in ages between oldest and youngest children; office coding)

Europeans	Turks	Persians	North Africans	Moslem Arabs	
26	7	1	7	2	1 - only one child
19	8	4	4	2	2 - 3 years or less
25	20	8	9	6	3 - 4–6 years
17	25	14	8	7	4 - 7–9 years
7	21	17	16	15	5 - 10–12 years
7	20	56	57	68	6 - 13 years or more
					0 - no children

19. (If one child) To what extent does your child need you? (If more than one child) Think about the child who needs you the most; to what extent does he need you?
    (Read aloud)

Europeans	Turks	Persians	North Africans	Moslem Arabs	
29	48	61	44	38	1 - needs you very, very much
20	20	15	18	16	2 - needs you to a great extent
41	20	14	23	29	3 - needs you
6	5	6	7	7	4 - doesn't need you so very much
3	8	4	8	11	5 - doesn't need you (skip to q. 21)
					0 - (no children)

20. What in particular does this child need you for?
    (Record verbatim)
    Office coding

Europeans	Turks	Persians	North Africans	Moslem Arabs	
11	29	33	17	42	1 - instrumental: routine household needs, e.g., child care, cooking, cleanliness
31	17	19	15	9	2 - affective: love, affection, emotional needs, attention, understanding, support (noneconomic), warmth, child tied to one
23	41	43	54	33	3 - global: as a mother, in general, for everything, to help
2	2	3	3	0	4 - care of grandchild(ren)
3	4	0	3	13	5 - economic support
3	2	2	3	0	6 - care in case of illness
27	5	0	5	3	7 - cognitive: advice, help in studies, education
0	0	0	0	0	8 - idiosyncratic, not included above
0	0	1	1	0	9 - nothing in particular
					0 - no answer, no children, respondent not needed

(N.B.: If more than one type of need is given, only the first one is coded, unless one of
the others is explicitly stated to be more important. Other needs are recorded
manually for subsequent consideration.)

21. As children grow up they need their mother for different things. Do the children, in
    general, need you now less or more than they did when you were aged 40?
    (Read aloud)

Europeans	Turks	Persians	North Africans	Moslem Arabs	
49	25	25	39	34	1 - in general they need you *less*
13	27	22	22	30	2 - in general they need you *more*
37	46	53	39	30	3 - no difference between now and then (for those whose children do need them: 1–4 in q. 19)
2	1	1	0	6	4 - no child needs her now and at forty none needed her
					0 - (no children)

22. As children grow up they become more independent. There are mothers who are sorry about this, and others who are not sorry. What is your feeling about your children? Are you:
(Read aloud)

Europeans	Turks	Persians	North Africans	Moslem Arabs	
2	5	2	8	7	1 - very sorry that they are becoming more independent
5	3	7	20	10	2 - quite sorry
11	8	1	13	7	3 - somewhat sorry
15	14	15	12	13	4 - not so sorry
67	70	75	47	62	5 - not at all sorry
					0 - (no children)

23. To what extent, in your opinion, do your children appreciate you? Do they:
(Read aloud)

Europeans	Turks	Persians	North Africans	Moslem Arabs	
36	39	39	41	44	1 - appreciate you very, very much
36	34	26	31	24	2 - quite a lot
21	19	27	20	25	3 - to some extent
7	8	8	8	7	4 - not so much appreciate you
					0 - (no children)

24. Many women say that the trouble with children these days is that they don't pay attention to their parents. Do you:
(Read aloud)

Europeans	Turks	Persians	North Africans	Moslem Arabs	
5	12	14	11	19	1 - definitely agree to this
11	14	16	21	18	2 - agree
26	33	26	27	32	3 - not so much agree
58	41	44	42	31	4 - not at all agree
					0 - (no children)

25. Are any of your children married? (If yes) Do they have children?

Europeans	Turks	Persians	North Africans	Moslem Arabs	
32	62	79	76	78	1 - married child(ren) with grandchild(ren)
14	10	6	8	7	2 - married child(ren) but no grandchild(ren) (skip to q. 30)
54	27	15	16	15	3 - no married children (skip to q. 30)
					0 - (no children)

26. How often do you see your grandchildren—or at least one of them? (Code highest frequency)
(Read aloud)

Europeans	Turks	Persians	North Africans	Moslem Arabs	
18	30	25	37	31	1 - every day, at least for an hour or two
1	3	5	6	40	2 - every day, but not for long
29	20	16	11	12	3 - not every day, but at least several times a week
18	34	26	21	8	4 - about once a week
16	5	15	12	3	5 - from time to time
6	3	10	10	6	6 - seldom
12	4	3	3	0	7 - (children abroad)
					0 - (no grandchildren)

27. Do you have a chance to do things for your grandchildren? (If yes) What sort of things? (Record verbatim)
Office coding

Europeans	Turks	Persians	North Africans	Moslem Arabs	
61	80	76	73	44	1 - instrumental: feeding, cooking, sewing, knitting, candy, presents
15	10	10	11	11	2 - affective: love, play, visit, child tied to one
3	0	0	1	7	3 - global: as a grandmother, I'm their grandmother
18	5	10	10	8	4 - mother substitute, care, raising

27. *(continued)*

Europeans	Turks	Persians	North Africans	Moslem Arabs	
0	0	0	0	0	5 - economic support
0	1	0	2	1	6 - care in case of illness
1	1	3	0	0	7 - letters or packages to grandchildren abroad
0	0	0	0	0	8 - idiosyncratic, not included above
3	4	1	3	29	9 - nothing in particular
					0 - no answer, no grand-children, respondent not needed

(N.B.: If more than one type of need is given, only the first one is coded, unless one of the others is explicitly stated to be the most important. Other needs are recorded manually for subsequent consideration.)

28. Did you have grandchildren when you were 40? (If yes) Do you get to see your grand-children now less or more than you did then?

Europeans	Turks	Persians	North Africans	Moslem Arabs	
97	73	54	44	57	1 - there were no grand-children then
0	1	10	13	5	2 - now sees grandchildren more
3	12	12	19	6	3 - now sees grandchildren less
0	14	23	23	32	4 - no difference
					0 - (no grandchildren)

29. Parents and their grown children don't always agree about the grandchildren, especially at first. Sometimes the children don't let the grandmother do things for the grand-children, and sometimes the children demand too much of the grandmother. How is this with you?
(Read aloud)

Europeans	Turks	Persians	North Africans	Moslem Arabs	
5	5	9	12	10	1 - do you want to do more for the grandchildren than they let you do
5	11	11	8	17	2 - do they demand too much from you
81	77	71	72	72	3 - are things as they should be
9	7	9	8	2	4 - other (What?)
					0 - (no grandchildren)

(Questions 30–34 are to be asked also of widows and divorcees)

30. How old were you when you married for the first time? Aged _____
(record and code)

Europeans	Turks	Persians	North Africans	Moslem Arabs	
0	1	22	17	8	1 - 13 or less
0	4	13	20	22	2 - 14–15
1	10	24	18	21	3 - 16–17
21	34	26	25	28	4 - 18–20
46	25	8	10	11	5 - 21–24
24	16	6	7	7	6 - 25–29
8	10	1	3	4	7 - 30 or more
0	0	0	0	0	8 - doesn't know
					0 - (single)

31. When you married (for the first time), did your family live in the same country you were living in? (If no, code 5; if yes) Who, mainly, determined your choice of husband, you or your family?

Mainly the family
Did you accept their choice?

Europeans	Turks	Persians	North Africans	Moslem Arabs	
4	31	40	41	80	1 - willingly
3	15	35	15	15	2 - not so willingly

Mainly you
Did the family accept your choice?

Europeans	Turks	Persians	North Africans	Moslem Arabs	
40	33	7	30	1	3 - willingly
14	8	7	13	1	4 - not so willingly
39	13	12	1	4	5 - (no family)
					0 - (single)

32. On the basis of your experience, what is your opinion now—who should determine a young girl's choice of husband?
    (Read aloud)

Europeans	Turks	Persians	North Africans	Moslem Arabs	
0	1	4	2	3	1 - the family, and there is no need to consider the girl's wishes
1	11	17	17	49	2 - the family, with the girl's agreement
89	78	61	66	46	3 - the girl, with the family's agreement
8	8	13	14	1	4 - the girl, and there is no need to consider the family's wishes
2	2	4	2	1	5 - the girl, even against the family's wishes

33. Were you younger than your (first) husband? (If yes) By how many years?

Europeans	Turks	Persians	North Africans	Moslem Arabs	
4	6	4	5	7	1 - the husband was younger
18	23	6	14	14	2 - he is older by less than two years (includes the same age)
32	32	27	31	25	3 - 2–5 years
32	30	37	34	21	4 - 6–10
14	9	26	17	33	5 - 11 years or more
					0 - (single)

34. (To a married woman) Are you still married to the same husband?
    (To a widow) Was it your first husband who died?
    (To a divorcee) Was it your first husband that you divorced?
    (Continue to take the details of the marital history.)

Marital history

	Married at age	Living with him? Yes No	Husband died She was aged:	Divorced She was aged:
First husband:	————	————————————	————————————	————————————
Second husband:	————	————————————	————————————	————————————
Third husband:	————	————————————	————————————	————————————
Office coding				

34. (Marital history: *office coding*) *(continued)*

Europeans	Turks	Persians	North Africans	Moslem Arabs	
75	83	82	73	74	1 - married once, still married
6	8	8	10	18	2 - married once, widowed
2	1	2	3	4	3 - married once, divorced or separated
7	3	3	5	3	4 - married twice: widowed; still married to second husband
7	3	3	5	1	5 - married twice: divorced; still married to second husband
0	1	1	1	0	6 - married twice: widowed twice
0	0	0	0	0	7 - married twice: divorced twice
0	1	1	2	0	8 - married twice: widowed once, divorced once
1	0	1	0	0	9 - married three times
					0 - never married

. . . .

(The following questions pertain to the present husband. In the case of a widow or a divorcee who has not remarried, skip to q. 39.)

35. In what country was your (present) husband born?
(Record) _____
Office coding

Europeans	Turks	Persians	North Africans	Moslem Arabs	
53	72	86	96	100	1 - in same country as respondent
44	20	7	1	0	2 - not in same country, but in same region as respondent (Regions: North Africa, Middle East, Europe, or Arab states)
3	8	7	3	0	3 - not in same region as respondent
					0 - not currently married

36. How many years did your husband attend school?

Europeans	Turks	Persians	North Africans	Moslem Arabs	
0	25	49	53	66	1 - 0–3 years
21	56	44	32	24	2 - 4–8 years
53	12	7	10	8	3 - 9–12 years
26	7	1	4	2	4 - 13 or more years
					0 - (no husband)

37. What is your husband's occupation? (If a businessman, manager, or clerk:) How many men does he employ (or have under him)?

Europeans	Turks	Persians	North Africans	Moslem Arabs	
16	4	4	6	6	1 - professional
16	0	0	2	1	2 - businessman or manager, employs 10 or more workers
11	3	1	2	0	3 - businessman or clerk, employs 3–9 workers
34	29	11	12	5	4 - businessman or clerk, employs 0–2 workers
16	18	9	20	4	5 - skilled worker
3	38	52	49	52	6 - unskilled worker, including agricultural laborer, unemployed, doesn't work
0	0	1	0	18	7 - agriculture: landowner
0	0	1	0	4	8 - agriculture: tenant farmer
5	9	22	10	9	9 - other (What?)
					0 - (no husband)

(N.B.: 1. A man who is self-employed, e.g., a truck driver, is coded a businessman;
2. "Retired": code by former occupation, if known. If not, code 9.)

38. In every family, even the best, there are quarrels between husband and wife. The difference is, that in one family there is more quarreling and in another less. How is this with you? Would you say that:
(Read aloud)

Europeans	Turks	Persians	North Africans	Moslem Arabs	
3	8	13	9	5	1 - you've quarreled very frequently over the years
9	10	8	6	5	2 - you've quarreled quite a lot over the years
31	21	20	25	27	3 - you've quarreled to a certain extent
25	25	29	24	32	4 - you haven't quarreled too much
33	35	29	36	31	5 - you've hardly ever quarreled
					0 - (no husband)

. . . .

(Ask every woman)

39. Let's suppose you've just had a serious quarrel with someone very close to you. How do you feel after a quarrel like this? Would it be more correct to say:

Europeans	Turks	Persians	North Africans	Moslem Arabs	
66	78	69	75	70	1 - that you get very angry—it's all the other one's fault, or
31	16	21	17	28	2 - that you feel that everything is your fault
3	7	10	7	3	3 - (never quarrels)

Which is more similar to your feelings?

40. And is it more correct to say that after a quarrel like that:

Europeans	Turks	Persians	North Africans	Moslem Arabs	
81	64	57	63	56	1 - you feel nervous and tense, or
18	30	36	32	42	2 - that you just feel simply sick
1	6	6	6	2	3 - (never quarrels)

41. And is it more correct to say that after a quarrel like that:

Europeans	Turks	Persians	North Africans	Moslem Arabs	
40	50	46	62	41	1 - you feel that this is how life is, or
59	43	47	32	56	2 - that you have to do something to get over your mood
1	6	7	6	2	3 - (never quarrels)

(For widows, divorcees, and single women, skip to q. 53)

. . . .

42. Compared to other husbands of women you know, how did your husband treat you over the years? Did he mostly treat you:
    (Read aloud)

Europeans	Turks	Persians	North Africans	Moslem Arabs	
1	8	16	5	6	1 - much less well than most husbands
6	9	9	8	5	2 - not as well as most husbands
33	36	41	39	43	3 - no better and no worse than most husbands
39	38	26	42	34	4 - better than most
21	9	8	6	12	5 - much better than most
					0 - (no husband)

43. To what extent do you feel that you need your husband now? Would you say that you:
    (Read aloud)

Europeans	Turks	Persians	North Africans	Moslem Arabs	
2	3	12	4	4	1 - don't need him
6	7	9	4	8	2 - don't need him so much
32	38	35	41	37	3 - need him
25	24	19	29	20	4 - need him quite a lot
36	29	26	22	31	5 - need him very, very much
					0 - (no husband)

44. To what extent do you feel that your husband needs you now? Would you say that he:
   (Read aloud)

Europeans	Turks	Persians	North Africans	Moslem Arabs	
0	1	6	3	5	1 - doesn't need you (skip to q. 46)
2	4	6	5	5	2 - doesn't need you so much
26	28	23	30	36	3 - needs you
31	33	25	30	24	4 - needs you to a great extent
40	34	41	33	31	5 - needs you very, very much
					0 - (no husband)

45. If you think about your daily life nowadays, for what in particular does your husband need you? (Record verbatim) _____
   Office coding

Europeans	Turks	Persians	North Africans	Moslem Arabs	
14	33	35	20	41	1 - instrumental: any need directly related to house-keeping role
65	18	13	10	25	2 - affective: love, comrade, affection, to speak with, to help
17	34	36	43	16	3 - global: as a "woman," without specification; for everything; for everything a man needs a woman for, without specification
0	6	9	13	5	4 - as mother of children, to bear children, to take care of children
1	1	2	3	2	5 - economic assistance, help at work (include in fields)

45. *(continued)*

Europeans	Turks	Persians	North Africans	Moslem Arabs	
2	4	2	6	8	6 - care in case of illness
2	4	4	4	3	7 - sexual needs, mentioned explicitly
0	0	0	1	0	8 - idiosyncratic needs, not included above
0	0	0	0	0	9 - nothing in particular
					0 - no answer, no husband, respondent not needed

(N.B.: If more than one type of need is given, only the first one is coded, unless one of the others is explicitly stated to be most important. Other needs are recorded manually for subsequent consideration. When "as a woman" is recorded *in addition* to other needs, it is interpreted as "sexual need.")

46. Does he need you now less or more than he did when you were 40?

Europeans	Turks	Persians	North Africans	Moslem Arabs	
7	13	19	16	12	1 - now he needs you *less*
30	39	37	31	26	2 - now he needs you *more*
63	48	42	53	58	3 - no difference between then and now (for those whose husbands need them: 2–5 in q. 44)
0	0	2	0	4	4 - now husband doesn't need her and then he didn't need her
					0 - (no husband)

47. Would you want your husband to need you *more* than he needs you now, *less* than he needs you, or are you satisfied with things as they are?

Europeans	Turks	Persians	North Africans	Moslem Arabs	
6	14	25	12	11	1 - wants her husband to need her more
9	7	14	9	7	2 - wants her husband to need her less
85	79	61	78	82	3 - satisfied
					0 - (no husband)

48. In general, do you and your husband spend your free time separately or together? Do you:
(Read aloud)

Europeans	Turks	Persians	North Africans	Moslem Arabs	
2	10	13	13	21	1 - almost always spend your free time separately
5	4	18	16	31	2 - mostly spend your free time separately
27	28	37	43	49	3 - mostly spend your free time together
66	58	32	28	0	4 - almost always spend your free time together
					0 - (no husband)

49. As you know, there are many couples who don't get along in sexual relations, although in other areas they get along very well. How was this for you over the years—was your husband very satisfied, satisfied, or not satisfied by sexual relations over the years?

Europeans	Turks	Persians	North Africans	Moslem Arabs	
27	34	54	41	30	1 - very satisfied
69	62	39	56	61	2 - satisfied
4	5	7	3	9	3 - not satisfied
					0 - (no husband)

50. And how is this now—do you think he is very satisfied, satisfied, or not satisfied?

Europeans	Turks	Persians	North Africans	Moslem Arabs	
23	26	30	23	31	1 - very satisfied
71	59	53	54	58	2 - satisfied
7	15	16	23	11	3 - not satisfied
					0 - (no husband)

51. And what about you? Over the years, were you very satisfied, satisfied, or not satisfied?

Europeans	Turks	Persians	North Africans	Moslem Arabs	
24	19	35	27	22	1 - very satisfied
64	61	44	64	67	2 - satisfied
12	19	21	8	11	3 - not satisfied
					0 - (no husband)

52. And how is this for you now?

Europeans	Turks	Persians	North Africans	Moslem Arabs	
21	17	19	15	26	1 - very satisfied
62	52	41	50	57	2 - satisfied
17	31	40	35	17	3 - not satisfied
					0 - (no husband)

. . . .

I:53–II:9. Now I will read you a list of problems women sometimes have. Please tell me, for each one, if during the past year you were troubled by the problem often, sometimes, or not at all.

53. Pounding heart
54. Dizziness
55. Nervousness and tension
56. Diarrhea
57. Constipation
58. Inability to concentrate
59. Crying spells
60. Feeling of tiredness
61. Feeling of depression
62. Pains in the back of the head or neck
63. Black spots before the eyes
64. Headaches
65. Breast pains
66. Irritability
67. Cold sweats
68. Forgetfulness
69. Numbness and tingling in the hands and feet
70. Trouble sleeping
71. Cold hands and feet
72. Hot flashes

KEY TO I:53–II:9

1 - Often
2 - Sometimes
3 - Never in the past year

DECK II

1-4: Respondent serial number
  5. Rheumatic pains
  6. Weight gain (Yes = 1, a little = 2)
  7. Feeling of fright
  8. Worry about going crazy
  9. Feeling of suffocation
     (See III:38–41 for menopausal symptom scores)

Mean symptomatology score
(higher score = lower incidence of symptoms)

Europeans	Turks	Persians	North Africans	Moslem Arabs
57.2	54.7	53.2	54.5	56.1

. . . .

10. About how often do you get a chance to really chat with your friends and neighbors (including by telephone)? Do you chat:
    (Read aloud)

Europeans	Turks	Persians	North Africans	Moslem Arabs	
18	20	25	37	16	1 - almost never really with neighbors or friends
9	6	5	6	12	2 - once or twice a month
21	19	19	20	17	3 - about once a week
22	13	16	13	13	4 - a number of times a week
23	32	25	18	36	5 - almost daily
7	11	10	6	8	6 - a number of times a day

11. Did you spend more time or less time at the age of 40 with your friends and neighbors than you do now?

Europeans	Turks	Persians	North Africans	Moslem Arabs	
13	16	9	8	15	1 - more now than at age 40
34	39	37	36	32	2 - less now than at age 40
53	45	54	56	53	3 - about the same

12. Would you want to spend *more* time now with your friends and neighbors, *less* time, or are you satisfied with things as they are?

Europeans	Turks	Persians	North Africans	Moslem Arabs	
32	40	47	37	27	1 - wants to spend more time
4	5	9	4	5	2 - wants to spend less time
65	55	43	59	68	3 - satisfied

. . . .

13. Now we'll talk about relatives in Israel—your or your husband's parents, brothers and sisters, sons- and daughters-in-law, cousins, and so on. Think about the relative who needs you the most.
    A. Who is it? _____ (Record: if none, code and skip to II:15)
    B. Does (this relative)
    (Read aloud)

Europeans	Turks	Persians	North Africans	Moslem Arabs	
8	13	9	8	6	1 - not need you so much
27	29	31	24	13	2 - need you
14	12	13	11	1	3 - need you to a great extent
15	20	18	16	2	4 - need you very, very much
23	21	19	36	64	5 - (no relative who needs her; skip to II:15)
12	6	9	5	13	6 - (no relatives of this sort in Israel; skip to II:18)

14. For what, in particular, does he (she) need you?
    (Record verbatim) _____
    Office coding

Europeans	Turks	Persians	North Africans	Moslem Arabs	
5	14	10	7	38	1 - instrumental: household help, care of children
57	61	66	68	29	2 - affective: love, ties, be together, visit, advise, worry about

14. *(continued)*

Europeans	Turks	Persians	North Africans	Moslem Arabs	
5	3	6	10	15	3 - global: "to help" without specification
15	9	8	1	2	4 - to maintain family ties: only sister, etc.
3	1	1	2	0	5 - economic assistance, financial advice
10	5	4	4	8	6 - care in case of illness
5	5	3	7	6	7 - live together with the relative
0	0	0	0	0	8 - idiosyncratic needs, not included above
1	2	3	1	2	9 - nothing in particular
					0 - no answer, no relative, respondent not needed

(N.B.: If more than one type of need is given, only the first one is coded, unless one of the others is explicitly stated to be most important. Other needs are recorded manually for subsequent consideration.)

15. Did relatives like these (not only this relative in particular who needs her now), in general, need you less or more when you were 40 than they do now?

Europeans	Turks	Persians	North Africans	Moslem Arabs	
7	9	14	16	12	1 - in general they need her now *less*
26	16	17	13	15	2 - in general they need her now *more*
50	55	55	51	32	3 - both then and now there were relatives needing her to the same extent
17	20	14	19	41	4 - both then and now there were no relatives needing her
					0 - (no relatives)

16. Would you want relatives like these to need you more than they do now, less than they do, or are you satisfied with things as they are?

Europeans	Turks	Persians	North Africans	Moslem Arabs	
5	11	25	23	11	1 - wants them to need her more
17	9	14	9	5	2 - wants them to need her less
78	80	61	68	85	3 - satisfied
					0 - (no relatives)

17. How frequently are you in touch (including by telephone or correspondence) with relatives like these (or a relative like these)?
(Read aloud)

Europeans	Turks	Persians	North Africans	Moslem Arabs	
60	55	41	35	22	1 - at least once a week
16	19	15	10	18	2 - once or twice a month
14	9	18	24	17	3 - from time to time
9	12	21	22	26	4 - infrequently
0	5	5	8	18	5 - never
					0 - (no relatives in Israel)

. . . .

18-27. Each one of us has pleasures and worries in life, joys and problems. I want to ask you, in connection with each of the following questions, to describe your feelings in terms of five answers.

18. For example. To what extent do you enjoy your work in the house? Do you enjoy it to a very great extent, to a great extent, to a certain extent, not so much, or almost not at all?

Europeans	Turks	Persians	North Africans	Moslem Arabs	
15	31	32	20	31	1 - to a very great extent
18	30	37	31	26	2 - to a great extent
38	27	18	30	27	3 - to a certain extent
16	8	8	13	10	4 - not so much
14	3	5	6	5	5 - almost not at all
					0 - (irrelevant: doesn't work, no husband, no children, etc.)

19. To what extent do you enjoy your *grandchildren?* (Read alternatives)

Europeans	Turks	Persians	North Africans	Moslem Arabs	
83	71	82	54	55	1 - to a very great extent
9	20	14	36	31	2 - to a great extent
5	8	3	8	12	3 - to a certain extent
1	0	1	1	2	4 - not so much
2	1	0	1	0	5 - almost not at all
					0 - (irrelevant: doesn't work, no husband, no children, etc.)

20. And to what extent do you enjoy your *children?* (or at least one of them)?

Europeans	Turks	Persians	North Africans	Moslem Arabs	
62	58	63	40	44	1 - to a very great extent
25	30	26	37	31	2 - to a great extent
10	8	7	17	16	3 - to a certain extent
2	4	3	5	6	4 - not so much
0	0	1	1	4	5 - almost not at all
					0 - (irrelevant: doesn't work, no husband, no children, etc.)

21. To what extent are you happy with your *husband*—to a very great extent, to a great extent, to a certain extent, not so much, or almost not at all?

Europeans	Turks	Persians	North Africans	Moslem Arabs	
41	29	26	22	46	1 - to a very great extent
27	29	20	30	29	2 - to a great extent
26	24	23	32	16	3 - to a certain extent
2	10	19	9	4	4 - not so much
4	8	12	7	6	5 - almost not at all
					0 - (irrelevant: doesn't work, no husband, no children, etc.)

22. And to what extent do you enjoy your (paid) *work?*

Europeans	Turks	Persians	North Africans	Moslem Arabs	
32	13	13	13	26	1 - to a very great extent
26	16	26	20	27	2 - to a great extent
29	34	28	30	23	3 - to a certain extent
5	22	22	21	16	4 - not so much
8	16	11	16	8	5 - almost not at all
					0 - (irrelevant: doesn't work, no husband, no children, etc.)

And now to the other side of the coin.

23. To what extent do you have worries and problems about your *husband?*

Europeans	Turks	Persians	North Africans	Moslem Arabs	
10	16	23	12	20	1 - to a very great extent
11	20	18	13	12	2 - to a great extent
28	16	20	27	17	3 - to a certain extent
12	11	13	11	11	4 - not so much
39	37	26	38	40	5 - almost not at all
					0 - (irrelevant: doesn't work, no husband, no children, etc.)

24. And to what extent do you have worries and problems in connection with your *children* (or at least one of them)?

Europeans	Turks	Persians	North Africans	Moslem Arabs	
9	9	15	12	12	1 - to a very great extent
9	13	24	17	10	2 - to a great extent
36	19	13	24	16	3 - to a certain extent
13	22	14	13	15	4 - not so much
33	37	34	33	46	5 - almost not at all
					0 - (irrelevant: doesn't work, no husband, no children, etc.)

25. What about the *grandchildren?*

Europeans	Turks	Persians	North Africans	Moslem Arabs	
4	4	1	3	9	1 - to a very great extent
4	2	5	4	9	2 - to a great extent
6	2	5	9	10	3 - to a certain extent
5	7	6	11	10	4 - not so much
81	84	83	73	62	5 - almost not at all
					0 - (irrelevant: doesn't work, no husband, no children, etc.)

26. To what extent do you have troubles and problems from your (paid) *work?*

Europeans	Turks	Persians	North Africans	Moslem Arabs	
8	9	8	2	11	1 - to a very great extent
7	9	6	17	6	2 - to a great extent
17	6	10	14	15	3 - to a certain extent
14	24	18	12	12	4 - not so much
55	52	57	55	55	5 - almost not at all
					0 - (irrelevant: doesn't work, no husband, no children, etc.)

27. To what extent do you have troubles and problems from your *work in the house?*

Europeans	Turks	Persians	North Africans	Moslem Arabs	
1	2	4	2	10	1 - to a very great extent
4	8	8	9	6	2 - to a great extent
11	15	14	27	14	3 - to a certain extent
14	16	12	16	16	4 - not so much
71	59	63	46	54	5 - almost not at all
					0 - (irrelevant: doesn't work, no husband, no children, etc.)

28-35. All of us have other worries as well. Are you especially worried, quite worried, not so worried, or almost not at all worried about:

28. Your husband's health

Europeans	Turks	Persians	North Africans	Moslem Arabs	
26	34	32	24	34	1 - especially worried
26	27	30	30	14	2 - quite worried
20	20	14	23	14	3 - not so worried
28	18	24	23	38	4 - almost not at all worried
					0 - (not relevant)

29. Your health

Europeans	Turks	Persians	North Africans	Moslem Arabs	
7	25	37	22	42	1 - especially worried
20	33	26	42	20	2 - quite worried
36	26	18	20	18	3 - not so worried
38	17	19	16	20	4 - almost not at all worried
					0 - (not relevant)

30. Matters of finances

Europeans	Turks	Persians	North Africans	Moslem Arabs	
6	28	33	26	30	1 - especially worried
17	19	28	35	18	2 - quite worried
23	23	23	21	24	3 - not so worried
54	30	16	18	28	4 - almost not at all worried
					0 - (not relevant)

31. Growing old

Europeans	Turks	Persians	North Africans	Moslem Arabs	
3	8	8	5	24	1 - especially worried
12	27	16	18	17	2 - quite worried
19	19	18	15	19	3 - not so worried
66	46	58	62	40	4 - almost not at all worried
					0 - (not relevant)

32. Security conditions in the country (Israel)

Europeans	Turks	Persians	North Africans	Moslem Arabs	
63	65	83	51	48	1 - especially worried
26	31	15	43	17	2 - quite worried
7	3	1	4	14	3 - not so worried
4	1	2	2	22	4 - almost not at all worried
					0 - (not relevant)

33. Concern for a family member in Israel Defence Forces (Jews only)

Europeans	Turks	Persians	North Africans	Moslem Arabs	
52	59	72	43		1 - especially worried
25	28	17	39	(not	2 - quite worried
11	7	4	11	asked)	3 - not so worried
11	6	7	7		4 - almost not at all worried
					0 - (not relevant)

34. Death (in any connection)

Europeans	Turks	Persians	North Africans	Moslem Arabs	
11	21	25	6	19	1 - especially worried
13	25	9	18	11	2 - quite worried
11	14	9	15	13	3 - not so worried
66	40	56	61	57	4 - almost not at all worried
					0 - (not relevant)

35. Debts

Europeans	Turks	Persians	North Africans	Moslem Arabs	
16	24	28	20	31	1 - especially worried
13	27	26	35	10	2 - quite worried
15	9	11	11	10	3 - not so worried
56	41	35	33	50	4 - almost not at all worried
					0 - (not relevant)

36. Are you worried these days by anything else? (If yes) About what?
    (Record verbatim) _____
    Office coding

Europeans	Turks	Persians	North Africans	Moslem Arabs	
11	14	12	15	27	1 - health and illness, self
9	26	17	19	12	2 - finances
9	11	9	3	10	3 - special needs of an aged, ill, infirm person, other
1	1	1	3	1	4 - death, including problem of adjustment to widowhood, anxiety about danger of someone's dying

36. *(continued)*

Europeans	Turks	Persians	North Africans	Moslem Arabs	
30	10	15	9	8	5 - national security situation
9	15	12	15	1	6 - concern for family member in Israel Defence Forces
27	21	33	31	39	7 - intrafamily matters: child's marriage, problem of relatives not included above, feeling of isolation with children leaving house
3	1	0	0	0	8 - social relations with neighbors, friends
3	2	1	6	2	9 - global: worried in general, about life
					0 - no other worries

(N.B.: If more than one type of worry is given here, only the first one is coded, unless one of the others is explicitly stated to be most important. Other worries are recorded manually for subsequent consideration.)

37. Does your personal appearance give you:
    (Read aloud)

Europeans	Turks	Persians	North Africans	Moslem Arabs	
15	14	11	10	41	1 - a great deal of satisfaction
29	35	21	35	22	2 - a certain amount of satisfaction
15	15	13	16	7	3 - a certain amount of concern
4	13	16	13	3	4 - a great deal of concern
36	23	38	26	26	5 - neither satisfaction nor concern

38. To what extent are you satisfied by what you have gotten out of life so far? Are you:
    (Read aloud)

Europeans	Turks	Persians	North Africans	Moslem Arabs	
9	17	18	11	13	1 - almost not at all satisfied
12	15	21	18	17	2 - not so satisfied
46	33	35	43	31	3 - satisfied to a certain extent
22	20	16	22	26	4 - satisfied to a great extent
10	15	10	6	14	5 - satisfied to a very great extent

39. Do you sometimes have the feeling that you are likely to break down under your problems? Do you have a feeling like this:
    (Read aloud)

Europeans	Turks	Persians	North Africans	Moslem Arabs	
5	12	17	18	12	1 - very frequently
5	10	15	9	10	2 - frequently
16	24	28	25	22	3 - sometimes
12	12	9	13	22	4 - seldom
62	42	30	34	34	5 - never

40. To what extent do you feel yourself free to do the things that you feel like doing?
    (Read aloud)

Europeans	Turks	Persians	North Africans	Moslem Arabs	
51	58	57	49	51	1 - very free
27	16	17	16	34	2 - free to a certain extent
15	12	7	15	10	3 - not so free
6	8	15	15	3	4 - not at all free
2	6	4	5	1	5 - (doesn't understand the question)

41. Do you feel less free or more free now to do the things that attract you than you felt at 40?

Europeans	Turks	Persians	North Africans	Moslem Arabs	
29	30	27	17	21	1 - freer than at 40
56	53	54	61	70	2 - no change
12	12	15	16	6	3 - less free than at 40
3	5	4	6	2	4 - (doesn't understand the question)

42. Do you work? (For pay or in a family business, including agriculture) (If yes) Full time or part time?

Does work

Europeans	Turks	Persians	North Africans	Moslem Arabs	
16	6	8	8	11	1 - full-time work for pay
19	10	20	15	8	2 - part-time work for pay (includes occasionally)
3	1	1	1	9	3 - full-time work in family business
4	5	1	1	7	4 - part-time work in family business (includes occasionally)

Does not work

Europeans	Turks	Persians	North Africans	Moslem Arabs	
58	78	71	75	65	5 - does not work

43. What kind of work do you do? 43. (No question 43)
    (Record) _____

Europeans	Turks	Persians	North Africans	Moslem Arabs	
6	0	1	0	0	1 - professional or kindred
3	0	0	0	0	2 - proprietor or managerial, employs or supervises 3 + persons
18	7	1	1	0	3 - clerical, sales
14	3	3	5	0	4 - skilled or semiskilled manual work, nonfarm
1	11	24	18	2	5 - unskilled manual work, nonfarm
0	0	0	0	34	6 - agriculture
57	78	72	76	63	7 - does not work

44. Did you work (for pay or in a family business) when you were 40? (If yes) Do you work now fewer or more hours than you did then?

Europeans	Turks	Persians	North Africans	Moslem Arabs	
9	6	6	3	7	1 - works more now (includes: did not work at all then)
10	8	10	8	14	2 - works less now
13	3	8	8	10	3 - works about the same amount

44. Did you work (for pay or in a family business) when you were 40?

Europeans	Turks	Persians	North Africans	Moslem Arabs	
19	12	20	11	17	4 - yes
48	71	56	69	52	5 - no

45. How much do you like your work? Would you say:
Does work
(Read aloud)

Europeans	Turks	Persians	North Africans	Moslem Arabs	
16	10	13	12	17	1 - that you like everything connected with your work
10	2	6	3	5	2 - that you like most of what is connected with your work
12	8	4	6	11	3 - that there are things you like and things you dislike about your work
2	2	3	2	2	4 - that you dislike most of what is connected with your work
2	1	3	2	3	5 - that there is almost nothing you like about your work

45. Would you like to work (for pay)?
Does not work

Europeans	Turks	Persians	North Africans	Moslem Arabs	
24	15	18	16	13	6 - definitely yes
10	6	5	11	5	7 - maybe
24	56	49	49	44	8 - no

46. During the past year, have you done things like taking courses, volunteer work, etc.? (If yes) Did you have something:
(Read 1–3 aloud)
Yes

Europeans	Turks	Persians	North Africans	Moslem Arabs	
18	5	3	4	0	1 - at least once a week
2	0	1	1	0	2 - once or twice a month
4	2	2	2	1	3 - only from time to time

No

Europeans	Turks	Persians	North Africans	Moslem Arabs	
76	93	94	93	99	4 - (no activities)

47. When you were 40, did you take part in any activities of this sort? (If yes) Are you less active or more active now than you were then?

Europeans	Turks	Persians	North Africans	Moslem Arabs	
6	1	3	1	0	1 - more active now (includes those not active at 40)
2	0	1	2	0	2 - less active now
6	2	1	1	1	3 - activity about the same

47. When you were 40, did you take part in any activities of this sort?

Europeans	Turks	Persians	North Africans	Moslem Arabs	
12	8	6	3	6	4 - yes
74	89	89	94	93	5 - no

48. To what extent do you like the things you do in these activities? Would you say that:
(Read aloud)

Europeans	Turks	Persians	North Africans	Moslem Arabs	
15	2	6	3	5	1 - you like everything about your activities
2	1	1	0	1	2 - you like most things about your activities
4	1	0	1	1	3 - there are things you like and things you don't like

48. *(continued)*

Europeans	Turks	Persians	North Africans	Moslem Arabs	
0	0	0	0	0	4 - that you don't like most things about your activities
1	1	0	0	1	5 - that there is almost nothing you like about these activities

48. Would you like to take part in activities like these?

Europeans	Turks	Persians	North Africans	Moslem Arabs	
27	19	18	20	15	6 - definitely yes
14	9	6	16	20	7 - maybe
37	68	69	60	56	8 - no

. . . .

49. What portion of the day, usually, do you give to homemaking, including things you do to make the house prettier, knitting and sewing, work in the garden, and so on? Do you give homemaking:
(Read aloud)

Europeans	Turks	Persians	North Africans	Moslem Arabs	
11	21	29	29	14	1 - most of the day
38	39	33	35	18	2 - quite a large part
35	34	27	26	42	3 - not such a large part
16	6	11	10	27	4 - or a very small part of the day

50. When you were 40 did you give less time or more time to homemaking than you do now?

Europeans	Turks	Persians	North Africans	Moslem Arabs	
10	19	14	17	18	1 - now gives more time than at 40
43	54	50	43	37	2 - now gives less time than at 40
47	27	36	39	45	3 - about the same

51. Is the time that you give to homemaking *more* than you would like, *less* than you would like, or about what you like?

Europeans	Turks	Persians	North Africans	Moslem Arabs	
15	20	24	19	13	1 - gives more time than she wants
23	19	30	24	22	2 - gives less time than she wants
61	61	47	58	65	3 - about what she wants

52. Does it ever happen that you feel you have nothing to do?
(Read aloud)

Europeans	Turks	Persians	North Africans	Moslem Arabs	
4	10	9	9	20	1 - very often
8	14	26	30	23	2 - sometimes
7	7	7	15	31	3 - seldom
81	69	58	47	26	4 - never

53. In general, how is your mood when you get up in the morning? Are you:
(Read aloud)

Europeans	Turks	Persians	North Africans	Moslem Arabs	
52	36	36	31	25	1 - generally in a good mood
28	35	41	50	35	2 - sometimes good, some-times not so good
11	12	13	9	12	3 - not such a good mood
9	17	10	10	28	4 - generally in a bad mood

54. In general, how is your mood at the end of the day? Are you:
(Read aloud)

Europeans	Turks	Persians	North Africans	Moslem Arabs	
48	28	37	27	38	1 - generally in a good mood
43	40	39	53	28	2 - sometimes good, some-times not so good
6	16	13	11	17	3 - not such a good mood
3	15	11	8	17	4 - generally in a bad mood

55. Let's suppose that you've had one of those awful days where nothing goes right, where from all your efforts, nothing comes. How do you feel at the end of a day like that? Would it be more correct to say:

Europeans	Turks	Persians	North Africans	Moslem Arabs	
43	47	40	62	74	1 - that you accept it, there's nothing to be done; or
57	53	60	38	26	2 - that you have to do something to make yourself better

Which is more similar to your feeling?

56. And would it be more correct to say, after a day like that,

Europeans	Turks	Persians	North Africans	Moslem Arabs	
89	75	65	70	56	1 - that you feel very nervous, or
11	25	35	30	44	2 - that you feel really sick

57. And would it be more correct to say, after a day like that,

Europeans	Turks	Persians	North Africans	Moslem Arabs	
24	31	41	40	34	1 - that you get mad at the world, or
76	69	59	60	66	2 - that you blame yourself that everything turned out like that

. . . .

Now we'll talk a little bit about the past

58. Where were you born?

Europeans	Turks	Persians	North Africans	Moslem Arabs	
0	0	100	0	0	1 - Persia (Iran)
0	100	0	0	0	2 - Turkey
0	0	0	72	0	3 - Morocco (including Spanish Morocco)
0	0	0	2	0	4 - Algeria
0	0	0	26	0	5 - Tunisia

58. *(continued)*

Europeans	Turks	Persians	North Africans	Moslem Arabs	
51	0	0	0	0	6 - Germany or Austria
35	0	0	0	0	7 - Czechoslovakia
14	0	0	0	0	8 - Hungary
0	0	0	0	100	9 - Palestine (*only* Arab women)
					0 - another country. (Including Israel for Jews) Which?_____

59. How old are you? (nearest birthday) Aged _____
(Record and code)

Europeans	Turks	Persians	North Africans	Moslem Arabs	
1	3	4	5	10	1 - 43 or less
3	9	16	13	18	2 - 44–45
25	20	18	20	8	3 - 46–47
23	19	17	19	14	4 - 48–49
17	13	21	16	23	5 - 50–51
17	18	16	11	5	6 - 52–53
14	16	6	14	10	7 - 54–55
1	1	1	2	12	8 - 56 or more

Median

Europeans	Turks	Persians	North Africans	Moslem Arabs
49	50	49	49	50

60. In what year did you immigrate to Israel? Year _____
(Record and code)

Europeans	Turks	Persians	North Africans	Moslem Arabs	
2	1	1	0	100	1 - born in Israel
51	22	21	0	0	2 - 1939 or earlier
10	24	2	0	0	3 - 1940–1945
10	3	1	5	0	4 - 1946–5/15/48
25	38	47	32	0	5 - 5/15/48–1952
2	11	27	42	0	6 - 1953–1962
0	1	1	21	0	7 - 1963 or later

61. (Age at time of migration to Israel)
    Office coding

Europeans	Turks	Persians	North Africans	Moslem Arabs	
0	0	0	0	100	1 - born in Israel (Arabs only)
1	4	12	0	0	2 - 5 or less
5	3	5	0	0	3 - 6–12 years
24	11	4	0	0	4 - 13–18 years
34	24	9	9	0	5 - 19–25 years
35	54	63	55	0	6 - 26–40 years
0	3	8	36	0	7 - 41 years or older

62. During World War II, were you in a concentration camp?

Europeans	Turks	Persians	North Africans	Moslem Arabs	
27	(not asked)	(not asked)	(not asked)	(not asked)	1 - yes
73					2 - no

63. Are you accustomed to observe the religious tradition?
    (Read aloud)

Europeans	Turks	Persians	North Africans	Moslem Arabs	
10	10	29	53	79	1 - yes, definitely try to observe all religious traditions
11	20	28	32	19	2 - to a great extent observes religious traditions
40	60	40	15	1	3 - observes traditions somewhat
39	10	3	0	0	4 - completely secular. Not at all observant.

64. How many years did you study in school? (If three or less, ask) Are you able to read? (any language)

Europeans	Turks	Persians	North Africans	Moslem Arabs	
0	29	61	60	96	1 - 3 years or less school; unable to read
0	7	12	5	1	2 - 3 years or less school; able to read
23	55	23	29	2	3 - 4–8 years
61	9	3	6	1	4 - 9–12 years
15	0	1	1	0	5 - 13 years or more

65. Please, try to remember the very first time you menstruated. Of the following words, which are the two which are closest to your feelings then? (Circle the two words)
(Read aloud)
happiness, fear, unpleasantness, pride, natural, shame
(N.B.: Interviewer may record other words)
Office coding
Positive items: happiness, pride
Neutral items: natural
Negative items: fear, unpleasantness, shame
If only one word circled, code nonetheless. Additional words are evaluated in one of the three categories. If more than two words are noted, regard them all.

Europeans	Turks	Persians	North Africans	Moslem Arabs	
6	4	8	3	3	1 - only positive item(s)
25	18	10	14	3	2 - positive and neutral items
17	4	6	5	14	3 - neutral item(s) only
4	18	15	17	9	4 - positive and negative items
0	0	0	0	0	5 - positive, neutral, and negative items
23	12	14	8	8	6 - neutral and negative items
25	44	46	53	64	7 - only negative item(s)
					0 - no answer

66. Which two of the following words best describe the time when you were aged 13–18 approximately?
hopeful, moody, merry, fearful, dreamer, shy, suffering
(N.B.: Interviewer may record other words.)
Office coding
Positive items: hopeful, merry
Neutral items: moody, dreamer, shy
Negative items: fearful, suffering
If only one word circled, code nonetheless. Additional words are evaluated in one of the three categories. If more than two words are noted, regard them all.

Europeans	Turks	Persians	North Africans	Moslem Arabs	
40	39	32	30	49	1 - only positive item(s)
33	39	37	44	30	2 - positive and neutral items
11	9	11	13	7	3 - neutral item(s) only
4	0	4	3	4	4 - positive and negative items
0	1	0	0	0	5 - positive, neutral, and negative items
9	9	13	9	6	6 - neutral and negative items
3	3	3	1	4	7 - only negative item(s)
					0 - no answer

67. a. When you were a *young girl,* and until the time you married, to what extent was
    menstruation something:
    (Read aloud)
   b. And how did you feel from the time you married *until about age 40?*
    Was menstruation:
    (Read aloud)
   c. And what about during your 40s? Was menstruation:
    (Read aloud

> KEY TO 67
> 1 - very, very unpleasant
> 2 - quite unpleasant
> 3 - somewhat unpleasant
> 4 - there was no unpleasantness

Office coding

Europeans	Turks	Persians	North Africans	Moslem Arabs		Young girl	Until 40	Forties
62	57	57	58	67	1 -	3, 4	3, 4	3, 4
						(least unpleasant)		
6	7	8	8	7	2 -	3, 4	3, 4	1, 2
1	1	1	0	0	3 -	3, 4	1, 2	3, 4
10	13	11	24	5	4 -	1, 2	3, 4	3, 4
3	3	2	0	3	5 -	3, 4	1, 2	1, 2
2	3	4	0	1	6 -	1, 2	3, 4	1, 2
4	2	2	0	3	7 -	1, 2	1, 2	3, 4
13	11	14	8	12	8 -	1, 2	1, 2	1, 2
						(most unpleasant)		
0	1	1	2	2	9 - Reply to two periods, one			
						1, 2 and other 3, 4		
					0 - no answer			

(N.B.: If only one period is answered, code 0. If two periods are answered:
       a. If both are 3, 4, code as if the missing period was 1, 2
       b. If both are 1, 2, code as if the missing period was 3, 4
       c. If one is 1, 2 and the other 3, 4, code 9)

68. Generally, how many days does (or did) a menstrual period continue?

Europeans	Turks	Persians	North Africans	Moslem Arabs	
21	12	13	15	14	1 - 3 days or less
26	21	26	27	21	2 - 4 days
26	26	16	21	32	3 - 5 days
27	41	46	38	33	4 - 6 days or more

69. Did you generally menstruate regularly once every month, more often than once a month, or every few months? (Other than during childbearing)

Europeans	Turks	Persians	North Africans	Moslem Arabs	
84	83	84	89	79	1 - generally regularly
4	4	5	4	4	2 - generally oftener than once a month
3	5	4	3	5	3 - generally every few months
9	8	8	4	12	4 - there were times of irregularity (give details) ____

70. Every woman has positive and negative things to say about menstruation. What is the *best* thing for you about menstruation? *(Record verbatim)* _____
Office coding

Europeans	Turks	Persians	North Africans	Moslem Arabs	
27	60	73	71	68	1 - physical health: it's healthy, you feel better, it reduces pressure, the body is liberated (excluding code 7)
8	8	1	2	3	2 - emotional health: reduces tension, it's liberating in general
18	7	8	7	7	3 - global: menstruation is good, is natural
9	6	3	10	2	4 - sign of fertility
4	1	0	3	0	5 - sign of feminity; any sexual connotation
6	1	1	1	0	6 - sign of youth
4	6	3	2	14	7 - cleanses the body
10	3	4	2	0	8 - it means one isn't pregnant
15	8	8	1	6	9 - there's nothing good about menstruation (N.B. If something specifically negative is mentioned, this is used in coding q. 71.)
					0 - no answer

(N.B.: If more than one reason for menstruation being good is mentioned, only the first is coded, unless another is clearly stated to be more important.)

71. And what is the *worst* thing about menstruation? (Record verbatim) _____
    Office coding

Europeans	Turks	Persians	North Africans	Moslem Arabs	
42	37	39	31	42	1 - physical health: pains, weakness, suffering, you don't feel good, uncomfortable, (excluding code 7)
9	4	3	0	1	2 - emotional health: tension, nervousness, shame
14	9	3	10	1	3 - global: menstruation is unpleasant, not nice
1	1	0	0	0	4 - it means you still can conceive (which is undesirable)
3	0	1	1	1	5 - any sexual connotation: inhibits intercourse, prevents you from being a woman
11	2	9	3	7	6 - it limits your activities (excluding intercourse), including religious restrictions
8	22	19	24	27	7 - it's dirty
1	1	0	0	0	8 - not pregnant
11	24	26	30	21	9 - nothing bad about menstruation
					0 - no answer

(N.B.: If more than one reason for menstruation being bad is mentioned, only the first is coded, unless another is clearly stated to be more important.)

DECK III

1–4: Respondent serial number

5. Has your menstruation ceased?
   (If no) Has menstruation become irregular?
   (If yes) Was this the result of surgery?

Europeans	Turks	Persians	North Africans	Moslem Arabs	
34	26	33	23	30	1 - still menstruates regularly (includes pregnant women) (skip to q. 7)
23	18	17	19	9	2 - still menstruates, but menstruation is becoming irregular (skip to q. 7)
33	51	40	51	54	3 - menstruation ceased completely, naturally
10	5	10	6	7	4 - menstruation ceased as a result of surgery

6. (To those who have ceased menstruating) How old were you when menstruation ceased completely? Aged _____
   (Record and code)

Median age:				
Europeans	Turks	Persians	North Africans	Moslem Arabs
48.4	46.9	45.7	46.7	45.3

7. Different women have told us different things which were important to them about "change of life" (Hebrew: *gil hama'avar,* the age of transition). What is the most important thing for you about change of life? (Record verbatim)
   Office coding

Europeans	Turks	Persians	North Africans	Moslem Arabs	
35	35	60	23	29	1 - physical health: physical suffering; weakness; bodily changes, either positive or negative
18	15	6	8	5	2 - emotional health: crisis (without explanation); it's a difficult time; tension; you don't know what's happening to you; more quiet or peaceful; one is more free

7. *(continued)*

Europeans	Turks	Persians	North Africans	Moslem Arabs	
4	9	8	3	20	3 - anything related, positive or negative, explicitly to cessation of menstruation per se
2	3	0	8	10	4 - anything related to fertility or pregnancy
1	2	0	1	0	5 - femininity, sexuality
10	11	6	20	19	6 - social or familial implications
9	2	4	3	5	7 - aging
1	0	0	0	0	8 - change per se
20	22	16	33	12	9 - there's nothing important about it
					0 - no answer

(N.B.: If more than one answer is given, code only the first unless another is clearly more important.)

8–30. Here are some of the things women have told us about change of life and menopause. I would like to know to what extent you agree, or do not agree, with these opinions.

(N.B.: If the subject asks "What woman?" or says "It depends on the woman," etc., explain that we are talking about most women she knows, women like her.)

8. For example: Do you definitely agree, agree, not agree so much, or not agree, with this opinion: A woman is pleased that after menopause she cannot become pregnant.

Europeans	Turks	Persians	North Africans	Moslem Arabs	
25	39	50	42	48	1 - definitely agree
54	43	32	23	20	2 - agree
7	4	4	10	14	3 - don't so much agree
14	14	14	25	18	4 - do not agree

9. A woman has a feeling of better health and more abundant strength after menstruation has stopped.

Europeans	Turks	Persians	North Africans	Moslem Arabs	
2	9	8	7	23	1 - definitely agree
13	14	12	14	19	2 - agree
23	23	18	15	20	3 - don't so much agree
62	54	62	64	38	4 - do not agree

10. As a result of menopause, a woman becomes more nervous and moody.

Europeans	Turks	Persians	North Africans	Moslem Arabs	
20	34	38	22	21	1 - definitely agree
39	37	28	38	13	2 - agree
13	18	21	15	32	3 - don't so much agree
28	11	13	24	34	4 - do not agree

11. At middle age, a woman is given less respect than before.

Europeans	Turks	Persians	North Africans	Moslem Arabs	
7	15	21	7	18	1 - definitely agree
16	23	19	33	11	2 - agree
21	27	28	23	26	3 - don't so much agree
56	35	32	37	45	4 - do not agree

12. At change of life, a woman begins to suffer from weakness and disease.

Europeans	Turks	Persians	North Africans	Moslem Arabs	
17	39	47	34	35	1 - definitely agree
40	42	38	48	27	2 - agree
17	7	9	8	25	3 - don't so much agree
26	12	6	9	13	4 - do not agree

13. A husband is more interested in his wife at middle age than he was before.

Europeans	Turks	Persians	North Africans	Moslem Arabs	
3	26	22	12	35	1 - definitely agree
16	27	19	17	24	2 - agree
30	22	27	26	25	3 - don't so much agree
51	25	32	45	16	4 - do not agree

14. In middle age a woman is given more respect than before.

Europeans	Turks	Persians	North Africans	Moslem Arabs	
4	26	33	25	56	1 - definitely agree
19	40	36	31	31	2 - agree
33	19	19	17	9	3 - don't so much agree
43	15	12	27	3	4 - do not agree

15. So long as she is still menstruating, a woman's body is released every month from pressure and harmful materials.

Europeans	Turks	Persians	North Africans	Moslem Arabs	
32	52	56	55	70	1 - definitely agree
46	39	38	38	17	2 - agree
7	5	5	2	9	3 - don't so much agree
14	4	1	4	4	4 - do not agree

16. A woman is sorry she has no chance for additional children after menopause.

Europeans	Turks	Persians	North Africans	Moslem Arabs	
7	15	13	16	16	1 - definitely agree
16	15	10	18	7	2 - agree
16	17	16	12	27	3 - don't so much agree
60	52	61	53	50	4 - do not agree

I want to remind you that all these opinions and feelings are things different women have told us, and it is important for us to hear your opinion, whether you definitely agree, agree, don't so much agree, or do not agree that:

17. A woman in change of life has more strength than before.

Europeans	Turks	Persians	North Africans	Moslem Arabs	
3	9	12	4	15	1 - definitely agree
10	17	9	11	17	2 - agree
19	25	20	16	31	3 - don't so much agree
68	49	59	69	38	4 - do not agree

18. At middle age a woman feels freer to do the things that attract her than she did formerly.

Europeans	Turks	Persians	North Africans	Moslem Arabs	
10	23	29	19	39	1 - definitely agree
32	40	24	33	24	2 - agree
18	16	14	18	25	3 - don't so much agree
40	21	34	30	13	4 - do not agree

19. A man is less interested in his wife at middle age than he was before.

Europeans	Turks	Persians	North Africans	Moslem Arabs	
3	10	16	7	14	1 - definitely agree
17	20	33	30	11	2 - agree
19	22	23	19	31	3 - don't so much agree
61	47	29	44	44	4 - do not agree

20. After menopause a woman feels more peaceful and tranquil.

Europeans	Turks	Persians	North Africans	Moslem Arabs	
10	11	16	16	33	1 - definitely agree
35	35	37	47	22	2 - agree
19	23	16	19	26	3 - don't so much agree
36	31	31	18	19	4 - do not agree

21. After menopause a woman enjoys sexual relations less.

Europeans	Turks	Persians	North Africans	Moslem Arabs	
8	26	35	11	21	1 - definitely agree
22	33	31	30	28	2 - agree
13	18	20	16	30	3 - don't so much agree
56	23	15	43	21	4 - do not agree

22. A woman is sorry that after menopause she can no longer become pregnant.

Europeans	Turks	Persians	North Africans	Moslem Arabs	
5	12	13	11	18	1 - definitely agree
10	14	10	21	7	2 - agree
12	14	14	10	21	3 - don't so much agree
72	61	63	58	54	4 - do not agree

23. A woman is pleased that after menopause she no longer needs to suffer the pains and complications of pregnancy and birth.

Europeans	Turks	Persians	North Africans	Moslem Arabs	
32	48	56	31	48	1 - definitely agree
43	33	34	44	25	2 - agree
9	7	3	8	17	3 - don't so much agree
17	12	7	18	10	4 - do not agree

24. At middle age a woman has more chance than before to take good care of herself and her appearance.

Europeans	Turks	Persians	North Africans	Moslem Arabs	
22	30	26	18	36	1 - definitely agree
41	43	33	37	28	2 - agree
17	8	12	15	23	3 - don't so much agree
20	19	28	30	13	4 - do not agree

25. After menopause, a woman is sorry because her husband would have wanted more children.

Europeans	Turks	Persians	North Africans	Moslem Arabs	
2	10	11	7	26	1 - definitely agree
9	13	·13	26	11	2 - agree
14	17	19	13	20	3 - don't so much agree
75	60	57	54	43	4 - do not agree

26. A woman begins to age suddenly during change of life.

Europeans	Turks	Persians	North Africans	Moslem Arabs	
10	29	40	23	35	1 - definitely agree
33	45	30	50	23	2 - agree
19	15	16	9	22	3 - don't so much agree
39	11	14	18	20	4 - do not agree

27. A woman in change of life is pleased to be finished with the unpleasantness of menstruation.

Europeans	Turks	Persians	North Africans	Moslem Arabs	
24	27	34	25	48	1 - definitely agree
35	29	27	49	24	2 - agree
12	10	8	5	17	3 - don't so much agree
29	34	31	21	11	4 - do not agree

28. As a result of menopause, a woman is liable to go crazy.

Europeans	Turks	Persians	North Africans	Moslem Arabs	
6	17	8	3	7	1 - definitely agree
35	22	12	6	3	2 - agree
12	11	10	16	18	3 - don't so much agree
47	49	70	75	72	4 - do not agree

29. A woman is pleased there are no chances for additional children after menopause.

Europeans	Turks	Persians	North Africans	Moslem Arabs	
22	31	45	32	35	1 - definitely agree
54	48	39	34	23	2 - agree
7	6	4	9	22	3 - don't so much agree
17	16	12	26	20	4 - do not agree

30. After menopause a woman enjoys sexual relations more.

Europeans	Turks	Persians	North Africans	Moslem Arabs	
8	7	10	6	13	1 - definitely agree
35	21	12	18	32	2 - agree
18	22	18	18	32	3 - don't so much agree
39	50	60	59	23	4 - do not agree

31. Of all the things we have spoken about in connection with menopause and change of life, which, in your opinion, is the best thing from the woman's point of view? (Record verbatim) _____

Europeans	Turks	Persians	North Africans	Moslem Arabs	
9	11	13	5	12	1 - physical health
18	18	20	21	11	2 - emotional health, including greater freedom
14	16	24	11	22	3 - cessation of menstruation per se, including matters directly related to menstruation itself, e.g., pains
12	11	8	13	25	4 - anything related to fertility or pregnancy
8	4	2	1	2	5 - anything related to femininity or sexuality
21	14	11	26	20	6 - social or familial implications (more independence, freedom from child care, social status)
1	4	1	6	3	7 - release from religious limitations
5	2	1	1	2	8 - no particular changes involved in this period of life
11	19	20	17	5	9 - there's nothing good
					0 - no answer

(N.B.: If more than one answer is given, code only the first unless another is clearly more important.)

32. Of all the things we have spoken about in connection with menopause and change of life, which, in your opinion, is the worst thing from the woman's point of view? (Record verbatim) _____
Office coding

Europeans	Turks	Persians	North Africans	Moslem Arabs	
22	50	61	43	47	1 - physical health: illness, unpleasant sensations
16	10	5	4	5	2 - emotional health: nervousness, tension, crisis, mental illness, "it has an effect" (with no other specification)
2	4	2	0	3	3 - cessation of menstruation per se, including that it stopped too soon
4	3	1	4	8	4 - anything related to fertility or pregnancy
4	2	0	2	0	5 - anything related to femininity or sexuality
4	5	2	14	4	6 - social or familial constellation (cut off from children, etc.)
40	19	17	17	19	7 - aging or death
3	1	1	0	2	8 - no particular changes involved in this period of life
7	6	11	15	12	9 - there's nothing good
					0 - no answer

(N.B.: If more than one answer is given, code only the first unless another is clearly more important.)

33. There are women who see menopause as a most important thing in their lives; for other women, it has no effect at all on their lives. For you, personally, is menopause an important change? Would you say that it is:
(Read aloud)

Europeans	Turks	Persians	North Africans	Moslem Arabs	
7	20	20	11	11	1 - most important
9	31	25	30	10	2 - very important
25	19	10	21	18	3 - somewhat important
25	16	23	20	19	4 - not so important
33	14	22	19	42	5 - not at all important

34–36. Here is a picture of a ladder. Let's suppose that the top step of the ladder (point) represents the best possible life for you, and the bottom step (point) represents the worst possible life for you.

34. Where on the ladder (move finger rapidly up and down length of ladder) do you feel you, personally, are now? Step no. _____

Europeans	Turks	Persians	North Africans	Moslem Arabs
6.2	5.4	5.6	5.4	6.2

35. And where on the ladder were you at age 40? Step no. _____

Europeans	Turks	Persians	North Africans	Moslem Arabs
6.2	5.8	5.8	6.1	6.5

36. Where do you think you will be in another five years? Step no. _____

Europeans	Turks	Persians	North Africans	Moslem Arabs
6.9	5.9	5.6	6.4	6.4

Code key for 34–36:

1 = 1, 2 = 2, . . . 9 = 9
0 is coded as 1; 10 is coded as 9
No answer = 0

. . . .

37. We've been talking about all kinds of changes at "change of life," about joys and problems. Is there anything else you would like to add in order for us to get a complete picture? (Record verbatim)

THANK YOU VERY MUCH

38–42. Menopausal symptom scores, based on interview questions (I:53–II:5–9).
Office coding

The series contains 25 symptoms, each of which is classified as psychosomatic, psychic or somatic. Respondents are asked whether, in the past year, they have had the symptom often (scored 1), infrequently (scored 2), or never (scored 3).

38. *Psychosomatic:* items I:53, 54, 60, 63, 64
    Score

Europeans	Turks	Persians	North Africans	Moslem Arabs	
11.11	10.27	10.00	10.07	11.58	1 - 5, 6 (highest symptomatology)
					2 - 7
					3 - 8
					4 - 9
					5 - 10
					6 - 11
					7 - 12
					8 - 13
					9 - 14, 15 (lowest symptomatology)
					0 - no score

39. *Psychic:* items I:55, 58, 59, 61, 66, 68, 70; II:5, 6
    Score

Europeans	Turks	Persians	North Africans	Moslem Arabs	
23.00	22.29	21.40	22.13	24.07	1 - 10–12 (highest symptomatology)
					2 - 13–14
					3 - 15–16
					4 - 17–18
					5 - 19–20
					6 - 21–22
					7 - 23–24
					8 - 25–26
					9 - 27–30 (lowest symptomatology)
					0 - no score

40. *Somatic:* items I:56, 57, 62, 65, 67, 69, 71, 72; II:5, 6
    Score

Europeans	Turks	Persians	North Africans	Moslem Arabs	
23.9	23.7	22.9	23.0	22.8	1 - 10–12
					2 - 13–14
					3 - 15–16
					4 - 17–18
					5 - 19–20
					6 - 21–22
					7 - 23–24
					8 - 25–26
					9 - 27–30
					0 - no score

41–42. *Total menopausal symptom score*
       Exact score is punched. The higher the score, the lower the symptomatology.

Europeans	Turks	Persians	North Africans	Moslem Arabs
57.2	54.7	53.2	54.5	56.1

00 _____ no score

43–44. *Interviewer's name*

45. Status of medical exam

Europeans	Turks	Persians	North Africans	Moslem Arabs	
54	52	63	64	69	1 - examined
36	48	37	36	31	2 - not examined

Bibliography

1. THE START OF THE STUDY: GUIDING REFERENCES

Anderson, John E. Psychological research on changes and transformations during development and aging. *Relations of Development and Aging.* Edited by James E. Birren. Springfield, Ill.: Charles C. Thomas, 1964.

Arey, Leslie B. *Developmental Anatomy.* 6th ed. Philadelphia: W. B. Saunders Co., 1954.

August, Harry E. Psychological aspects of personal adjustment. *Potentialities of Women in the Middle Years.* Edited by Irma H. Gross. East Lansing: Michigan State University Press, 1956.

Bart, Pauline. "Depression in Middle-Aged Women: Some Socio-Cultural Factors." Ph.D. dissertation, U.C.L.A., 1967.

Benedek, Therese. Climacterium: a developmental phase. *Psychoanalytic Quarterly, 19* (1950), 1–27.

Cohen, Sidney; Ditman, Keith S.; and Gustafson, Sarah R. *Psychochemotherapy: The Physician's Manual.* Rev. ed. Los Angeles: Western Medical Publications, 1967.

Deutsch, Helene. *The Psychology of Women.* Vol. II, *Motherhood.* New York: Grune and Stratton, 1945.

Erikson, Erik H. *Childhood and Society.* New York: W. W. Norton, 1950.

Frenkel-Brunswick, Else. Adjustments and reorientations in the course of the life span. *Middle Age and Aging.* Edited by Bernice L. Neugarten. Chicago: University of Chicago Press, 1968.

Glick, Paul C.; Heer, David M; and Beresford, John C. Family formation and family composition: trends and prospects. *Sourcebook in Marriage and the Family.* 2nd ed. Edited by Marvin B. Sussman. Boston: Houghton Mifflin Co., 1963.

Havighurst, Robert J. Changing roles of women in the middle years. *Potentialities of Women in the Middle Years.* Edited by Irma H. Gross. East Lansing: Michigan State University Press, 1956.

_____. The sociologic meaning of aging. *Geriatrics, 13* (1958), 43–50.

Kraines, Ruth J. "The Menopause and Evaluations of the Self: A Study of Middle-Aged Women." Ph.D. dissertation, University of Chicago, 1963.

Kuhlen, R. G. Age differences in personality during adult years. *Psychological Bulletin, 42* (1945), 333–58.

MacFarlane, Catharine. Physiological changes and adjustments from the standpoint of a physician. *Potentialities of Women in the Middle Years.* Edited by Irma H. Gross. East Lansing: Michigan State University Press, 1956.

Mishnaot: Nashim; Taharot. [The Mishnah: Women; Cleannesses.]

Myrdal, Alva, and Klein, Viola. *Women's Two Roles: Home and Work*. 2nd ed. London: Routledge and Kegan Paul, 1968.

Neugarten, Bernice L. A developmental view of adult personality. *Relations of Development and Aging*. Edited by James E. Birren. Springfield, Ill.: Charles C. Thomas, 1964.

Neugarten, Bernice L., and Kraines, Ruth J. Menopausal syndromes in women of various ages. *Psychosomatic Medicine, 27,* 3 (May–June, 1965), 266–73.

Neugarten, Bernice L.; Wood, Vivian; Kraines, Ruth J.; and Loomis, B. Women's attitudes toward the menopause. *Vita Humana, 6* (1963), 140.

Nimkoff, M. F., ed. *Comparative Family Systems*. Boston: Houghton Mifflin Co., 1965.

Patai, Raphael. *Israel between East and West*. Philadelphia: The Jewish Publication Society of America, 1953.

Selye, Hans. *The Stress of Life*. New York: McGraw-Hill Book Co., 1956.

Wilson, Robert A., and Wilson, Thelma A. The fate of the non-treated post-menopausal woman: a plea for the maintenance of adequate estrogen from puberty to the grave. *Journal of the American Geriatric Society, 11,* 4 (1963), 347–62.

2. HISTORICAL BACKGROUND OF THE FIVE SUB-CULTURES

The Central European Women

Fraenkel, Josef, ed. *The Jews of Austria*. London: Vallentine-Mitchell, 1967.

Learsi, Rufus. *Israel: A History of the Jewish People*. New York: The World Publishing Co., 1966.

Marcus, Jacob R. *The Rise and Destiny of the German Jew*. Cincinnati, Ohio: Union of American Hebrew Congregations, 1939.

Roth, Cecil. *A History of the Jews*. New York: Schocken Books, 1961.

Sacher, Howard Morley. *The Course of Modern Jewish History*. New York: Dell Publishing Co., 1958.

Society for the History of Czechoslovak Jews. *The Jews of Czechoslovakia*. New York: The Jewish Publication Society of America, 1968.

The Turkish Women

Lerner, Daniel. *The Passing of Traditional Society: Modernizing the Middle East*. Glencoe, Ill.: The Free Press, 1958.

Thon, Hanna Helena. *Edot Beyisrael*. ("Ethnic Sub-Cultures in Israel.") Jerusalem: Rubin Mass, 1957.

Woodsmall, Ruth. *Women and the New East*. Washington, D.C.: The Middle East Institute, 1960.

The Persian Women

Institute of Jewish Affairs. "Jews in Moslem Lands." New York: World Jewish Congress, 1959. Mimeographed.

Learsi, Rufus. *Israel: A History of the Jewish People.* New York: The World Publishing Co., 1966.

Thon, Hanna Helena. *Edot Beyisrael.* ("Ethnic Sub-Cultures in Israel.") Jerusalem: Rubin Mass, 1957.

Woodsmall, Ruth. *Women and the New East.* Washington, D.C.: The Middle East Institute, 1960.

The North African Women

Sacher, Howard Morley. *The Course of Modern Jewish History.* New York: Dell Publishing Co., 1958.

Thon, Hanna Helena. *Edot Beyisrael.* ("Ethnic Sub-Cultures in Israel.") Jerusalem: Rubin Mass, 1957.

Willner, Dorothy. *Nation-Building and Community in Israel.* Princeton: Princeton University Press, 1969.

Wolkowicz, Steven D. "Mission to Morocco: A Report on Moroccan Jewry." Jerusalem: Institute for Contemporary Jewry, 1947. Mimeographed.

The Moslem Arab Women

Antoun, Richard E. On the modesty of women in Arab Muslim villages: a study in the accommodation of traditions. *American Anthropologist, 70* (1968), 671–97.

Cohen, A. *Arab Border Villages in Israel.* Manchester: Manchester University Press, 1965.

Datan, Nancy; Maoz, Benjamin; Antonovsky, Aaron; and Wijsenbeek, Henricus. Climacterium in three cultural contexts. *Tropical and Geographical Medicine, 22* (1970), 77–86.

Fuller, Anne. *Buarij: A Muslim Village in Lebanon.* Cambridge, Mass.: Harvard University Press, 1960.

Granqvist, Hilma. Marriage conditions in a Palestinian village. Helsinki: *Societas Scientarum Fennica Communitas Humanarum Literatas, 6, 8,* 1947.

Patai, Raphael. *Sex and Family in the Bible and the Middle East.* Garden City, N.Y.: Doubleday and Co., 1959.

Rosenfeld, Henry. Change, barriers to change and contradictions in the Arab village family. *American Anthropologist, 70,* 4 (1968), 732–52.

_____. *Hem Hayu Felahin.* ("They were Peasants.") Tel Aviv: Hakibbutz Hameuhad, 1964.

3. RELATED PUBLICATIONS: DATAN, ANTONOVSKY, AND MAOZ

Datan, Nancy; Maoz, Benjamin; Antonovsky, Aaron; and Wijsenbeek, Henricus. Climacterium in three cultural contexts. *Tropical and Geographical Medicine, 22* (1970), 77–86.

Maoz, Benjamin; Datan, Nancy; Antonovsky, Aaron; and Wijsenbeek, Henricus. Female attitudes to menopause. *Social Psychiatry, 5,* 1 (1970), 35–40.

Maoz, Benjamin; Wijsenbeek, Henricus; Antonovsky, Aaron; and Datan, Nancy. The climacterium and non-psychotic disturbances in women. *Mental Health in Rapidly Changing Society.* Edited by L. Miller. Jerusalem, 1970, pp. 355–57.

Antonovsky, Aaron; Maoz, Benjamin; Datan, Nancy; and Wijsenbeek, Henricus. Twenty-five years later: A limited study of the sequellae of the concentration camp experience. *Social Psychiatry, 6,* 4 (1971), 186–93.

Datan, Nancy. "Women's Attitudes Towards the Climacterium in Five Israeli Sub-Cultures." Ph.D. dissertation, University of Chicago, 1971.

Datan, Nancy. To be a woman in Israel. *School Review, 80,* 2 (February, 1972), 319–32.

Antonovsky, Aaron. Breakdown: a needed fourth step in the conceptual armamentarium of modern medicine. *Social Science and Medicine, 6* (1972), 537–44. Reprinted in Spanish by CIDOC Dossier, Cuernevaca, Mexico.

Datan, Nancy. Your daughters shall prophesy: ancient and contemporary perspectives on the woman in Israel. *Israel: Social Structure and Change.* Edited by M. Curtis and M. Chertoff. New Brunswick, N.J.: Transaction Books, 1973.

Maoz, Benjamin. "The Perception of Menopause in Five Ethnic Groups in Israel." Ph.D. dissertation, University of Leiden, Netherlands. Kupat Holim publication, 300 pp., 1973.

Antonovsky, Aaron. The utility of the breakdown concept. *Social Science and Medicine, 7* (1973), 605–12.

Maoz, Benjamin. Perception of menopause among five ethnic groups in Israel. *The Family Physician, 4,* 2 (1975), 1–8.

Datan, Nancy. Ecological antecedents and sex-role consequences in traditional and modern Israeli sub-cultures. *Emergent Women.* Edited by A. Schlegel. New York: Columbia University Press, 1977.

Maoz, Benjamin; Antonovsky, Aaron; Apter, A.; Wijsenbeek, Henricus; and Datan, Nancy. Ethnicity and adaptation to climacterium. *Archiv fur Gynikologie, 223* (1977), 9–18.

Maoz, Benjamin; Antonovsky, Aaron; Apter, A.; Wijsenbeek, Henricus; and Datan, Nancy. The perception of menopause in five ethnic groups in Israel. *Acta Obstetricka Gynecologicka Scandanavia 65* (1977), 69–76.

Maoz, Benjamin; Antonovsky, Aaron; Apter, A.; Datan, Nancy; Hochberg, J.; and Salomon, Y. The effect of outside work on the menopausal woman. *Maturitas, 1* (1978), 43–53.

Antonovsky, Aaron. *Health, Stress, and Coping.* San Francisco: Jossey-Bass, 1979.

Index

Additional page references for asterisked entries are found under individual subcultures: Arabs, Central Europeans, North Africans, Persians, Turks. Page numbers appearing in *italic* type refer to items in the interview schedule found in Appendix 2.

Abortion(s), 113; *of sample women, *131*
Adolescence(s), 1, 14; *of sample women, *169*
Adultery, 14, 15, 16–17, 93
Ages: *of sample women, 2, 24, 27, 43, 59, 61, 62, 75, 77, 79, 95, 117–18, *167;* *of sample women's children, 2, 18, *134–35*
Aging, *as concern of sample women, *157, 173, 174, 178, 180*
Anti-Semitism: in Europe, 24–25; in North Africa, 74; in Persia, 59–60; in Turkey, 44; relief from, in Israel, 62
Appearance, *as concern of sample women, *159, 178*
Arabs: abortions of, *131;* adolescences of, 101, *169;* ages of, 95, *167;* ages of children of, 3, 18, 22, 95, 96, 98, *135;* choice of husbands of, 12, 18, 22, 95, *140–41;* cultural stability of, 2, 22–23, 96, 110, *141, 168;* deaths of children of, 3, 95, 96, *131;* education of, 3, 4, 8, 12, 18, 22, 95, 96, 113, *168;* education of children of, 4, 8, 113; ethnic identities of, 94, *129, 166–67;* family planning of, 111, 113; history of changing life in Israel of, 22–23, 91, 92, 96, 113; husbands of, 18, 95–96, *142–43, 155, 156, 175, 177;* marital histories of, 18, 22, 95, 96, 97–98, 100, 101, 104, 105, *140, 141, 144–48, 154, 155, 175, 177;* marital statuses of, 95, 96, *129, 142;* menopausal statuses of, 68, 103, *173;* menopausal symptomatologies of, 103, 104, *149, 150, 157, 181–83;* menstrual histories of, 101, *169, 170–71, 173;* miscarriages of, 3, 22, 95, 96, 102, *131;* modernity of, 18, 96, *141, 148, 166–68;* number of children of, 2, 3, 18, 22, 95, 96, *130;* orthodoxy of, 12, 18, 22, 96, *168;* personality variables of, *144–45, 166;* psychological well-being of, 104, 105, 106, 109, 110, 113, *153–60, 165, 173, 175, 177, 178, 180–81;* socioeconomic

statuses of, 105, *143, 157–58;* stillbirths of, 3, 22, 95, 96, 102, *131*
— attitudes of, toward: childbearing, 102, *131–33, 177;* choice of husbands, 18, 22, 95, 96, *140–41;* family size, 2, 18, 102, 104, *133–34;* loss of fertility, 102, 103, 104, *174, 176, 177, 179, 180;* menopause, 2, 5, 85, 103–4, 110, 115, *173–80;* menstruation, 101, 102, 103–4, *170, 171–72, 174, 176, 178*
— concerns of, over: aging, 103, 105, *157, 173, 174, 178, 180;* appearance, 106, *159, 178;* death, 103, 105, *158, 180;* husbands' health, 105, *156;* national security, 105, *157, 159;* own health, 101, 103, 104, 105, 106, *157, 158, 171, 172, 173, 175, 179, 180*
— sexuality of: past, 101, 104, *140, 145, 148, 169–72;* present, 101, 104, *141, 145, 148–49, 173–80*
— social roles of: employee, 18, 22, 99, 100, 105, *154, 156, 161–62;* extended family member, 18, 22, 81, 99, *151–53;* friend and neighbor, 99, 100, *150–51, 159;* grandmother, 18, 22, 95, 98–99, 100, 105, *138–39, 153, 155;* homemaker, 98, 99, 101, 105, *153, 156, 164–65;* matriarch, 98, 104, 115, *137, 175;* mother, 18, 22, 95, 98, 100, 105, *135–37, 154, 155;* volunteer, 100, *163–64*

Bath, ritual, 10, 13, 14, 15, 16, 93. See also *Mikvah*
Bigamy, 75. *See also* Polygyny
Biology: egalitarianism of, 116; freedom from, for modern women, 1
Bride-price, 8, 15, 22, 92, 95

Central Europe, 8, 16, 24–26
Central Europeans: abortions of, 19, 28, 29, 35, 69, 111, 113, *131;* adolescences of, 27, 34,

189

Central Europeans *(continued)*
51, *169;* ages of, 24, 27, *167;* ages of
children of, 18, 19, 28, 29, 31, 32, *135;*
choice of husbands of, 12, 18, 27–28,
140–41; cultural stability of, 2, 19, 28, 110,
141, 168; deaths of children of, 18, 28, *131;*
education of, 3, 12, 17, 18, 27, *168;* effect
on, of feminist reforms, 8; ethnic identities
of, 27, 129, *166–67;* family planning of, 4,
12, 18, 19, 28, 36, 111, 113; as Holocaust
survivors, 1, 27, 41, 42, *168;* husbands of,
18, 28, 29, *142–43, 156;* immigration to
Israel of, 9, 17, 24–26, 27, 29, *167–68;*
marital histories of, 18, 27, 29, 30, 34, 35,
37, 38, 39, 40, 48–49, 56, 80, 98, 110, *140,
141, 144–48, 154, 155, 175, 177;* marital
statuses of, 28, *129, 142;* menopausal
statuses of, 36, *173;* menopausal symptomatologies of, 4, 36, 37–38, 111, *149, 150, 157,
181–83;* menstrual histories of, 34, 36, *169,
170–71, 173;* miscarriages of, *131;* modernity of, 3, 18, 27, 29, *141, 148, 166–68;*
number of children of, 2, 3, 4, 12, 18, 29,
130; orthodoxy of, 12, 18, 19, 29, *168;* personality variables of, *144–45, 166;*
psychological well-being of, 4, 37–38, 39,
40, 41, 42, 57, 109, 110, 111, 113, *153–60,
165, 173, 175, 177, 178, 180–81;* socioeconomic statuses of, 3, 12, 19, 28, 47, 56, *143,
157–58;* stillbirths of, 35, 53, *131*
— attitudes of, toward: childbearing, 35,
131–33, 177; choice of husbands, 18, 28, 29,
140–41; family size, 2, 18–19, 35, 38, 53, 84,
85, 111, 133–34; loss of fertility, 35, 36, 37,
38, 70, 85, *174, 176, 177, 179, 180;* menopause, 2, 4, 5, 35, 36, 37–38, 54, 69, 85, 110,
113, *173–80;* menstruation, 34, 37, 38, 51,
52, *170, 171–72, 174, 176, 178*
— concerns of, over: aging, 36, 38, 40, *157,
173, 174, 178, 180;* appearance, 38, 159,
178; death, 36, 40, *158, 180;* husbands'
health, 40, *156;* national security, 40, *157,
158, 159;* own health, 36, 37, 38, 40, *157,
158, 171, 172, 173, 175, 179, 180*
— sexuality of: past, 34, 35, *140, 145, 148,
169–72;* present, 30, 34–35, 37, 52, 54, 104,
141, 145, 148–49, 173–80
— social roles of: employee, 3, 12, 18, 19, 30,
32, 33, 39, 40, 56, 105, 110, *154, 156,
161–62;* extended family member, 18, 19,
31, 33, 50, *151–53;* friend and neighbor,
31–32, 33, 50, *150–51, 159;* grandmother,
18, 19, 28, 31, 33, 39, 40, 50, 56, *138–39,
153, 155;* homemaker, 31, 33, 56, *153, 156,
164–65;* matriarch, 5, 30, 38, *137, 175;*
mother, 18, 28, 29, 30, 32, 33, 39, 40, 49,
81, *135–37, 154, 155;* volunteer, 32, 33, 110,
164–65

Change of life. *See* Menopause
Childbearing: as affected by Israel public health
care system, 92; *attitudes toward, of sample women, 109, 112, *131–33, 177;* effect of,
on friend and neighbor role, 32; effect of,
on psychological well-being, 113; as expression of biblical tradition, 16; history of, and
response to loss of fertility, 5, 6, 35, 36–37,
38, 54, 69, 70, 85, 86, 104; planned and
restricted, 4, 114; as shaped by cultural
values, 2. *See also* Number of children, of
sample women
Childbirth: *attitudes toward, of sample
women, 177;* of daughters, as disappointment, 7, 92; effects on, of modern medicine,
8, 28, 92; first, as psychosexual index, 124;
ritual periods of uncleanness after, 8, 13;
rituals of, involving sex of child, 7, 13,
15–16, 76; subsequent, as psychosexual
index, 124–25
Climacteric indices, 125–27
Cultural context, 110
Cultural stability, 110, 113; *of sample women,
141, 168*

Death(s): *as concern of sample women, *158,
180;* *of sample women's children, *131*
Deutsch, Helene, 5
Double standard, 16–17. *See also* Sex roles;
Subordination of women to men

Education: compulsory, in Israel, 8, 92; disparity of, for Moslems and non-Moslems in
Turkey, 43–44; history of, for North
African Jews, 75; history of, for Persian
Jews, 60; in index of modernity, 3, 122, 127;
level of, and socioeconomic status, 117; *of
sample women, *168;* *of sample women's
children, 113; as social victory, 46
Employee role, 2, 3; *of sample women, 18,
154, 156, 161–62
Ethnic identity(ies), 12, 117, 127–28; *of sample
women, *129, 166–67*
Evil Eye, 76
Extended families: affected by degree of
modernity, 92; *of sample women, 18,
151–53
Extramarital relations. *See* Adultery

Family life, 10, 44
Family life cycle, 17, 28, 46, 114
Family size, 18; *attitudes toward, of sample
women, *133–34;* relation of, to traditional
values, 84, 92. *See also* Number of children,
*of sample women
Family stability, 2, 113, 115
Femininity, 5, 103